Ninon,

A Courtesan of Quality

LILLIAN DAY

Doubleday & Company, Inc.
Garden City, New York

1957

To the memory of Norbert Lederer

Library of Congress Catalog Card Number 57–10451
Copyright © 1957 by Lillian Day
All Rights Reserved
Printed in the United States of America
First Edition

Preface

THERE are two qualifications considered necessary for the success of a courtesan: avarice and frigidity. Ninon de Lanclos possessed neither, nor was she a beauty. Yet she was, perhaps, the best-loved woman in a profession noted for its illustrious following . . . certainly the best liked.

She lived during *Le Grand Siècle*, the century that bridged the age of fanaticism and the age of reason. When heresy was treason she raised her voice for freedom of opinion; she asserted the rights of her sex, she fought the anti-vice crusaders and defied the clergy by taking a daily bath.

Hers was an age of letter writing before the telephone came to deprive biographers of their most prolific source of information. People bared their hearts in such flowery rhetoric that one cannot but suspect that they entertained hopes of their missives being read by posterity; to this end, no doubt, they tied them in packages with scarlet ribbon and hid them in secret compartments of fine furniture where they were sure to be discovered.

Hers was an age of journals and memoirs. Saint-Simon, Cardinal de Retz, Tallemant des Réaux, Dangeau, Bussy-Rabutin, Montespan and other reporters of delicious scandal have found their way to the shelves of solemn reading rooms in libraries throughout the world, forming a literature *en déshabillé* which affords, perhaps, a more authentic picture of the epoch than we get from the historians.

There is a copious series of letters purporting to be written by Ninon to the young marquis de Sévigné. Although they capture her style and philosophy, since I believe they are a hoax, I am not including them.

Preface

There is hardly a collection of *femmes fatales*, enchantresses, gallant ladies or wicked women that does not contain a piece about Ninon. She emerges from them all not only as a symbol of seduction but as an example of integrity.

When Edwige Feuillère played *La Dame aux Camélias* in London, the critic of *The Times* complained that she portrayed the heroine as a great lady. Her reply was: "The courtesans of France were the only *grandes dames*."

L.D.

Chapter I

It was as black as midnight and only the sound of an approaching bell warned her that dawn had come. Ninon jumped out of bed, bundled herself into a warm robe and ran to open the window. The clang of the bell drew nearer, accompanied by a mournful voice:

> "Awake, sleeping people, awake!
> Pray for the souls of the dead."

She leaned out, the better to see the tall figure clothed in black with a white skull and crossbones on his tunic. He carried a lantern in one hand and in the other a bell. As he passed along the middle of the narrow street the few people abroad in the chill November morning stopped to make the sign of the cross. Even the blasphemous old ragpicker of the quarter, decked out in the accumulated skirts of years, paid grumbling respect to the Bell Ringer of the Departed.

Suddenly church bells from towers near and far rang out their matins as dawn crept in between the leaning houses. Windows began to open and heads in white nightcaps came out cautiously, lest the baneful miasmas of night be lingering in the air. Another day had begun in the crooked little street, a very important day. It was the third of November in the year 1629 and Ninon de Lanclos [1] was nine years old.

She watched young country-bred maids as they scurried by, their wooden shoes clopping on the slippery paving stones, warming their hands on the newly baked loaves that they clutched. Shopkeepers hailed one another as they opened their

---

[1] She signed her name Anne de Lanclos, which is used here except when quoting letters or passages where it is spelled otherwise.

shutters. By leaning out she could see Pierre, the waiter in the wineshop on the corner, turning his benches right side up and sprinkling the floor with sawdust. The valet of the lodging house across the street was singing as he emptied the slop jars and chamber pots into the brown gutter stream, swollen to a rivulet by the dirty water each householder threw out before his door.

Soon cartwheels from the rue du Temple croaked an obbligato to the cries of foodmongers, water carriers, old-clothes merchants. Each huckster chanted his unintelligible words to the melody he had learned with his trade. Cold as she was, Ninon waited to hear the high-pitched, plaintive reed of the goatherd as he drove his nanny goats from door to door.

She poured cold water into a basin and washed herself bravely, and then did her morning dance to get warm. When she heard her mother moving about she quickly put on her underclothes as Maman had said a naked body was a wicked thing.

Her parents slept in the next room, the one without a window. She had heard them quarreling far into the night, and, as usual, she herself had been the subject. Papa had brought her a lute and had given her the first lesson, and Maman had said that music was a devil's instrument.

"But, Maman," she had protested, "you told me the angels played heavenly music."

Her father had chuckled. "The child takes after me."

"The good God forbid!" Madame de Lanclos had exclaimed, and that had started them all over again.

Whenever she listened to their quarrels she was torn by opposing loyalties. Her affection for her mother was tempered by the constant restrictions she imposed; she knew her father for what he was, yet she adored him.

She put on the petticoats, and the skirt that reached her ankles, and then the pointed bodice like her mother's. She arranged her curls as best she could, for the only mirror in the house was hung out of reach.

Papa came home so seldom now. Maman believed that his long absences were due to his duties at the Hôtel Saint-Luc but Ninon knew better. She had noticed that the neighbors stopped their gossip on her approach, and she understood only too well the innuendoes of Jeanne, the old servant. Her father had a mistress. More than once her vivid imagination had kept her awake, the tears of jealousy pouring down her cheeks. Yet never for a moment had she considered telling her mother. She would protect her father by telling lies if necessary.

Captain Henry de Lanclos and his daughter understood each other. On their long walks he had told her how he fought for Henri IV. There was a king who had been a man as well!

One day they had gone to the new church of Saint-Gervais to hear a young organist named Couperin, and another time they had crossed the Seine to go to the Fair of Saint-Germain-des-Prés, and another time they had spent a whole afternoon on the green Ile des Vaches right in the middle of the river. The best of all was when he had taken her to the Palais d'Orléans to see the wonderful paintings of Queen Marie which a great artist named Rubens had come from Flanders to make. That day he had bought her books which she had read eagerly, that she might talk to him about them when he came home again.

But he came less and less, and when he did he was preoccupied and silent and anxious to get away. But he hadn't forgotten her birthday. In spite of her mother's protest he was taking her to the Pont-Neuf to buy a silver necklace.

Madame de Lanclos came in to bring her daughter a gift, a leather-bound treatise on the Love of God by François de Sales.

As Ninon drank her broth that morning she pondered over her father's creed which offered so much: music, dancing, books, pretty dresses, and fun without a sense of sin. To the child, happiness on earth offered a serious challenge to the possibility of a seat in heaven.

The Pont-Neuf was crowded with people whose dress proclaimed not only their nationality or the provinces from which they came, but their trades and professions as well. The somber costumes of the Huguenots contrasted with the ornate dress of the aristocrats; clergymen in black, white, gray, brown or scarlet dotted the throng. Men of the medical faculty were distinguished by their pointed caps, and those of the old school rode donkeys while the doctors who believed in modern methods rode horses.

A man in a red fez with one gold earring was draped in rugs which it broke his heart to give away so cheap; a gypsy woman was reading cards for a young man who seemed to hang on every word. There was an astrologer with the sun and the moon and the stars on his blue cap, and an alchemist with a retort containing a green liquid. There were jugglers, and potboys in leather aprons, and *crocheteurs*, or street porters, intent on confidential errands. There were medicine men with large enemas or saws; there were flower girls with baskets slung around their necks, and beggars everywhere with real or simulated afflictions.

The crowd pushed its way in and out of the little booths where velvets from Lyon and laces from Brittany and smuggled gold and silver brocades from Venice were displayed; in and out of the stalls piled high with gleaming fish and coiled eels. Rabbits were strung up by the ears and open carcasses of oxen gaped from their hooks. There were fruits and nuts and greens; there were casseroles and baskets, pewter plates and tankards, pitchers and brooms. Housewives, accompanied by their kitchen maids, pinched the fowl and the fish and harangued the hucksters, who answered back with nimble wit. Gossip and laughter issued from the pastry cook's kitchen along with the delicious smell of tarts. And for those who had eaten too many there was a pretty girl outside with a brass kettle of boiling water on her back and packets of herb teas in her hand.

On the sidewalks of the bridge . . . the first in Paris . . . were barkers for holy relics and unholy nostrums, for elixirs and amulets, protection against the evil eye or the plague.

Henry and Ninon joined a group gathered around an old man who was playing a rebec. When he had finished his tune he began to promote his secret formula, guaranteed to cure wrinkles and rupture, impotence, griping of the guts, and to turn Negroes white. It also removed corns, to which His Majesty's *valet de chambre* would gladly testify, were he here. Soon his voice was drowned by that of a tooth extractor who, wielding a large forceps, cajoled and threatened, using big words.

A little farther on another merchant burned his finger in a flame and then applied his miraculous unction which not only would heal the burn in a few moments, if the ladies and gentlemen would have the kindness to wait, but was good for running sores, pimples and the itch.

"In addition," he cried, "this Balm of Jerusalem kills fleas and lice and prevents the hair from falling out. You, there, monsieur, with the bald pate. You could grow locks like Samson with my ointment. If you don't hurry you'll have no hair at all, and then you will sprout horns." He paused for the laugh, for Frenchmen through the centuries have found nothing funnier than a husband who is made *cocu.*

Ninon skipped and danced beside her father to a bazaar with gold and silver jewelry. A tray of necklaces was placed in front of her. She chose a simple one of delicate craftsmanship. She did not miss the look that passed between the shopkeeper and her father.

"So that is your choice," said Henry. "I don't think that one is suitable for a little girl."

Ninon guessed that he had bought a similar one for his mistress.

"I don't want it," she cried, "I don't want any of them."

Because her father insisted, she chose another. He fastened it around her neck.

"Maman doesn't approve of jewelry," she said.

"Tell her to sprinkle it with holy water," Henry said as they left the shop.

At the center of the bridge they paused to drink water from La Samaritaine, the large fountain with its sundial and clock surmounted by the figures of Jesus and the woman of Samaria. It was here that forbidden pamphlets were sold under cover to customers who were known. They tasted bits of cheese from different provinces, bought sweets and soap' balls, and a medal for Madame de Lanclos that had been blessed by His Holiness.

Across from the Place Dauphine stood a bronze statue of

Henri IV, the *Vert Galant*. Henry told his daughter about a day long ago, his first in Paris, when the beloved monarch had been foully murdered in the street.

At the other end of the bridge Mondor, king of the mountebanks, and his troupe was performing *The Love Life of the Empress Theodora*, the lover dressed as a goose. Across the road Jean Salomon, known as Tabarin, was aping the mannerisms of celebrated people known to be homosexuals. Recognized now as the prototype of the *farceur*, he was then just a puller-in for his brother, a quack doctor and tooth extractor.

One hardly knew where to look, there was so much that was exciting. The little Ninon did not understand, her father explained. It was a liberal education for a little girl.

Light-fingered pickpockets plied their trade, and a cloak snatcher was well out of sight before his victim realized that his back was chilly and started up a cry for the Watch. Jugglers tossed red and blue balls and nuns appealed for charity, while in and out of the crowd rascals tried every sort of confidence game short of selling the bridge.

The tumult continued to mount until noon was announced by the carillon of the Samaritaine. With amazing speed the merchandise that had not been sold was packed, the stalls folded, and a corps of sweepers with brooms made of twigs shoved the debris together; pedestrians had to step fast to avoid the pails of cold water that were splashed about. The crowd debouched at both extremities of the bridge.

As Ninon and Henry walked home along the quay they heard the swish of the river, the cries of the bargemen and the creaking of rusty wrought-iron signs as they swung on their hinges.

For two hours, just as today, business stopped. Paris was at lunch.

Chapter II

ONE afternoon in May in the year 1610 a young man of about nineteen arrived in Paris from his home in Champagne. At the Porte Saint-Antone he showed his passport: Henry de Lanclos, lord of La Duardière, squire and gentleman of Touraine. He was a gentleman because he came of the lesser nobility and possessed a duly recorded coat of arms.[1] He had received the education of a gentleman: mastery of horsemanship and dexterity with the rapier. He had already fought in the service of his king. Manhood began early in the seventeenth century. When he was searched for contraband his saddlebags revealed implements of less manly pursuits . . . a lute and a volume of the essays of Montaigne.

He rode past the Bastille into the Marais.[2] From her windows and her rooftops Paris waved the white standard of the Bourbons for Marie de Medici, the Florentine banker's fat daughter, as her husband called her, having borne her royal spouse six children, had at last been crowned queen of France.

Young Lanclos had difficulty finding lodgings. The population, some five hundred thousand residents and thirty thousand transients, was already squeezed into flimsy, precarious dwellings hastily constructed on filled-in ditches and in the crooked streets.

[1] Party per pale; (1) or, three chevronels gules; (2) azur a lion's head erased, lampassé, or the tongue supporting a ring of the same.

[2] So called because it was once a swamp. The quarter extends from the outer ramparts south to the Seine and west to the rue Saint-Denis. It was fashionable in the seventeenth century, containing the *hôtels* of the aristocracy and the princes royal. It was also the center of liberalism and the arts. It is rich in historical landmarks: the Carnavalet, the Hôtel de Ville, Tour Saint-Jacques, Les Halles, et cetera.

The upper stories leaned crazily toward each other. The *meublés*, or furnished flats, were jammed and dirty, and the bare unfinished attics, crouching among the chimney pots, housed the lower class of servants. Everywhere, even in the magnificent *hôtels particuliers* of the aristocracy, Paris was bursting at the seams.

Eventually he found makeshift quarters and accommodation for his horse. If he ventured forth after dark that night he took his life in his hands, for the unlighted, unpoliced streets were an invitation to roving marauders who did not hesitate to exchange a stab in the back for a purse.

Early next morning he set forth to explore the city that was to become his home. Crossing the inner fortifications, he strolled through the rue des Mauvais Garçons, past the wheat market to the Hôtel de Ville on the Place de Grève. In the square before the City Hall most of the gibbets were empty. Only one poor devil swung and twisted in the breeze. Henry strolled along the embankment to the Pont-Neuf, the new, uncovered bridge where special sidewalks permitted pedestrians to loiter without fear of being run down or splattered by cartwheels. Toward the east two bridges spanned the Seine like strands of a giant girdle, buckled in the middle by an oval island, studded with churches, one great dazzling jewel that was Notre-Dame, and a small, exquisite gem that was Sainte-Chapelle. The morning sunlight lit up the twin towers of the great cathedral which the Protestant Henri de Navarre, now Catholic monarch of France, had been forbidden to enter for the consecration of his own marriage to Marguerite de Valois.

Henry had a liking for this king whose Christian name he bore, this hero of a few battles and many assignations, who loved his bastards quite as much as his legitimate brood, and who had done so much to improve and beautify this great city. True, he had changed his religion, but only to heal the breach that cut the nation in two. For a decade there had been peace and prosperity. The king had been right, Paris was indeed "worth a mass." It was said that he had surreptitiously sent food to the suffering population he was besieging; and to insure religious tolerance, had he not signed a special edict at Nantes?

Not so long ago, in the time of Henry's father, the sparkling stream below had been tinged with the blood of men stabbed in their beds, and hurled, half alive, from those very windows along the banks. The past, thought Henry, lives side by side with the present, and the same tocsin from Saint-Germain-l'Auxerrois that now called the good people to prayer had sounded the signal for human slaughter one Saint Bartholomew's day.

But such horrors were over. The last century had been one not only of renaissance but of bloody reform. Hatred and torture had come out of a difference in the manner of worshiping God. Montaigne had written, ". . . skepticism as a means of tolerance, and through tolerance serenity." Let people worship God any way they chose, or not at all.

Moreover, Henry suspected that the frenetic spirit of the people had been exploited for plunder as well as for piety, for many who had been poor suddenly became rich, with possessions they had neither inherited nor earned.

He strolled over to the students' quarter on the other side of the river where print shops clustered around the colleges. He bought a few books, then stopped to eat at a cookshop on the rue de la Harpe near the Hôtel de Cluny. It was crowded with those students who could afford to supplement the meager fare offered them at the college refectories to the accompaniment of sermons on the virtue of abstemiousness. The air was thick with controversy in many tongues.

After luncheon Henry wandered through the rue de la Huchette. Some of the pretty girls who smiled at him were honest prostitutes, while others were decoys to lure men into dark doorways where they would be robbed if they didn't resist, and murdered if they did. Henry had been warned of the pitfalls of the great city; moreover, wenching was not his vice.

In the late afternoon he found himself in the rue Saint-Denis, tired and in need of refreshment. As he was entering a wineshop he was stopped by two soldiers with arquebuses and requested to show his credentials. The place seemed strange, the occupants whispering or eying each other furtively. He ordered a dry sack and had scarcely tasted it when a rumble arose in the street, as if words were being rolled from mouth to mouth, gathering volume. Those inside who were seated rose, for they knew what was being said, even before the bell tolled. In silence they removed their caps and made the sign of the cross.

The soldiers who had been at the door burst in. "The king is dead," cried one, "God rest his soul."

Bit by bit Henry learned that scarcely three hours before His Majesty had driven past this very door. He was returning from a visit to Sully, his minister, and on his way to see the beautiful Angélique Paulet. He was reading a letter as his open carriage turned into the rue de la Ferronnerie. Suddenly a madman . . . a stranger from Angoulême, named Ravaillac, who had been loitering around the quarter for days . . . sprang out from nowhere and plunged a dagger twice into the monarch's heart.

The proprietor raised his tankard. "The king is dead; long live the young king, thirteenth of his name, Louis the Just."

"Why 'the Just'?" asked Henry. "He is but a child of nine."

"Because, monsieur, he was born under the sign of Libra, the Balance. The astrologers cannot be wrong."

The body of Henri IV lay in the Salle des Cariatides at the Louvre while most of the nation mourned. Those of his mistresses who were alive . . . history has recorded some fifty-six . . . his many children and his divorced wife, Marguerite, wept sincerely. What his widow felt is not easy to determine. Was it a document he was reading, another one of Sully's requests for repairs, bridges or canals? Or was it a love letter that had absorbed him when he met the blow of the assassin's knife?

Ravaillac was duly tried, drawn and quartered, and the nation settled down to unrest under the reign of a delicate, peevish boy and the regency of his mother, who could scarcely speak French, and who was under the domination of that sinister Italian couple, the Concinis. Leonora Concini, it was said, seldom left her apartments in the palace for fear of encountering the evil eye.

Chapter III

IN a short time Henry found proper lodgings near the Place Royale.[1] He soon made friends to his taste, for the Marais was the rendezvous of the freethinkers, or *esprits forts*. He enjoyed the fashionable gathering places as well as the lowest dives with the adaptability of youth. He ate well, drank moderately, played his lute, bought books and never missed a performance of the Strolling Players of the Marais. He kept himself and his horse well groomed and carefully avoided work. This happy life was interrupted by a short exile from Paris for the use of obscene and blasphemous language.

When his money ran out he joined a group of itinerant musicians composed of idlers and petty thieves with a jailbird or two in the woodwinds. They were under the leadership of a well-known musical family called Gaultier. Denis and Jacques were the virtuosi and Ennemond, called Gaultier le Vieux, was the conductor. When the ensemble had no regular engagements they were not above playing in courtyards, passing the hat around and picking up coins thrown from the windows.

After a time Henry tired of this vagrant life. He began to cultivate people who might be of use to him. Soon his charm

[1] In the sixteenth century this place was occupied by the Palais de Tournelles and it was there that Henri II met accidental death in a jousting match. His widow, Catherine de Medici, had the palace razed. In 1605, Henri IV transformed it into a park enclosed in a square of pink pavilions intended as ateliers for the manufacture of silk. For two centuries the arcades housed the finest shops and restaurants, and the park was the gathering place of the fashionable world and the site of many duels. In 1799 the name was changed to the Place des Vosges. It is now a workmen's quarter, but every year on the birthday of Henri IV a torchlight festival is held there with banquet tables under the arcades.

and his knowledge of horses procured him the place of equerry to the duc d'Elbeuf, a prince of the house of Lorraine.

Under the regency tolerance began to diminish; the hounds of fanaticism strained at the leash. The Catholic Church began introducing monastic orders from Spain and Italy and the uneasy Protestants banded together. *Libertinage*, a philosophy of free thought whose leader was Pierre Gassendi,[2] tried to reconcile Epicurean doctrine with Christian faith. Leonora Concini managed to dodge the evil eye well enough to amass a fortune and make her husband a marshal of France, maréchal d'Ancre. When the king became sixteen he manifested his manhood by having the marshal murdered, and when the deed was accomplished he cried:

"Now I am king. Of course I have always been king, but in future I shall be king more than ever."

The household of a nobleman when in Paris consisted of his troops, his entertainers, his rich friends and poor relations, many of whom ate at his table and rode his horses. He had an immense staff of servants—coachmen, footmen, cooks, kitchen maids, *maîtres d'hôtel*, butlers, stableboys and pages. The lackeys, often of dubious character, were ill paid, ate the leavings of the great hall and slept wherever they could find an unoccupied corner. But like the rest of the ménage, they were under the protection of the master whose livery they wore. In return for his protection they owed his allegiance. They were, in a sense, his subjects first, and the king's after. They often grew old and died in his service.

In addition, there were the pensioners, retired soldiers, chaplains, almoners, physicians; men of letters, painters and musicians, whose duties consisted of praising their lord in verse or paint, of furthering his intrigues, hating his enemies, writing his love letters, supplying him with wit and saving his soul.

One of the requirements of Henry's new position was to become a snob. Since professional musicians enjoyed a status little better than that of upper servants, he looked down his nose at his former associates, avoiding encounters with them and refer-

[2] The discoverer of atmospheric pressure.

ring to them as "scum." For a time he even convinced himself that he despised music, and put aside his lute.

As his duties were light, he enjoyed a considerable amount of freedom in his new position. There were a number of young matrons whose husbands were away, or enjoying the company of their mistresses, and Henry had a few minor episodes, but he did not fall seriously in love. He was invited to a number of homes where he conducted himself with due decorum.

He found an especially warm welcome at the house of Nicolas de Gouge, where he was regarded as one of the family. Two daughters, Marie and Lucrèce, were then ten and eight years old. He brought them gifts, fondled them and treated them as would an indulgent uncle, not realizing that the younger girl soon began to develop romantic notions about him.

When Henry was about twenty-four he decided that a respectable marriage with a suitable *partie* would further his career. He chose Marie-Barbe de la Marche, the timid, devout daughter of an influential family.[3] Marie-Barbe had learned to read, but she used this accomplishment only in the interest of saving her soul. She was utterly unworldly, with the quiet obstinacy that often accompanies meekness. She married Henry because her parents wished it, and because she looked forward to giving joy to heaven by leading at least one sinner to repentance.

A marriage could hardly have been worse. In a short time the Lanclos household became a battlefield for opposing doctrines. There were occasional truces after each of which, in due time, a child was born. The eldest, Charles, had as godparents the duc d'Elbeuf and the comtesse de Fiesque, and two years later Léonor was sponsored by the marquis de Saint-Luc and the duchesse d'Elbeuf.[4]

[3] Influential because the elder daughter, Madeleine, had married a man whose younger brother, Charles-François d'Abra de Reconis, had his feet planted on the first rung of the ladder of success: he was a favorite of the clever bishop of Luçon, Armand du Plessis, destined to become Cardinal Richelieu.

[4] These boys have never again been mentioned and it is reasonable to assume that they died in infancy or very early childhood. The infant mortality rate was so high that it was hardly worthy of comment.

The family moved from the rue des Petits-Champs to an apartment in the parish of Saint-Jean-en-Grève, and Henry quit the service of Elbeuf and entered that of Timoléon d'Epinay, maréchal de Saint-Luc, His Majesty's governor at Bourges. He was made a lieutenant and later promoted to a captaincy in charge of infantry.

The marshal was a generous, crude, lusty Norman who preferred revelry to battle and Paris to the provinces. He sang off key and wrote bad verse. At his *hôtel* on the Place Royale he gathered all the good fellows and bad women of the Marais: petty noblemen, soldiers of fortune, scholars and ruffians. The common denominator was some education and much wit.

Dinners lasted four or five hours. The tables were loaded with game and joints; often one kind of meat would be served cooked in three different ways. There were three or four soups and every fish and vegetable the season offered. In addition there were complicated stews and *pâtés*, for the French cuisine under two Medici queens had taken on an Italian flavor. There were sausages from every province and birds stuffed with smaller birds. It was quite in order for a guest to reach for a morsel with his fingers, examine it and exchange it for another more to his taste. Mouths were greasy and hands were wiped on the edge of the tablecloth or on the back of a passing dog.

In this company Henry found compensation for the austerity of his home. Here his music was welcome. He improvised verses to his own accompaniment and distinguished himself by table conversation that made the harlots blush.

In the year 1619 Henry had a good subject for his ballads. There was rejoicing in the streets; the young king had after four years of marriage begun to make love to the queen. There was hope of a dauphin. Louis XIII at the age of fourteen had married the fourteen-year-old Anne of Austria, daughter of the king of Spain. Split by the growing rift between the great nobles on the one hand and the regent, Marie de Medici, the boy king and the corrupt Concinis on the other, France needed the assurance of an heir to the throne. Ears were glued to the door of the royal bedchamber. It was good material for ribald verse. In a few months, however, the joy subsided, for there was a miscarriage at the palace.

In the year 1620 Ferdinand II reigned over the Holy Roman Empire, Philip III over Spain, Gustavus Adolphus over Sweden and James I over Great Britain. In November of that year a girl was born to the Lanclos family and on the tenth she was christened in the church of Saint-Jean-en-Grève. Her godparents were Nicolas de Villetret, King's Counselor and Treasurer General Extraordinary for War, and his daughter Anne. The baby performed her part of the ceremony with no accidents, and it is said that her career of charming people began about this time. "Anne" soon became affectionately Annine, Nannine and finally Ninon. The name Anne was used only by her mother and when Mademoiselle de Lanclos signed documents.

Her father was devoted to the child, and when at an early age she manifested qualities resembling his own, he took charge of her education. He taught her Italian and a little Spanish; mathematics and philosophy followed. She read what she chose, and in their discussions he never talked down to her. Soon Henry began to enjoy in his daughter the companionship he missed with his wife, and when she showed an interest in music, he began her instruction on the lute.

To counteract this, Marie-Barbe made the girl read sacred books, dressed her in somber colors with ill-cut bodices that flattened the growing young breasts. She made her cover her throat and hide her lovely chestnut curls in a calico kerchief.

Chapter IV

NINON would practice a new piece on the lute, or compose a verse that might merit her father's praise, but when at long last he came he scarcely noticed. He was secretive, preoccupied and eager to get away, and it did not escape her that a name he had so often mentioned in the past, that of Lucrèce de Gouge, no longer passed his lips.

Henry had continued his visits to the Gouge family. Marie, the elder daughter, married a retired officer of the Scots Guards, Simon Le Tellier, but Lucrèce refused all offers, nursing a secret passion for Henry. When she was twenty-five, however, realizing that the desultory attentions of a married man could lead to nothing but unhappiness, she yielded to the suit Jean de Riberolles, an advocate from Périgord, who seemed to her parents to be a good match.

It was not long after the wedding that Riberolles manifested his dour disposition with leanings toward brutality. Lucrèce had not seen Henry since her marriage, and it was quite natural that she should magnify his virtues, compare him to her husband and indulge in daydreams of what might have been. She persuaded Riberolles that a man in Henry's position might be useful to him, and suggested that he renew the acquaintance. Henry accepted the advocate's advances without enthusiasm, visited the house occasionally when invited, but took no initiative in furthering the friendship.

Riberolles had to return to Périgord on business and decided to leave his young wife behind. Lucrèce managed to conceal her delight as she kissed him good-by. As he left her without maintenance, she was obliged to take up her residence with her sister

24

and brother-in-law. She began at once to enjoy the freedom which marriage had prohibited and, as is frequently the case, used her new freedom for a new entanglement.

Captain de Lanclos became a frequent visitor to the Le Tellier apartment on the rue Saint-Anastase. There were cozy dinners for four, and toasts were often drunk to the prolonged absence of the advocate. Both Marie and Simon were fond of Henry, and had little liking for the tricky Périgourdin. Soon Henry, for the first time in his life, was deeply in love.

At night he would ostensibly leave the house, closing the door noisily. Then he would wait in a doorway until all the lights had been extinguished. He would creep back, boots in hand, to a door that had been cautiously unlatched. In time, however, all subterfuge was abandoned, and he spent every hour that he could spare with his mistress. When the nights proved all too short, he would remain in Lucrèce's chamber all day, and if callers arrived unexpectedly he would hide doubled up under the staircase.

From time to time the lovers found it necessary to use the sordid lodgings of Lucrèce's maid, Françoise du Charme, where they installed a new and clean bed. The devotion of this servant was somewhat motivated by curiosity or prurience, because years later, when testifying, she asserted that "Captain de Lanclos had fondled Madame de Riberolles's breast under her nightgown, and that furthermore the said Captain had slapped the aforementioned Madame de Riberolles on the thigh, which action she had not appeared to resent." These gestures could hardly have been witnessed without benefit of keyhole.

The rue Saint-Anastase was a short street mainly inhabited by shopkeepers, whose dull evenings were enlivened by peering from behind shutters or strolling beneath windows to catch stray bits of conversation. The lovers grew careless, and it was not long before everyone in the neighborhood knew of the affair except, of course, Marie-Barbe, who believed her husband busy recruiting men to invade the Rhine provinces of the Holy Roman Empire.

Richelieu had forced on the king an alliance with Gustavus

Adolphus, and Catholic France found herself fighting on the side of the Swedish and North German Protestants. Ninon knew her father was still in the Marais occupied with his own private skirmishes. Whenever she could, she went to the vicinity of the Hôtel Saint-Luc, hoping to run into him, but as this did not happen she decided to give fate a little push. She wrote a letter which was dispatched to him by Jeanne, who promised to keep her secret.

> My honored Father:
>
> I am nearly eleven. I am big and strong. But I shall certainly become ill if I attend three masses a day, especially the ones said by a gouty, fat canon who takes ages to get through the Epistles and the Gospel, and whom the choir boys have to put back on his feet after every genuflexion. In the interest of your only daughter, it is time to put an end to this state of affairs. How, you will ask, is this to be done? Nothing more simple.
>
> Let us suppose that if, instead of me, Heaven had sent you a boy. I should have been brought up by you instead of my mother. You would have already instructed me in arms and mounted me on a horse. This would please me much better than twiddling along the beads of a rosary to *Aves, Paters* and *Credos.*
>
> I inform you now that I have decided to be a girl no longer, but to become a boy.
>
> Will you please arrange to send for me to come to you in order to give me the education suitable to my new sex.
>
> I am, with respect, my very honored sire,
>
> Ninon

Years later she wrote to Boisrobert, "Men enjoy a thousand privileges which women never have. From this moment, I have become a man."

Henry, amused and also touched by this childish appeal for attention, returned home. He took Ninon to his tailor and had her outfitted with a doublet and breeches of pale blue, and a short cloak of burgundy velvet. His *cordonnier* made her a pair of riding boots, and at a fashionable *chapellerie* on the Place Royale they bought a beaver, turned gracefully up on one side, with a little plume . . . her *panache*. He could not resist showing her off at the Hôtel Saint-Luc. She learned to ride and to fence and soon became the darling of the guardsmen. She also enriched her vocabulary with the jargon of the stables.

As Paris was suffering from the plague, Henry took Ninon to spend the summer at Loches, where his sister had a château. The lady welcomed her niece, who arrived dressed as a nephew.

There are stories that she met the eighteen-year-old prince de Marcillac, later the duc de la Rochefoucauld, at Loches, and that they enjoyed a happy companionship, exploring the caves, going on picnics and fighting mock duels. Some even claim that there was a sentimental attachment.

This is highly improbable. The author of the *Maxims* had then been married for three years. Doubtless it was one of those child marriages arranged by families of the nobility and not yet consummated; he and Ninon may well have met, but neither one ever mentions it.

Years later they became good friends but were never lovers. La Rochefoucauld's three distinguished mistresses are well known to history.

Chapter V

For two years Lucrèce had no word from Riberolles; then, all at once, abusive letters began to arrive. Someone had told.

One day, with no warning, he turned up at Le Tellier's apartment. Just as unexpectedly, he implored his wife's forgiveness for his letters and for not having provided her with the necessary maintenance during his absence. With protestations of devotion he persuaded Lucrèce to return to him. No sooner were they under one roof than his motive became apparent. He had found a way of making a living which was easier than practicing law. If his wife pleased one man, why not others? Lucrèce let loose a volley of abuse which he meekly accepted. After that he alternated between threats and cajolery and when money ran out he pawned her dowry silver.

One day he brought a chancellor home and, crudely pointing to the bed, told her to enjoy herself with the gentleman. Frightened, Lucrèce pleaded indisposition and the man left, crestfallen. Thereupon Monsieur Riberolles grabbed her by the hair and began searching for his sword which he managed not to find. She thereupon left his bed and board and took up her residence with a Mademoiselle Marchand in the house where her sister lived. She then entered a complaint at the Châtelet for a legal separation.

Lucrèce and Henry became reckless; nothing mattered but being together. To this end relatives, friends and servants connived. The husband took no steps except to keep himself informed. The legal mind was at work. One day he met his wife on the Place Royale and loudly denounced her as a whore, whereupon a chivalrous passer-by drew his sword and put him to flight.

When Riberolles realized that there was no possibility of earning his living as his wife's panderer, he embarked on a cunning project that cast its shadow over many lives for years to come.

He took into his service Françoise du Charme, Lucrèce's former maid, who had been in the confidence of the lovers. He then gathered information from neighbors, servants and tradespeople and drew up a set of affidavits based on truth and embellished with falsehood. Then he brought the case before the *prévost*. For a year the parties thereto brought accusations and counteraccusations. As many of the witnesses had disappeared, or seemed to have lost their memories, the case was dismissed.

He then took it to the criminal court and dragged everybody into it. Pages of interrogations have been recorded which read remarkably like the court records of a modern divorce trial. The defendants denied the allegation. The suit dragged on for three years, during which time Henry's devotion never wavered. Eventually the Court ruled that "nothing that had been alleged could be found."

The lawsuit had been the breath of life to Riberolles and after the verdict he was completely deflated. He tried transferring it from one jurisdiction to another, continued his search for new witnesses and started a campaign of slander including the accusation that the lovers had eaten meat during Lent.

Paris had been devastated by plague, famine and fire. The bodies of newborn infants were found in holes and ditches; robbers and assassins flourished. The aristocracy had fled from infection to their châteaux or closed themselves in behind the walls of their *hôtels;* the poor could only pray to what they believed to be a wrathful God. And through it all Maître Jean de Riberolles lay awake night after night plotting his revenge.

Henry realized his danger and never went out unarmed. Unlike Siegfried, he slept with Lucrèce on one side and his sword on the other.

A group of Périgourdins took up the Riberolles cause. Their leader, Louis de Chabans, was an unscrupulous man, influential by virtue of his property. To defend the honor of Périgord he hired a band of ruffians under the leadership of a man he had helped to get out of jail.

One night as Henry was returning to the Hôtel Saint-Luc he noticed a man flattened against the wall, and on the other side of the gate Riberolles crouching between two of his brothers. Suddenly the stranger sprang from the darkness with a drawn sword, but Henry was ready and put the whole band to flight.

His nerves on edge, Henry decided to take the offensive. He sought out the witnesses who had testified against him, threatening their lives if they did not retract. He carried his campaign of terror up and down the rue Saint-Anastase. He dragged a woman who had invented a few gratuitous details to the street. He threatened to kill her unless she admitted that she had lied to the judge, and "gave her several blows with his foot, his hand, and a stick," until her screams brought the neighbors to her aid. She filed a complaint and he was arrested and confined in the Conciergerie. Fuming at his incarceration, he flooded the magistrate with appeals, claiming that the witness was "a debauched girl and the whore of Riberolles, having borne an illegitimate child, due to the work of the latter."

As pummeling (*frotter*) a woman was not a major offense, he was soon released. Chabans and his gang continued to harass him in the interests of Périgourdine cuckoldry. Henry's hatred was deflected from Riberolles to Chabans and he sought in all the haunts of the Marais, but in vain. Since he was a general of the Republic at Venice, Henry conceived the idea that sooner or later he would visit the Venetian Embassy behind the Minimes, and it was there that he lay in wait. Lying in wait took up a good deal of his time.

On the day after Christmas, in 1632, a carriage drove up to the embassy and Chabans alighted and entered the building. Henry hid behind the vehicle, and when the general returned, he ran him through. His revenge accomplished, he fled Paris, and no attempt was made to bar his way.

Madame de Chabans appealed to the Crown to avenge her husband's death, but the culprit had already crossed the frontier.

Tallemant des Réaux, a contemporary chronicler and later a neighbor of Ninon, wrote:

. . . her father was obliged to flee France for having slain Chabans in circumstances that might pass for an assassination, for the other had his foot still in the doorway when l'Enclos thrust his sword into him.

and then continues:

During his absence the girl became quite big. . . . She never had any great measure of beauty, but she had always much pleasantness.

Chapter VI

AT fifteen, Ninon was a brat. Neither her mother nor the curé could influence her. She made the most of her developing figure, and she wiggled her hips. She read indiscriminately and was interested in the wrong things: dancing, secular songs and pretty clothes. Some of the hostesses of the neighborhood, therefore, found that their receptions were more successful if they invited the little Lanclos girl to entertain their guests not only with her drawing-room accomplishments but with her precocious conversation as well.

To placate her mother Ninon accompanied her to mass at the Minimes, but instead of being influenced in favor of the Church, what she saw there had quite the opposite effect. The latest fashions were displayed. Women in dazzling jewels and daring décolletés flirted openly with swains who obviously regarded the church as an antechamber to the alcove. Love notes were passed in hymnals and quick caresses stolen under the noses of the priests.

When Ninon's eyes were discreetly lowered to her breviary, it was because between its covers she had concealed some pages of Rabelais or *Les Contes de la Reine de Navarre*.

On Palm Sunday a guest preacher of renown delivered a sermon on the Passion. The church was crowded to capacity. Dramatically the priest evoked the scene of Calvary, the torture of the Divine Crucified. He described Jesus taken down from the cross, wrapped in linen and laid in the sepulchre. In a low but penetrating voice he closed with: "Our Lord is dead."

The frivolous congregation was deeply moved. There was a moment of silence and then a sound of sobbing was heard. But before the organist could begin the chords which were to accompany the offertory, a soft clear voice sang:

> ". . . et pourquoi pleurer?
> S"il meurt
> Qu'importe?
> Devant votre beauté
> Il sera résuscité."

(". . . and why cry? If he (it) should die, what does it signify? Before your beauty he (it) shall rise again.")

This was the refrain of a Spanish song popular at the time. It was hummed by women to their lovers with an obvious double meaning.

There were a few nervous titters and heads began to turn in the direction of the voice. Ninon lowered her eyes, but she could not control the blush that rose to her cheeks. Madame de Lanclos, though she did not understand the allusion, was horrified. After the service she took Ninon to the vestry to apologize to the reverend father. The interview turned into a theological discussion in which the priest was not always the interrogator. Marie-Barbe's hope that her daughter might eventually take the veil received a serious setback.

The next best thing would be a suitable, respectable marriage. Ninon was beginning to get out of hand, seeming to manifest the traits of her father. Madame de Lanclos realized, however, that good families would not encourage an alliance with a girl who had no dowry, and whose father had fled the country in disgrace. She hoped, however, that Anne's charm and lively disposition would attract some worthy young man.

The group that surrounded Ninon were for the most part of the lesser nobility. The lack of money in the royal coffers forced the Crown to create and sell offices, both military and civil. The titles which accompanied these posts enabled their holders in turn to negotiate advantageous marriages for their children. The young generation looked down their noses at the class from which they had sprung. With their new titles, serious occupation, outside of battle, was unthinkable. Intrigue was the order, adventure an end in itself. Patriotism and loyalty were at a low ebb and young men frequently switched sides in a controversy for quite trivial reasons. Yet paradoxically, they sacrificed their lives readily.

Madame de Lanclos welcomed these young visitors at her new apartment on the rue des Trois Pavillons.[1] They were well dressed, had courtly manners and were too young to show the effects of their dissipation. She gave Ninon more liberty than was the custom, taking for granted that her daughter would hold what she thought of as the "supreme sacrifice" for the conjugal bed.

"My mother," Ninon wrote years later, "was a good woman with no sensory feeling. She procreated three children, scarcely noticing it."

The atmosphere of Paris was charged with love-making. On the slightest provocation, or none, men wrote sentimental verse, and no woman dropped a glove or a handkerchief unintentionally. The Place Royale, with its high privet hedges trained in the forms of love symbols, was known as *le centre voluptueux* of Paris. Despite the prohibition, duelists sought its seclusion at midnight, parrying and thrusting by the light of lanterns. On fine afternoons in spring it was a veritable drawing room under the sky. The *grand-monde* and the *demi-monde*, not always distinguishable, strolled in its shaded paths, scarcely remarking the couples locked in embrace. Chatter and laughter rivaled the song of the birds in the well-clipped elms overhead.

Beauties, sometimes with velvet hoods over their elaborate coiffures, walked seductively in their bouffant skirts, slashed in front to reveal puffed and beribboned petticoats. Their court-plaster patches, or *mouches*, indicated what they had to offer. Worn near the left eye or the right, at a corner of the mouth, or on the chin, each signaled a specific promise. The most daring, known as an *assassine*, was worn low on the breast. Bows of satin and velvet also spoke a language. The *favori* was worn in the hair, the *mignon* on the heart, while one suspended from a fan was called a *badin*. Flowers, as well as fans, were important

[1] Now the rue de l'Elzévir.

accessories, to this art of mute communication. The dandies, with lace ruffs beneath their long, curled hair, with plumes and slashed sleeves, flowing ribbons and elaborate garters, were all conversant with the idiom. Flirtation was a serious occupation.

The old cookshops had developed into restaurants serving the finest produce of the surrounding farms and the best vintages of the *Halles-aux-vins*. Some were known as *restaurants discrets*. These had private dining rooms where a lady might go cloaked and masked, and where the waiters, after knocking, counted ten before entering. Some of the crude wineshops and gambling houses were becoming fashionable, and a great deal of money changed hands. The most notorious was the Pomme de Pin. Entrance to the Place Royale was prohibited to beggars and vagrants, so that one could enjoy the afternoon undisturbed by the sight of poverty.

Ninon watched and listened to everything with mingled excitement and envy. She caught snatches of conversation which she understood only too well, and when a cavalier's eyes left his lady long enough to rest on her fresh face or luscious figure, she turned pink, but by no means resentful.

There were days when she visited the Jardin des Apothicaires.[1] Sometimes she wandered among the bookstalls near the Sorbonne, way over on the other side of the river.

Music and dancing, books and young friends helped to pass Ninon's days during the waiting period of youth, but on the long summer evenings, when her admirers were at the gaming houses, or making love to women whose husbands were at the gaming houses, Ninon found the sanctimonious atmosphere of her home very trying, and her mind wandered from her mother's conversation about household and church matters. The *gros point* which most young ladies found absorbing bored her. She considered handiwork a waste of time. Sometimes she sat at the window watching young housemaids and laundresses strolling by with their lovers' arms about their waists; in a shadowy doorway or beneath a tree she often saw two figures pressed close, and then she found it difficult to concentrate on her book. Music,

[1] Now Jardin des Plantes.

which usually gave her so much pleasure, now sometimes made her cry. But these moods passed. Innately gay, she found occupations to improve her mind and distract her thoughts; and in the afternoons she lent herself with a little more abandon to surreptitious embraces.

Charles-Claude de Beaumont, vicomte de Chaumusy, sieur de Saint-Etienne, may have been handsomer, wittier or more pleasing than the other young men who tried to make love to her. He was certainly more importunate, and he was her mother's favorite. He intimated to Madame de Lanclos that his object was matrimony. Ninon had no wish to disillusion her mother. Saint-Etienne became Ninon's first lover, and her emotions at this time have been a matter of conjecture. No doubt she fancied herself "in love." But there was also curiosity, sensuousness, a desire to overcome the obstacle of virginity; perhaps resentment at her mother's restrictions played a part in her surrender, if a considerable amount of co-operation can be so called.

After a short time Madame de Lanclos noticed that Saint-Etienne's attentions diminished. He came less often, and Ninon mentioned nothing about a marriage. She assumed a lovers' quarrel, and put herself out to be pleasant to the young man, unaware that he was not always quite sober. Besides being a drinker and a gambler, he had a loose tongue, and he boasted of his conquest at the Pomme de Pin. A rumor reached Madame de Lanclos which she could not believe. She questioned Ninon, who admitted the truth.

Had her daughter confessed her sin tearfully, had she been pregnant but repentant, she would have forgiven her. She might even have experienced a secret joy that her child, who, alas, was showing the blood of her father, having learned of the perfidy of men, might now turn to God. But she was shocked at this strange girl who showed no remorse, who bore no ill will toward her seducer, who accepted equal responsibility with him for her conduct. Her own flesh and blood was a stranger.

Ninon was disillusioned with her lover, but not with love. Saint-Etienne had served his purpose. She just hoped for better luck next time.

Chapter VII

PARIS was expanding. The crumbling fortifications had given way to broad, tree-lined boulevards. Streets of misshapen dwellings near the Louvre had been ruthlessly demolished by Richelieu to build his Palais Cardinal, ten years under construction. The shops, behind windows of rounded glass, began to display the treasures of Europe and the Orient. Wrought-iron signs, swinging at right angles above the doors, pictured dwarfs, mermaids, dragons, bicornes and fleurs-de-lys; there were signs with devils and angels, with boots, gloves, or candles; the taverns displayed red lions, black cats, white horses or golden cockerels.

Ladies might leave their sedan chairs to make purchases without splattering their voluminous skirts with mud, for now tumbrels drove daily through the main thoroughfares to collect such refuse as their drivers could shovel up, and the shopkeeper who did not sweep and wash before his door was fined. If a gentleman went about on foot, however, he stopped in the courtyard of a dwelling to change his boots for satin slippers before paying a call. It was considered vulgar to enter a lady's drawing room smelling of the gutter.

Paris was growing not only in size and beauty but in its opportunities for enjoyment and culture as well. The establishment of the royal printing press had made the Sorbonne, which had been the gathering place of scholars from the time of Abelard, the greatest center of learning in Europe. *La Gazette de France*, a weekly, had made its debut in 1631, and in 1635 the group of intellectuals surrounding Valentin Conrart made themselves heard through the canon Boisrobert, who was a favorite of Richelieu, and L'Académie Française was born.

In the salons, the gardens and the restaurants, people were discussing the campaign, the intrigues against His Eminence, Marie de Medici's exile by her son and such scientific matters as the recently discovered sunspots and the manner in which the blood circulated, according to a new theory by an English physician.

The Marais continued to be the center of social and cultural activities. The old *hôtels* of the aristocracy were rivaled by the opulent new ones of the wealthy merchants and taxgatherers.

The theatre had come a long way. The mystery plays of the sixteenth century had been forbidden by *parlement*.[1] No longer did the Holy Ghost descend in a flare of burning brandy, nor was the priest raised on a cross while the antics of devils formed the comic relief. The opening of the seventeenth century saw the Strolling Players of the Marais giving somewhat extemporary performances based on the Italian commedia del' arte, and soon this gave way to real plays performed in theatres.

Bucolic pieces known as *bergeries* were popular. Le Théâtre de l'Hôtel de Bourgogne in the parish of Saint-Eustache, so well portrayed in Rostand's *Cyrano de Bergerac*, rented its license to a new group devoted to low comedy and obscene farce as well as tragicomedy. The scenes of the play were set simultaneously running from left to right across the stage, and in this medium Hardy had written some six hundred pieces, but he had added a new element: conflict and suspense. His plays remained in the repertory for over thirty years.

The Théâtre du Marais on the rue Vieille-du-Temple was under the direction of Mondory. He had produced a series of comedies by Pierre Corneille, and had encouraged the playwright to venture into more serious fields. In 1636, *Le Cid* was produced, with Mondory playing Rodrigue. This play added the element of inner conflict, the struggle of man, not against his fate or his enemies, but against himself.

At the beginning of the century the theatre was strictly the sport of man, but gradually a few bold women began to attend, wearing masks. They sat, chaperoned by duennas, in the upper

[1] A purely judicial body with no legislative power but the power of remonstrance.

boxes, watching the spectacle in the pit below, which was illuminated by hundreds of candles in sparkling lusters. Near the
door sat a woman, who "had to be clean and civil," selling cider
and beverages of syrup in summer, and in winter liquors, Spanish
wine and *rivesalts*.[1] The pageants and crude satires attracted an
audience of ruffians, but the better plays brought a mondaine
public in *grande toilette*.

In the intermissions someone might decide to practice a musical
instrument, or a duel might be fought on the spot over the relative
merits of two playwrights. And all the time love messages went
back and forth between beribboned cavaliers and their lady loves
in the gallery. The theatre was as good a place as the church for
arranging assignations.

Madame de Lanclos did not approve of the theatre. She had
never been in one, but she recognized the work of the Devil
whatever its manifestation. Her failing health kept her at home
much of the time, and the friends who came were as little interested in the arts as she. The most frequent visitor was the
curé, who brought her consolation and gossip.

With no formal instruction, Ninon seemed to have a gift for
absorbing knowledge. In an age where most women and many
men could neither read nor write, when spelling was a matter
of discretion, and culture confined to the salons whose doors
were closed to her, she managed to pick up a serious education.
She spoke both Italian and Spanish, read the Greek classics in
translation, and some of the Latin in the original. Later on her
education was continued by the three men she called her "eman-
cipators," but at this time her instinctive taste was her only guide.
She could manage to buy and to borrow books, but going to the
theatre was not easy.

Nevertheless, on a blustering afternoon in February she managed to attend a performance of *Le Cid* at the Marais, leaving
Jeanne, her chaperone, in a tavern warming her old bones with
eau-de-vie and gossiping with her cronies. Ninon was enchanted
by the poetry, and gripped by the story. It was some minutes
after the curtain fell that she was brought back to reality.

[1] A white wine from the Pyrenées.

39

As she was leaving the theatre she noticed a group of men having a heated discussion about the play. The center of the group was a man in his late twenties. He was rather short, well built; he wore the habit of a canon, but his language was anything but canonical. It was witty and impious, and Ninon stopped to catch what he was saying. He was having an argument with a man who apparently did not like the play, and who said he agreed with Richelieu that it was an outrage to have a Spanish hero when France was at war with Spain. The canon replied that art was above politics, and went into an analysis of the drama. Moreover, he said, His Scarlet Eminence was jealous because his own plays were not so good, and annoyed because Corneille had refused to follow the rules he had laid down. Then someone called out, "Beware, Monsieur Scarron, the trees have ears."

The name Paul Scarron was not unknown to Ninon. The poet and satirist already had some reputation in the Marais. As she turned to go she caught sight of the chevalier de Raré, one of the young men who came to her house.

"I see Monsieur Scarron's wit pleases you," he said. "Would you like to meet him?" He turned to the canon. "Monsieur Scarron, this is Mademoiselle de Lanclos. She has been admiring you. May I present her?"

"The young lady shows taste," said Scarron, smiling. "You are not the daughter of Henry de Lanclos?" Ninon nodded. "I knew him by reputation. He was a fine musician, I understand. How did you like the play?"

"It was the most wonderful play I ever saw," said Ninon, and then added, "It was the first one I ever saw."

Scarron laughed and paid her a compliment. The group dispersed, and as she walked away with Raré, she noticed that Scarron limped a little. They walked to the tavern where Jeanne was waiting, and on the way he told her something of the poet.

His father had been a councilor of *parlement* and the young man was a canon at Le Mans. But he was not very pious and managed to spend much of his time in the Marais, where he was one of the leading spirits. With the income from his post, and a small inheritance, he was able to enjoy life and in his spare time he wrote.

The previous year, at the carnival at Le Mans, he had masqueraded as a rooster. Stripped, he had rolled in honey and then feathers. As he walked among the revelers he began to molt. The honey trickled away and the feathers dropped, and just when his nakedness was becoming embarrassing, he saw two of the elders approaching. Because of his worldliness he was not in their good graces anyway, but this would have been the end. Before they recognized him he turned and fled and the crowd, amused at his plight, pursued him. As he was crossing a bridge they gained on him and he jumped into the river. He swam toward shore and waited until the crowd dispelled and he could go home under cover of darkness. Soon after he was taken to bed with chills and a fever. The doctor tried bleeding, poultices and purging, all in vain. Rheumatism soon set in and was now beginning to cripple him.

Young Henri de Lancy, chevalier de Raré, was better-looking and better-mannered than Saint-Etienne. His father had been wounded in the service of Monsieur, and he had been raised at the Hôtel d'Orléans in an atmosphere of intrigue and treachery.

Soon, despite her mother's vigilance, Ninon had embarked on an affair with Raré. Clandestine meetings may have made love more piquant, but they certainly made it less comfortable.

One afternoon when Raré had promised to pass at four, Ninon sat at the window, impatiently waiting, trying to read but straining to discern his figure. He was nearly an hour late, but she was reluctant to leave her post. At last she recognized him and, making an excuse to her mother, ran eagerly down to the street. Oblivious of the passers-by, they exchanged embraces and tender words. As they were locked in each other's arms, a beggar approached and made an appeal for a few *sols*. At first they took no notice, but as his demands became more insistent Ninon told Raré to give him something. As usual, the young man had nothing to give. The mendicant stood there, looking from one to the other, and Ninon pulled out her lace handkerchief and gave it to him, saying, "Take this—it is worth at least ten *sols*—and leave us in peace." Whereupon the lovers returned to their established position.

If one dare draw a conclusion from so slight an episode it might be that Ninon was a sensuous, somewhat aggressive young lady, indifferent to public opinion and to material things like lace handkerchiefs.

The psychoanalyst might say, three hundred years after the fact, that she had a fear of being deserted and thereby reliving the painful experience of her father's disappearance.

Chapter VIII

MADAME DE LANCLOS's health continued to decline. In a niche alongside of her bed was a polychromed statue of Sainte-Geneviève, before which burned two wax tapers, and on a table were sacred books. The small window, through which little light entered, was kept tightly shut, and the fumes of tallow and camphor struggled for mastery over lamp oil and benzoin. Occasionally, when her mother felt well enough to sit up in the adjoining chamber, Ninon took the opportunity to open the window wide.

Now and then the doctor called for a bleeding or to administer a drug. When the parish priest came, Ninon knelt down with him at her mother's bedside, doing her best to concentrate on her orisons.

Three times a week she went to the Marché Saint-Michel or Les Halles accompanied by Jeanne. The servant was getting old and needed more and more *eau-de-vie* to warm her bones. As increasing responsibility fell on Ninon, she developed into an efficient housekeeper and a tender nurse.

Paris still stank in the wind and people lived in terror of the pox and the pest, but it never occurred to them to connect disease with dirt. The art and the philosophy of Greece were part of the life of the upper classes, but it was as if the sanitation of Rome had never existed.

Witch doctors and alchemists were consulted by the sick; palmistry, dreams and the stars were legitimate sources of advice. The ambitious, the lovelorn and the wicked resorted to charms, spells and magic, and Richelieu actually made an ordinance prohibiting the invocation of demons to help discover state secrets.

Ninon was exposed to idolatry on all sides, and to superstition. If the Seine overflowed its banks, the good people disinterred some saint's thighbone and carried it through the streets in solemn procession; when a bridge collapsed under the weight of its traffic, the officials invoked everything but engineers. The king placed France under the special protection of the Virgin so that "all our loyal subjects might be received into Paradise, such being Our good will and pleasure," and the members of *parlement* came to blows in the aisles of Notre-Dame to establish the order of precedence through the Golden Gates.

Amid bigotry and what Samuel Johnson called "alembicated metaphysicalities," Ninon planned her life on a basis of reason. She read Montaigne and Pierre Charron, a skeptic priest who had made a compendium of the religions and the philosophies of the age. He counseled tolerance and maintained that religion could exist without virtue, and virtue without religion. Descartes's *Le discours de la méthode,* in which he propounded a philosophy based on logic, had just appeared and people were reading and discussing it. Urfé's *L'Astrée* was still being devoured, and it set the fashion for an imitation of the bucolic life of ancient Greece. Ninon read indiscriminately, anything she could get hold of.

She was developing into a young woman whose attraction was less in regularity of feature than in gaiety and charm. Her dark intelligent eyes and her brilliant smile gave the impression of beauty and her complexion was described as "rose-petals in milk." Her brow, a little too broad, was softened by a fringe of bronze curls.

All around her she saw wanton extravagance in dress. Brocades and velvets were trimmed with silver and gold lace; even precious stones were used to embellish a costume. Yet the partition between splendor and filth was often just a petticoat. Ninon dressed simply, with little ornamentation; she used the finest materials in brilliant colors, and a brooch or jeweled clip only when it had a raison d'être.

If she had other love affairs at this time, they were of little importance, as she herself was of no importance; no one would have bothered to record them. It wasn't until much later that the keepers of journals and the chroniclers of juicy tidbits thought her activities worth noting.

A number of writers, including Voltaire, have stated that at this time Cardinal Richelieu asked Ninon to be his mistress. Some of them maintained that he requested her to use her profession to spy for him. There is a dramatic scene in which the prelate offers her fifty thousand *écus*, and she indignantly hands him his biretta and shows him the door.

Voltaire wrote:

> No less a person than the cardinal de Richelieu was one of the first to enjoy Ninon's favors, and we may rightly imagine that this lady was one of the last recipients of his love. I believe that this marks the unique occasion on which the same celebrated courtesan gave herself without consulting her heart. She was then about fifteen or sixteen.

He couldn't have been more mistaken. During these years Richelieu was at the height of his power; he was prosecuting a war abroad and trying to subdue rebellion at home; he was encroaching on the accepted privileges of the nobility, lining the royal coffers, rebuilding Paris and laying the ground for the absolute monarchy that was to come. He was also collaborating on plays with several writers, granting endowments, wreaking vengeance, frustrating plots, fomenting counterplots and causing heads to roll. He was busy being a great minister and founding an empire. Nevertheless, he found some time for dalliance. But it was hardly likely that it was with an unknown hussy in her teens. Moreover, he was quite dead before Ninon had a "profession."

Chapter IX

EARLY in the century France still regarded violence as a virtue. Chivalry had gone to sleep and education was suspect. Language was crude, rhetoric in its infancy and spelling purely individual. The men of the middle classes, however, could read and write. Women, even of "good family," had to be content with learning manners, the catechism, needlework and music.

About 1618 a revolt arose against coarseness and vulgarity, a movement which began in a salon on the rue Saint-Thomas-du-Louvre and spread throughout France.

Catherine de Vivonne, daughter of the French ambassador to Rome, married, at the age of twelve, Charles d'Angennes, later to become the marquis de Rambouillet. When she was about twenty she withdrew from court life, having found its manners and its morals intolerable. She had her *hôtel*, near the Louvre, remodeled according to her own plans, which were very much in advance of the times. She put her staircase on the side, instead of in the middle, had her walls painted various colors, and introduced other innovations which have now become a part of French architecture. Soon her home became the resort of famous people, and her gatherings were to continue for half a century.

The marquise de Rambouillet was intelligent, cultured and warmhearted. She spoke three languages and had an appreciation of science and of the arts, but her outstanding talent was for bringing out the talents of others. Soon she gathered a most distinguished company, aristocrat and bourgeois, scholar and artist, scientist and poet. Voiture, Vaugelas, Balzac, Chapelain, Conrart, Ménage, Méré, Gassendi, Malherbe, Rancan and the Scudérys, brother and sister. Descartes came, when in Paris, and it was here

46

that Pascal wrote his *Treatise on Love*, under the influence of the chevalier de Méré, one of Ninon's lovers. It was under this roof that Bossuet, at sixteen, wrote his first sermon, that Corneille read his plays for criticism before they were produced. Wit was valued above ideas, and conversation was cultivated for its own sake; debates were held on the questions of the day and symposiums conducted. On entering one might be greeted with: "Pray, what think you of love, madame?" or "Monsieur le Duc, in your opinion, of what does the soul consist?" Mingling with the learned were many of the aristocracy and princes of the blood, and women were encouraged to display their talents.

Food was plentiful and the service unobtrusive. There were napkins, the guests ate delicately and chewed mincingly, but it is doubtful if they used knives or forks. Sometimes the marquise received in her chamber, sitting up in her vast bed which was separated from the rest of the room by a low wooden railing. It was an honor to be received in this "Blue Room" and a special mark of distinction to be allowed to enter the spaces between the bed and the side walls, the *ruelles*. The word came, in time, to denote a salon.

On fine days the company strolled in the formal garden, keeping up the never ending talk. Although they discussed many things freely, certain words became taboo as "they gave unpleasant ideas" or seemed too commonplace. A hat was a "defier of the weather"; chairs were "indispensable of conversation"; teeth were "the furniture of the mouth"; tears were "pearls of Iris"; ears were "the gates of understanding." The cheeks were "thrones of modesty" and the moon was a "torch of silence." The brain was called "the sublime" and the feet "dear sufferers." A toilet, or *chaise percée*, was not mentioned unless absolutely necessary, and then it was "*une soucoupe inférieure*," or lower saucer. To blow up the fire was "to excite the combustible element" and one did not say, "Lackey, snuff out that candle," but "*Inutile, ôtez le superflu de cet ardent.*" "*La compagne perpetuelle des morts et des vivants*" was nothing more than a chemise.

These *précieux* and *précieuses* played parlor games to test the mind, the forfeits being gloves, fans or garters. They never tired

of written questions and answers on the contents of *L'Astrée*.
Although the hero and heroine of that pastoral allegory were a
young shepherd and shepherdess, living in a mythological Greece
peopled with nymphs and fauns, although they wore the ancient
costumes, they spoke like French courtiers. The influence of this
work on the literate world of France lasted more than half a
century. Arcadia became the fashion and love changed its manners. It was now proper for a suitor to sigh hopelessly at the
feet of his beloved . . . *"un amant inoffensif."* He dare not aspire
to her hand before proving his worthiness over many years, passing if necessary, through debauchery while the object of his
devotion remained chaste and remote. While the gentleman was
suffering, the beloved exercised the "correct rules of cruelty."

Madame de Rambouillet's oldest daughter, Julie d'Angennes,
was the most popular member of the circle. She had once said,
"Grandma, let's have a talk about affairs of state now that I'm
five years old." She kept her fiancé languishing twelve years
before rewarding him with herself. During the time that he was
dangling, the duc de Montausier, who was said to be very fastidious, made his contribution to civilization. He originated the
soup ladle so that the diners need not dip their own spoons into
the tureen for a second helping.

Improvising verse was another favorite pastime. The men
formed a circle around Julie, each reciting a poem in her praise.
The best ones won prizes. Only the poet, Voiture, who was in
love with her, did not contribute.[1]

Of all the brilliant company, the leading spirit was Vincent
Voiture, whom they named *el chiquito rey*, the little king. He
was the son of an itinerant wine merchant. The marquise secretly
made it possible for him and for many others of limited means
to dress and live decently. In the Hôtel de Rambouillet social
snobbery was dying out while intellectual snobbery was being
born. Sex was frowned upon, and a neo-Platonic form of love
taking its place.

---

[1] These verses, written on vellum by the finest scrivener of the time,
Jarry, and adorned with illuminated flowers, became the famous *Garland
of Julie*.

It is, therefore, not surprising that some of the *amants inoffensifs* repaired to the Cabaret des Lanternes on the corner of the rue Saint-Thomas-du-Louvre for a few drinks, and that a number of them, refugees from Rambouillet refinement, ended the night on the Place Royale making corporeal love to the most beautiful, the most distinguished, the most acquiescent and the most expensive courtesan in Paris, Marion Delorme.

After twelve years Julie d'Angennes decided to "crown the flame" of the marquis de Montausier, and so they were married. She had just turned forty. They left Paris for Saintonge where he was governor. Madame de Rambouillet spent much of her time in the country, and though the doors of the salon were not closed, it was the beginning of the end. In 1648 Voiture died. Beside his poems and letters, he left behind some additions to the language, among them the word *urbanité*, which might well have been coined during a debate on city versus country life.

Imitative salons sprang up where Boileau read his satires, Racine his tragedies and Pascal his *Provinciales*. Madame de Sablé reduced the neo-Platonic credo of love to an absurdity:

. . . that men without committing any crime might cherish the most tender feelings for women; but that women, on the other hand, who were the ornaments of the world and made to be served and worshipped, should never permit anything beyond respect on the part of men.

Born of a genuine need, preciosity had grown into a monstrous idiot child.

Chapter X

EPISODES in the life of Marion Delorme have been attributed to Ninon by careless chroniclers. The two women, though friends and neighbors and in the same profession, frequently even sharing the same lovers, were very different in appearance, character, education and outlook.

Marion, born Marie de Lon, was nine years older than Ninon. Her father, like Ninon's, was of the lesser nobility. Jean de Lon, seigneur de Lorme and baron de Champagne, was a councilor and the president of the royal treasury in his province. Unlike Henry de Lanclos, he was a pious and respectable citizen who expended a great deal of effort guarding his daughter's virginity. As she grew in beauty and in charm this became a major occupation. Marion was tall, distinguished by a queenly carriage and a low-pitched voice. Her manner was reserved, but her glance, under dark lashes, beckoning. She learned to read and write, to sing and to play the theorbo, a large lutelike instrument with two necks.

Jacques Valée, sieur des Barreaux, known in the Marais as "the Illustrious Rake," toured the countryside preaching materialism. It was said that he "inherited his incredulity" from a great-uncle, a sixteenth-century writer who had been consigned to the flames in the days when they burned the author as well as the book. When des Barreaux appeared in Touraine the vines froze and the peasants wanted to stone him to death. When, in Saint-Cloud, during Lent, he tranquilly ate an *omelette au lard* while a storm was raging and when a thunderbolt nearly struck the *auberge*, he cried out, "*Ventre Saint-Gris!* That is precisely the accompaniment for an *omelette au lard*," words which rang around the country.

Ninon de Lanclos

In the course of his tour des Barreaux visited Champagne and spent a week at the Château de Lorme, but owing to the growing antipathy of the baron, he spent the last few days of it in the woodshed, with Marion bringing him his meals under cover of the night, and the hayloft put to its traditional use.

To his own surprise, des Barreaux fell in love with the young girl, and she, being of a pious nature, used her influence to reform him. For a time he relinquished his blasphemy and his bottle. He even wrote a religious sonnet, *Recours d'un pêcheur à la bonté*, which has been highly estimated.

Soon after Papa died, and Marion and her mother, who had none of the scruples of Madame de Lanclos, took up residence in Paris, des Barreaux establishing a love nest near them in the Faubourg Saint-Victor. It wasn't long before the ladies realized that there were better fish in the Marais. Marion began to make clandestine visits to other houses, not, at first, for money, but for little presents of jewels and objets d'art. For a time she was installed at a *hôtel* in the rue des Tournelles by the maréchal de Bassompierre. Then all secrecy was abandoned and Madame and Mademoiselle Delorme set up house in a grand manner at number 6 Place Royale, the house that is now the Victor Hugo Museum.

Soon lackeys in the liveries of many of the great houses were seen arriving with packages and flowers. The tradesmen of the quarter vied for the custom of this corner house beneath whose portals passed the flower of French manhood.

Marion inspired painters as well as writers, and her portraits, including one by Le Nain, hang in a number of museums. Her one defect was that her nose had a tendency to be red. To counteract this she sat for many hours soaking her feet in hot water.

Duels were fought for Marion Delorme, and suicides threatened, if not accomplished. She was showered with attention, covered with jewels. She had none of Ninon's wit or perspicacity; she thought she was in love with each customer. But she was religious and kind, and not only self-supporting but the mainstay of her mother, three brothers and a sister.

A number of the nobility attached to the Hôtel Condé were

among "the twenty lovers who shared her extravagance" and poor old Des Barreaux had to take a back *fauteuil*. For a while he accepted the situation, but he soon grew weary of the overwhelming competition and stepped out to devote himself seriously to a life of the intellect and of sodomy.

While the Palais Cardinal, now the Palais Royal, was being built, Richelieu occupied a house at number 21 Place Royale and occasionally attended one of Marion's more discreet gatherings. That she visited him, dressed as a page, is testified to by the contemporary, Tallement des Réaux, an expert on the bedroom lore of the time:

> For fair ladies, he scarcely paid any better than he did for his paintings. Marion de l'Orme went twice to him. (I have been told that once she went there in man's dress, being passed off as a courier. She tells this herself.) On the first visit he received her in a costume of gray satin with gold and silver broideries, booted and with plumes. She declares that his pointed beard and his hair above the ears made the most attractive effect imaginable. After these two visits he presented her with a hundred *pistoles* through Bourmais, his *valet de chambre*, who had acted the procurer in the episode. She flung them away and jeered at the cardinal. Several times he was seen wearing face patches.

When Marion was felicitated upon her conquest of the great man, she replied: "A cardinal is a very little man when he no longer has on his biretta and his scarlet robe."

Marion's house became the center of espionage and of plots against Richelieu, and it is quite possible that the proposition made by the cardinal to spy for him was addressed not to Ninon but to Marion.

In his famous *Memoirs*, the comte de Gramont recounts how he entertained Charles II of England with an account of Marion Delorme:

> Sire, you must have known Marion de l'Orme, the most charming creature in all France; though she was as witty as

an angel, she was as capricious as a devil. This beauty having made me an appointment, a whim seized her to put me off and to give it to another. She therefore writ me one of the tenderest billets in the world, full of the grief and sorrow she was in by being obliged to disappoint me, as a most terrible headache obliged her to keep her bed.

The count, being suspicious, planted his servants around her house to spy and learned that one of her footmen had set forth and met another lackey to whom he gave a letter. Gramont concluded that she was allotting his time to someone else. He lay in wait for his rival's approach. At dusk a gentleman in a voluminous black cloak appeared, and he recognized a friend, Louis, duc de Cossé-Brissac.

"Brissac, my friend," Gramont quotes himself as saying, "you must do me a favor of the greatest importance." He explained that he had a visit to pay in the neighborhood which would not take long. He asked Brissac to lend him his cloak and to mind his horse. He thus obtained entrance into Marion's house in a disguise worthy of a Mozart opera. He found her "on a couch in the most agreeable and genteelest *déshabillé* imaginable; she never in her life looked so handsome nor was so greatly surprised."

" 'What is the matter, my fair one?' said I. 'Methinks this is a headache very elegantly set off.' "

Marion made excuses and was "as haughty as a woman of the greatest virtue" but she ended up in bed with the count while the duke remained outside walking Gramont's horse. When he finally told her the story of his entry she burst into laughter and, "throwing her arms around my neck, 'My dear Chevalier,' she said, 'you are too amiable and too eccentric not to be pardoned.' "

When Gramont left he found the duc de Brissac in the same place exercising the horse, which he held politely while Gramont mounted.

Several years later the duc de Rohan wrote to the prince de Condé: "I heard yesterday that Madame de Brissac has separated from her husband because of the money he spends on Marion." And Tallement des Réaux writes: "Monsieur de Brissac was so

Chapter XI

IT was at a party at Marion Delorme's that Ninon met a number of the men who were destined to play important parts in her life. The celebrated courtesan felt that this young girl, who was well bred, entertaining and not too pretty, would prove an asset to her gatherings, which were predominantly male.

The windows were open and the afternoon sunlight crept in to challenge the myriad candle flames. Spectra from the prisms of the many lusters were cast on the dancers. Ninon stood on a landing of the stair, halfway between two floors, and watched through the wooden balustrade the graceful figures of a *courante*. Lackeys with silver trays were moving around the edge of the dance floor, and a few couples, as they passed the open door, quietly withdrew to the tree-shaded courtyard. In a recess at the far end was a couple locked in each other's arms. This was what life should be always: music, dancing, love.

She heard a voice calling, "Mademoiselle de Lanclos!" She looked down over the railing and there was Monsieur Scarron smiling his crooked smile at her. He was leaning on a cane and he wore a short black cape to hide a slight deformity. "Come down and talk to me," he said. They found a place in the room next to the dancers where Scarron installed himself in a *fauteuil* with Ninon on a *tabouret* at his side. Many of the guests stopped to speak to the canon. "This is the daughter of Lanclos," he would say, and add a complimentary word or two, and as soon as the guest had turned his back he would fill her ear with gossip about him.

"The curé there is Boisrobert. Not a bad fellow, even if the Scarlet Eminence likes him. Posterity will build a monument to

Richelieu for founding the Academy, but it was a fellow called Conrart who conceived the idea, and Boisrobert who whispered it into the cardinal's ear. The man he's talking to is Gassendi, a philosopher who is having a private war with Aristotle. The tall fellow in the corner is Claude de Chauvigny, baron de Blot l'Église. In spite of his name he's a rampant atheist. You must know his verse, he writes under the name of Blot. If it weren't that Monsieur is his protector, he'd have lost his head. Oh, here comes the Lord Chief Gossip of the Marais; beware of Monsieur d'Elbène; no one borrows with more charm."

"Who is that young man who looks so miserable?" asked Ninon. She indicated a gentleman with unruly hair, a beaked nose and rather prominent teeth, who was standing in a corner, obviously unhappy.

"That's Louis de Bourbon, duc d'Enghien," said Scarron. "He's the eldest son of the Prince de Condé and the beautiful Charlotte de Montmorency, the one whose brother lost his head."

"Is that why he is so sad?" asked Ninon.

"Oh no," said Scarron. "He's in love, desperately in love, with his cousin, but they want him to marry a niece of the cardinal who lives in the provinces and can neither read nor write. Come, let us pay our respects. I'll present you to His Highness."

Enghien greeted them graciously. He asked Ninon to dance. He held her loosely. They said not a word. When he returned her to Scarron's side he said, "Thank you, mademoiselle, for your silence."

Marion was everywhere, dancing, greeting new arrivals, moving from one group to another. When she spied Scarron she came over to him accompanied by a middle-aged gentleman of at least thirty with strong features and burning dark eyes, whom she introduced as Monsieur de Saint-Evremond. The name was not unknown to Ninon.

"Scarron," said Marion, "you've been whispering into Mademoiselle de Lanclos's ear all afternoon. You haven't even noticed my gown."

Ninon's eyes were round with admiration. The gold satin gown, the blue *paniers* lined in gold, might have been draped on a Greek statue. At Marion's breast was a brooch of pearls and sapphires, and in the middle of her forehead, where her dark hair was parted, was a smaller, matching one, held in place by a fillet of pearls. It was said that she always had the stones weighed before thanking their donors.

Suddenly Marion seemed to lose the thread of the conversation. Ninon followed her gaze, which was fixed on the entrance of the room. A young man, very young indeed, stood looking over the company. He was dressed in white satin, his breeches slashed to reveal cloth of silver, his light blue cape attached to one shoulder with a diamond buckle. When his glance encountered Marion's they made their way toward each other on a simultaneous impulse. Her face had turned red, nose and all, and she seemed unaware of the eyes that followed her. She led the young man back to the group and presented him to Ninon. He was Henri Coëffier, marquis de Cinq-Mars, His Majesty's equerry. As he bent over Ninon's hand she caught a whiff of ambergris and musk. Soon he and Marion turned away and were accosted by a dark gentleman with a short, pointed beard. Ninon caught a few words in Spanish. Cinq-Mars looked around furtively and the three disappeared in the crowd.

Saint-Evremond turned to Scarron. "Caesar had better beware the Ides of Mars," he said in English. Ninon caught the play on words and guessed that some conspiracy was afoot, but in an age of conspiracies she gave it little thought. She was to recall the incident before the year was out.

"They are very much in love," she said.

"Dangerously," said Saint-Evremond. "His Majesty is so jealous that when the court is at the Louvre Marion has to decamp to Baye."

"His Majesty's real interest is in raising green peas," said Scarron. "It took him twenty-two years and hundreds of novenas to make one dauphin, and at that they say the child was born with an Italian accent."

Ninon danced with Gaspard de Coligny, whom she liked, and

Bussy-Rabutin, whom she did not. As she passed Marion on the arm of Particelli d'Emery she heard the Director of Finance say, "Have pity on me, dear Marion, my wife does not understand art."

When darkness came the footmen drew the draperies and lighted the fires, and the company adjourned to a large room where two oblong tables were laid. The center of each was covered with game, each bird decorated in its own plumage. In geometrical patterns around these were the side dishes and the sauces. Napkins were served, folded to represent different animals according to a method invented by Hester, the master folder of the day.

Ninon was seated between Saint-Evremond and Brissac, with Scarron opposite. Madame Delorme sat at the head of her table, while Marion played hostess at the other one. A procession of servants in green and gold livery heaped the silver plates while wine stewards with chains around their necks presided over the side tables, going back and forth with ewers that were masterpieces of the silversmith's art. In desperation at the country's threatened ruin, the king had proclaimed an edict prohibiting more than three courses to a meal, with only six dishes to each course.

Ninon ate with great appetite, enjoying the unaccustomed delicacies. Brissac was silent, his eyes constantly on Marion, but Saint-Evremond exerted himself to be entertaining. He spoke of Descartes's voyage, and his conclusions on the effects of travel in promoting tolerance of other peoples. Ninon reminded him that in the previous century Montaigne had also made a voyage "to read the book of the world" and had also concluded that every custom, however different from one's own, has its reason.

Charles de Marguetel de Saint-Denis de Saint-Evremond was not good-looking. His wit was not as mordant as Scarron's, but it seemed to her more profound. He knew English history and literature as well as French, had studied law, served in the armed forces and written essays, which had not been published. He did not employ the usual fatuous flattery, yet she felt he was trying to gain her admiration by a display of his learning.

A gentleman in a long curled wig with a small mustache arrived late, the prince de Marcillac, duc de la Rochefoucauld. The writers who tell of the childhood friendship of Ninon and the prince at Loches maintain that La Rochefoucauld did not remember her and she had to recall the incident to him.

Ninon was so excited by the gay company that she forgot the time. Suddenly she remembered, and became uneasy about her mother. She spoke a word to Scarron. He looked tired and was glad of an excuse to slip away.

She tried to enter her apartment noiselessly, but Madame de Lanclos was awake, waiting for her and tossing about with a fever.

Chapter XII

FOR many months Madame de Lanclos was confined to her bed and Ninon left the house for only the most necessary errands. She went to no more parties, nor did her friends come to the house where the routine of illness prevailed. She was an efficient and tender nurse, and when at last her mother died in her arms she was overcome with grief.

Relatives who had kept away during the difficult years came ceremoniously to the funeral. Ninon arranged an elaborate cortege, as her mother would have wished. The coffin was carried in an open hearse drawn by two black horses. Priests followed, carrying lighted tapers and chanting dolefully to the swinging censer. Friends and relatives trudged slowly behind in the mud.

They returned from the cemetery in the rain, and after the few friends had left the apartment Ninon was suddenly faced with the fact that she had no one to look after, and her sense of desolation overwhelmed her. She felt not only grief but guilt for having caused any unhappiness to a woman who had experienced so little joy and so much pain. Her own health had suffered during the last trying months; she was pale and had lost weight. She had no appetite, and little strength to make decisions, and there was no one to make them for her. Most of her friends were youths who readily offered their lacy bosoms for her tears, trusting that her sorrow would be assuaged by their kisses.

Fortunately her sound instinct for self-preservation came to her aid. She applied for permission to make a retreat at the Carmelite convent on the rue Saint-Jacques. It was easily obtained. The white sisters welcomed her and asked no questions. She was given a small, clean, austere room, simple fare and the luxury of indulging her grief in solitude. All that was demanded of her was an outward observance of ritual.

She was permitted to choose books, to write letters and to receive visitors, but she chose to see no one. She walked in the garden unmolested, and when she felt the need of companionship the gentle nuns were only too willing to talk. They grew fond of her and she lent variety to their ordained lives. In time the kindness, the routine and the beautiful sacred music had their effect, and as her health improved she began to wonder what was going on in the Marais. Had Marion married Cinq-Mars? How was poor Scarron? What were they playing at the theatres? When would she have a lover? Who would it be? As she knelt in the dim chapel thoughts crept into her mind which would have made her white-robed companions blush.

The small amount left by her mother would soon be gone. No one had asked her in marriage, perhaps no one ever would. Marriage, her father had said, was an unfair institution: the woman sacrificed everything, while the man remained free. She had seen many instances where lovers became husbands, and then lovers again . . . of some other woman. At Marion's the prince de Marcillac had said, "There are some good marriages but no delicious ones."

There were no remunerative occupations open to women except menial ones. To become a rich man's mistress would be to accept the restraints of marriage without receiving its benefits. Two lovers, or three, who could share in her maintenance would be best. She would not then be dependent on any one of them; having only a share of her, they would each be less demanding. In time she might even build up quite a respectable clientele. It was a profession for which she knew she had aptitudes, an honorable profession that required little investment.

That evening, during vespers, she made her decision.

No doubt when Ninon returned from the Carmelites she opened the windows wide, rearranged the furniture and gave the statue of Sainte-Geneviève to some neighbor who would provide it a more fitting abode. She also swept out a few young blades who were only too willing to buy, with flattering words, her favors and her hospitality. But a woman doesn't enter the oldest profession by dusting the parlor and hanging out a sign. No one was in love with her, but she had a few admirers who had been kept at bay during her mother's last illness. She let it be known that she was in business, and as gossip was the second largest industry in the Marais, she soon had a number of applicants, none of whom was to her taste. However, she was realistic enough to realize that she would have to begin in a modest way.

Of all the candidates, Jean Coulon, a member of *parlement*, seemed the least impossible. At any rate he was the most importunate. When not on duty at the High Chamber, he could be seen weaving about the Marais from wineshop to cabaret, hurling abuse at priests and ugly women. Everyone knew he had a sorrow to drown. His attractive wife had a number of lovers, the dean of whom was Particelli d'Emery, Superintendent of Finance, who had charge of the tax on all foodstuffs entering Paris. His secret sorrow, as he had told Marion Delorme, was that his wife didn't love art. Coulon complained to his fellow tavern-flies that everyone slept with his wife but himself, yet with all this collaboration he could not obtain a son. His conduct was so reprehensible that at one time *parlement* considered having him whipped.

Obviously, if Ninon had had a wide choice, she would not have selected Coulon. She realized, however, that he was basically a decent sort, that he had a good mind and that he was devoted to her. Moreover, he was willing and able to pay.

For a regular income of five hundred *livres* a month, Ninon granted him limited rights. He became the first of what she termed her "payers." She warned him that the arrangement was not exclusive, and that either party had the right to terminate the relationship at any time. He asked only that the other shareholders be men of honor. Ninon refused to promise anything.

Coulon was delighted with Ninon. Being a man who sang his

joys as well as his sorrows, he boasted of his happiness in the
taverns, and soon one of the rhymers, who were as anonymous
then as the inventors of off-color jokes are today, brought forth
a verse on the subject:

> Chacun sait l'étroite union
> D'entre Monsieur et Madame Coulon. . . .
> > Si d'Emery
> > Fait cocu le mari,
> L'autre en conte à Ninon.

(Everyone knows the slim union between Monsieur and
Madame Coulon. . . . If d'Emery makes a cuckold of the
husband, the latter tells it all to Ninon.)

This and other rhymes circulated not only in the taverns but
in the drawing rooms as well, and soon they came to the ears
of Madame Coulon. With the indignation of a deceiver deceived, she turned her fury on Ninon. Since Emery was largely
financing her household, the fact that her husband was keeping
a mistress with her lover's money added to her wrath. She
spread a report that Ninon de Lanclos was a dangerous woman,
a menace to the sanctity of the home. She naturally regarded
the woman as the seducer and her husband as the poor victim.
A number of doors were closed to Ninon, but she maintained
her dignity and her few real friends, and Coulon rose to the
occasion by openly proclaiming himself her protector. In fact
he continued the allowance for quite some time after their relationship had come to an end.

The question of whether Ninon could be classed as a prosti-
tute has occasionally arisen, and according to the definition of
our times, "a woman who gives herself for hire," she might.
But we must judge her in her milieu, not in ours. The courtesans
of France were respected even more than the hetaerae of ancient
Greece, and far from being social outcasts, they were sought
after.

Prostitutes were classed with criminals. An ordinance of 1635
provided that, without trial, they should be shaved, whipped and

banished for life. Nevertheless, they did a thriving business.

The women of the pavements were recruited largely from the servant class . . . poor country girls who, tired of scrubbing pots, tried to pick up an easy living. The prettiest among them, *les chèvres coiffées*, followed the court, and the *petrels*, or chatterboxes, with less showy headdresses, were at the disposal of the bourgeoisie. Lower on the scale were the miserable *pierreuses*, so called because they lodged in stone basements. These women often acted as decoys for their pimps. The virginity of a young girl might be sold twenty times. On the rues Saint-Victor and Saint-Jacques "academies" held girls of all nationalities without police supervision.

Ninon, it is true, accepted money for her favors, but she also turned down rich customers. She really enjoyed her work, which gave her amateur rather than professional standing. She soon divided her men into "payers," "martyrs" and "favorites." The martyrs desired her in vain, and the favorites, who gave her pleasure, often gave her nothing else. These candidates she selected herself, and while the affair lasted she shut the door to all others, but as soon as the "first, fine, careless rapture" began to wane she dismissed the man. If he happened to possess a quality of mind that pleased her he was promoted to the drawing room, but the love-making was definitely over. It is a tribute to her that all of these gentlemen were grateful to be allowed to see her on any terms.

The second candidate to present himself as a payer was François d'Amboise, comte d'Aubijoux. He was a soldier devoted to the oblique causes of Monsieur. Like Coulon, he was a *bon vivant*, good-natured and self-indulgent. Unlike Coulon, he was handsome and had good manners. Coulon approved the choice, and if there was any jealousy between them, Ninon managed matters so tactfully that it soon disappeared and the gentlemen became boon companions.

Ninon was now modestly established, her basic needs taken care of, and with enough time to read and enjoy her many friendships. She was mistress of her home, an expert and thrifty housekeeper. Little by little her circle was enlarged, and while a few insecure wives closed their doors to her, other doors were opening. She and Marion were friends, as good friends as a beautiful, successful, rich demimondaine and a modest neophyte can become. Ninon was careful not to poach, but there were men of discernment who realized that she had more to offer; they believed that an intelligent woman might be sexually delectable, and a few who had patronized the house on the Place Royale now came to the rue des Trois Pavillons.

Chapter XIII

THE king gave his jester twenty gold *écus*. Doucet took them and, patting his purse, cried, "There, sire, be quiet, it will come back to you quickly; you'll just put some more taxes on the poor people." The cardinal-minister, even while laying the foundations of a great empire, was making himself hated. Even as he approached the grave, conspiracies sprang up faster than they could be suppressed, and the most dangerous had its headquarters at the house of Marion Delorme. Ninon was not yet politically minded, but she could not help noticing the overtones when she went to the house on the Place Royale. Richelieu did not come, but when any of his henchmen were there the conversation became stilted and uneasy. Marion, not an independent thinker, was the kind of woman who could only be involved in a cause through a man she loved, and young Henri de Cinq-Mars was the spearhead of the rebellion.

He had entered the court at fifteen as captain of the Guards, and a few years later, in order to divert Louis's attention from Marie de Hautefort, Richelieu had presented the attractive young man, who soon became Grand Ecuyer and the favorite. There was gossip about the young marquis and the enigmatic monarch. Louis had been deliberately uneducated by his mother. He never opened a book but he showed a propensity for carpentering, printing, forging metal and raising green peas; he larded meat and cooked preserves. One day he amused himself by shaving off the beards of several of his officers. He seemed afraid of close relations with women, yet when the cardinal saw he was becoming too friendly with Mademoiselle de Hautefort, he became uneasy lest she have some influence which he could not control.

Richelieu's project was all too successful. Cinq-Mars anointed himself with perfumed oil before receiving a visit from the monarch. He was the best-dressed courtier, owning three hundred pairs of shoes. He slept in the royal antechamber and sometimes, after Louis had fallen asleep, he would creep out, saddle his horse and ride at top speed to Paris to spend a few hours with Marion Delorme, thereby deceiving not only his monarch but the woman he intended to marry, Marie-Louise de Gonzague. He was careful, however, to be back at Saint-Germain in time for His Majesty's *lever*. Louis would sometimes ask, with a touch of sarcasm:

"How did you sleep last night, Henri?" And then a period of sulking would follow. Tallement des Réaux says, "Louis XIII knew none of the emotions of love save jealousy."

Cinq-Mars distinguished himself at the siege of Arras, but when he asked for a command he was refused by Richelieu. This added to his growing resentment and he joined the cabal of conspirators who had for their objective the elimination of the cardinal. A number of nobles were involved, including Monsieur, the king's brother, and, it was even said, the queen. Because of his easy access to Louis, Cinq-Mars was used as a tool for gaining information. He requested to be present at a meeting of the King's Council and his wish was granted, the wily minister making sure that nothing serious would be discussed in his presence. "Affairs of the state should not be entrusted to boys," he said. The conspirators even went so far as to make an agreement with Spain in which that power promised them troops and money. Richelieu's spies succeeded in obtaining a copy of the treaty, which the cardinal showed to Louis. In the midst of war, this was high treason.

The king, in poor health, went south to the battlefield. The cardinal followed, partially paralyzed but indomitable, inspiring more terror than ever. At Narbonne, "less in body and corrupting visibly," he made his will. It was there that he received final proof of the secret treaty with Spain; his murder was to have taken place on the journey. While Cinq-Mars was fighting at Perpignan, the king and the cardinal discussed the young man's fate from adjoining sickbeds. "For six months, the man has turned my stomach," said Louis.

When Cinq-Mars was at Narbonne a message was slipped into his hand, warning him of danger. He spent the night in hiding in a closet with two farm wenches. History says that he was frightened and "one of the king's *valets de chambres tapissiers* hid him in a closet."

Brander Mathews speculates, with some evidence, that young Poquelin (Molière) might well have been the one to hide Cinq-Mars. He writes:

In all the travels of the King there were in attendance on his person two of the eight *valets de chambres tapissiers* (upholsterers) whose duty it was to see to the comfort of the monarch wherever he might tarry. The quarterly term of service of Molière's father extended from the beginning of April to the end of June; it was during these three months that the arrest of Cinq-Mars took place. A *valet de chambre tapissier* had the privilege of substitution; he could get one of his colleagues to take his place. He could also send in his stead his future successor, the possessor of the survivor of the post.

He concludes that, as Poquelin Senior was proved to be in Paris at the time, it was quite likely that his son went on this journey.

Cinq-Mars was arrested, and with him his friend, de Thou, who had not entered the conspiracy but had known of it. Richelieu was towed up the Rhône on a barge canopied in royal purple. Troops of cavalry followed on one bank and the prisoners on the other. Monsieur had got out from under by turning on his associates.

The trial took place at Lyon. The cardinal presented proof, and Cinq-Mars, having faith in his monarch's bounty, confessed his guilt.

The execution took place the following day. The marquis was dressed for the occasion in a Flemish waistcoat ornamented with gold lace, white pantaloons, a scarlet cloak, green silk stockings and a black Catalonian hat with plumes. As the moment approached the king looked at his watch and was heard to say, "Monsieur le Grand is passing a bad quarter of an hour." During the strokes of noon the heads fell into the basket. Cinq-Mars was not yet twenty-three.

Both men died courageously, but France was stricken with terror. No one knew where the blade would fall next.

The Grande Mademoiselle, who adored her father, noted in her *Memoirs* years later that the memory of that day was so painful she could not bear to write about it; she nevertheless did:

Monsieur came to have supper at my house where thirty-four violins were playing. He was as gay as if Messieurs Cinq-Mars and de Thou had not been left by the roadside. I confess that I could not look at him without thinking of them, and that happy as I was at seeing him again, his gaiety caused me real grief, nor am I praising myself too highly when I say that I showed more emotion over this disgrace for which my father was highly responsible than another person of my age would have done.

Her age at the time was fifteen.

Chapter XIV

MARION mourned Cinq-Mars in costly widow's weeds; she had masses said, received calls of condolence and curtailed her professional activities for several weeks. Ninon was most sympathetic.

The year was one of public as well as private mourning, and Paris was perpetually draped in purple and black. In July, Marie de Medici died at Cologne. In her shabby clothes she had been the guest of Rubens, who had appealed to Richelieu on her behalf. In response, the cardinal had offered him ten thousand *louis d'or* for *The Descent from the Cross*. The painter declined and Richelieu provided a small maintenance for the king's mother, and invented a new tax to pay for it.

The cardinal had reached Paris from Lyon on a litter on the shoulders of his guards; he was eaten up with ulcers; pneumonia set in. To the question of his confessor: "Do you forgive your enemies?" he replied, "I have no enemies save those of the state." Whereupon His Majesty handed him a cup of egg yolks. Tallemant des Réaux wrote, "The king only went to see the cardinal just before he died, and having found him very ill, he came away cheerful." The vicar of Saint-Eustache, who had baptized him, administered the last sacrament. On December 4, 1642, Richelieu died.

The Pope said a strange thing for a pope: "If there be a God, the cardinal de Richelieu will have much to answer for; if there be none, he lived a successful life." History has evaluated the greatness of the minister's role, but at his death there was more rejoicing than sorrow. The queen and Monsieur were relieved and Louis's first act of independence was to withdraw the pensions the cardinal had granted to men of letters. "We have more important things than that," he pronounced.

On the first of the year Scarron, as was his custom, distributed his *étrennes rimées* to his friends. The one addressed to Marion was a banal tribute to a beautiful courtesan. But for Ninon he wrote:

> O belle et charmante Ninon,
> A laquelle jamais on ne répondra non,
> Pour quoi que se soit qu'elle ordonne,
> Tant est grande l'autorité
> Que s'acquiert en tous lieux une jeune personne
> Quand, avec de l'esprit, elle a de la beauté,
> Puisque, hélas! à cet an nouveau
> Je n'ai rien d'assez bon, je n'ai rien d'assez beau
> De quoi vous bâtir une étrenne.
>
> Contentez-vous de mes souhaits.
> Je souhaite donc à Ninon
> Un mari peu hargneux, mais qui soit bel et bon,
> Force gibier tout le carême,
> Bon vin d'Espagne, gros marron,
> Force argent sans lequel tout homme est triste et blême
> Et que chacun l'estime autant que fait Scarron.

(Oh, beautiful and charming Ninon, to whom no one can say no, to whatever it is that she commands, so great is the power wielded by a young woman who possesses beauty as well as wit. Alas, at the beginning of another year I have nothing good enough, nothing beautiful enough to offer you. Content yourself, therefore with my wishes. I wish for Ninon a husband who will not be bad-tempered but handsome and kind, plenty of game during Lent, good Spanish wines, fat chestnuts and a great deal of money, for without it one is miserable and handicapped; and that the whole world should esteem her as much as does Scarron.)

The Palais Cardinal was bequeathed to the Crown, becoming the Palais Royal, but Louis had little time left to enjoy it. That he survived thirty bloodlettings in a year is a miracle, but in May 1643, at the age of forty-two, he succumbed. During his last illness he had composed music for the *De Profundis* which was sung in his chamber.

Louis was mourned sincerely by his own people, if not by his family, and a five-year-old boy, for whom the soothsayers had predicted a long and brilliant reign, became Louis XIV, under the regency of his Spanish mother and the domination of her Italian adviser and lover, Mazarin, whom she nominated Chief of Council.

During the period of mourning there was rejoicing everywhere. Serenades were played in the gardens, there was dancing in the streets and there were concerts at the Louvre and the Tuileries Palace, though the Grande Mademoiselle observes, "It was not in accordance with the proprieties to listen to violins in a room draped with mourning." The queen and her two little boys established residence at the Louvre with a secret staircase connecting her rooms with those of Mazarin.

During a season so gay Marion could not afford to mourn long.

Maurice and Gaspard de Coligny, the du Vigeans, the comte de Gramont, Saint-Evremond and the duc d'Enghien disported themselves at her house, and even Monsieur came occasionally, though he was not addicted to the opposite sex except for the purpose of marriage. These gallants with long curls covering their falling lace ruffs, with jeweled sword hilts, and fine lace dangling from their garters, brought with them their poets and musicians. The house became a temple of pleasure, and Marion had more lovers than she could accommodate, kind as was her heart. La Rochefoucauld occasionally lent his presence when he was not at the Salon de Rambouillet admiring Enghien's beautiful sister, who had become the duchesse de Longueville. George Villiers, second duke of Buckingham, wandered in and out, a dignified presence who was seeking the philosopher's stone. Ninon met them all.

Marion could take admiration for granted; Ninon had to work for it, but it wasn't long before the more discerning members of the circle began to appreciate her superiority. But of all the galaxy Ninon's pulse quickened only at the proximity of one man, a thoroughly unworthy character.

Gaspard de Coligny, seigneur de Chastillon, marquis d'Andelot, was the overt lover of Marion and the secret wooer for the hand of Isabelle-Angélique de Montmorency. He was a frivolous young man with a round boyish face and long curls. He was descended from the younger branch of the great Huguenot family. Protestantism was the bone and fibre of the Colignys; his great uncle was the admiral who was butchered by the henchmen of the duc de Guise at dawn on Saint Bartholomew's day.

But Marion had promised him and his friend Chavanac that if they embraced Catholicism she would reward them. Young Gaspard's conversion had a triple motive: he would not only possess Marion, he would placate the Catholic family of Isabelle-Angélique, and he would please the king. Therefore, with his friend, he took instruction in the tenets of the Roman Catholic Church. They threw dice to see who should make the first confession, and the day they received baptism and the eucharist they dashed off together to the Place Royale to receive their reward, no doubt drawing lots as to precedence.

Chavagnac soon lost interest in Marion, but Coligny continued the relationship for several months before cooling off. Marion confided to Ninon that his ardor was diminishing and attributed it to his being the type who lost interest in a woman after he had won her. Ninon thought, or wished to think, that Marion lacked the skill to hold him. Since her friend was losing him anyway, she reasoned, she might as well try her luck. She wrote him a letter which was an emotional outburst, guilelessly revealing her passion and inviting him to visit her.

Scarron, who missed nothing, wrote her a verse of warning:

> N'engendrez jamais de querelle
> De peur qu'il n'en arrive autant;
> Tâchez de n'en pas blesser tant
> Et commandez à vos œillades
> De faire un peu moins de malades.

(Never start a quarrel for fear it will go too far; try not to wound so much, and command the glances of your eyes to make fewer victims.)

Tallemant des Réaux expressed it:

She wrote to him and gave him an assignation. He went there. But as he was a faithless fellow, he soon left her. She deemed this treatment insufferable, although, as you will see from what follows, she was, herself, rather of a humor to leave than to be left; and she made complaint to Moussaye, who made peace betwixt them and brought the fugitive back to her. It has been said that in order to avenge herself she had suffered herself to take a malady wherewith she peppered him so thoroughly that it was long before he could be restored: he had a delicate blood and caught the illness with great ease. This, perhaps, saved his life, for if he had not been thus disabled, he would have been at the battle of Honnecourt and no doubt would have paid with his life.

This was written some time after the fact, and the author prefixes the part about venereal disease with "It has been said." That Ninon would do such a thing deliberately is unthinkable. She took the utmost care of herself, and if she ever was infected, it was despite the best hygienic precautions of the time. Moreover, her nature was never a revengeful one. Such an act would not only have been reprehensible, it would have ruined her business.

Coligny's marriage to the Catholic girl was considered a calamity by his family; his father withdrew his support and the young man exiled himself to Holland. He was killed at the battle of Charenton nine years later.

Ninon made a resolution not to let herself become emotionally involved again.

Chapter XV

NINON could not afford anything like the hospitality offered at the Maison Delorme. Her drawing room was small and she had only two servants, but they were devoted to her interests. At first she gave little supper parties where the guests brought their own food, but as her circumstances improved she abandoned this custom and provided her intimate friends with dinners which were delicious, wholesome, well appointed, but not wantonly lavish.

It has often been said that she had but to crook her little finger to bring the most distinguished adorers to her feet; that she had the choice of the aristocratic and literary worlds. This was true of the Mademoiselle de Lanclos of a later date, but not of the Ninon of this period.

Her rooms were filled with men of rank and title, it is true, but when we consider her lovers at this time, the young men must have been a pretty poor lot. With neither the patriotic nor the religious motives of their grandfathers, they enjoyed battle as a game and a change from the skirmishes of the alcoves. Many were disloyal to the Crown, yet were not protectors of their own feudal subjects. Since work would have made them *déclassés*, they lived on their parents, who in turn lived on the tax money wrung from the peasants on their lands, or on salaries from government posts entailing no work. "There are in Paris more than twenty thousand gentlemen who have not a sou; they live on gambling and on women; one day they arrive on foot, the next day they are in a carriage." Many of these wastrels found their way to Ninon's house.

Careless of human life, including their own, the young aristocrats had a certain reckless courage, but they had gallantry without chivalry, pride without honor; they cheated in politics, in love and at cards. A popular saying was, "Without money, honor is a disease." The Salon de Rambouillet was but a little candle in a naughty world.

Among the guests who crowded into Ninon's apartment were a few distinguished and interesting men, and as many distinguished and interesting rogues. She began to enjoy life thoroughly. Sensuality governed her sexual relations which she accepted as a delight that would only be diminished by sentiment. How much rationalization there was in this attitude no one can say, but it has been cited as evidence of her "masculine mentality." This interpretation assumes that women are more sentimental than men.

She went merrily from one caprice to another. To Antoine de Rambouillet, sieur de la Sablière, she said, "I think I shall love you for three months, which is eternity for me."

The marquis de Jarzé, a dandy and rich, was one of her clients, and César-Phoebus, comte de Moissens, a most formidable character, was another. Being an Albret (the family of Henri IV's mother), he had entree to the great *hôtels* and palaces, where he conducted himself in anything but a princely manner. He was savage and inarticulate, and rather than stutter his pleas he would chase his prey with lowered head, butt into her and grab her. When he entered a room the women pulled their scarves close around their necks, except, of course, the few who were thrilled by this technique. The duchesse de Rohan, it was said, paid him to beat her. This gentleman later became the maréchal d'Albret, getting his baton as a reward for arresting three of his best friends.[1]

Tallemant des Réaux asserts that Ninon had a child by Moissens. It is, of course, possible, but no mention of it can be found. The duc de Luynes, a most unreliable source, claims that she also had a child by Jarzé who was brought up from infancy as the nephew of the marquis.

[1] The Hôtel d'Albret still stands in the Marais, at 24 rue Pavée. It is at this writing occupied by a wholesale lighting-fixture company.

The lover most worthy of Ninon's admiration at this time was a man ten years older than she, Antoine Gombauld, chevalier de Méré. He was a cultured, gentle soul whose credo was the fundamental virtue of man and his ability to rise above circumstances. He was a Knight of Malta with a distinguished record in the navy, a writer whose style achieved such clarity and conciseness that it is used today as an example for students. It was he who took Pascal to the Rambouillet salon, and who influenced the mathematician in his "worldly period." Saint-Cyr wrote that Méré was "one of the first exponents of a new calling: the professional diners-out."

Ninon did not find in Méré the thrill that she was always looking for, so the affair was brief, but he was promoted to the drawing room and remained her friend and mentor. It has also been said, with little supporting evidence, that she had a child by Méré.

The matter of unwelcome maternity was a serious problem for a courtesan. Midwives and "witches" performed abortions under horrifying conditions with blunt and septic instruments, and they risked hanging if discovered. There were abortive medicines based, as they are today, on ergot which could be purchased in the same dark places that sold aphrodisiacs compounded of mandrake and cantharides as "love potions" and compounds of arsenic as "powders of succession." Moreover, a product called "Death to Rats" was openly on sale. La Fontaine wrote:

> Avait-on un amant?
> Un mari vivant trop au gré de son épouse?
> Une mère fâcheuse, une femme jalouse?
> Chez la devineresse on courait. . . .

(Has one a lover? A husband living too long to suit his spouse? A mother who is a nuisance, a jealous wife? To the seer one runs. . . .)

In spite of the difficulties of controlling the birth rate, a rise in population was held in check by the high degree of infant mortality, intentional and inadvertent. Little bones were discovered everywhere . . . in ditches, under crumbling walls and in shallow graves. So many live infants were found in churches and on doorsteps that Monsieur Vincent founded an asylum for *Les Enfants Trouvés*.

Venereal disease also acted as a deterrent to the increase of the birth rate, but it added its own serious problem. Syphilis had broken out in epidemic form at the siege of Naples in 1494. The Italians had blamed it on the French and the French had blamed it on Columbus. It spread north during the first decade of the sixteenth century, wiping out great numbers of its victims. A cure of gold and mercury had been introduced by Paracelsus, but it wasn't until 1684 that the city of Paris awoke to the necessity of treating diseased prostitutes; however, as prostitutes were beaten without mercy, they would hardly come forth and officially acknowledge their calling.

Moreover, the lack of the simplest sanitation made prevention of disease almost impossible. In the early 1640s, when Ninon set up her establishment, the *hôtels* of the aristocracy, the rich and the high functionaries received water through special canalization and by special license. For the rest of the city there were only thirty public fountains. Water was more precious than wine and people used it more sparingly. They purchased it by the jar from passing water carriers, or sent their servants to the nearest fountain where backstairs gossip enlivened the hours as they waited their turn.

Parisians cleaned themselves with moist towels, and to avoid body and foot odors used pastes and oils, essences and sachets. If a man reached the point when a bath became a necessity, he went to the *barbier-étuviste*, where he was put into a steam room to sweat out the dirt.

Ninon, from her earliest childhood, had been dainty and immaculate. She spent on water what other women spent on deodorants and cosmetics. A contemporary wrote, "Costly garments did not suit her but she was always of the most elegant simplicity and the most exquisite freshness." It was also said that she wore a pair of gloves but once.

78

Scrupulous cleanliness is not, of course, insurance against
venereal disease, but there seems evidence of her freedom from
infection in the fact that she enjoyed robust health all her life,
dying at last of old age.

Chapter XVI

"They never quarreled over me," wrote Ninon, "they had confidence in my inconstancy. Each awaited his turn."

And the turn of Louis de Bourbon, duc d'Enghien, prince of the blood, cousin of the king, scion of the great houses of Condé and of Montmorency, and known in history as the Great Condé, eventually came.

He had been in love with his cousin Marthe du Vigean ever since he had danced with her at her father's château. She returned his passion but, being a *précieuse,* had only permitted him to kiss her hand. His father, Henri II, prince de Condé, had for reasons of state forced him to marry one of Richelieu's nieces, a country-bred girl of fifteen who could neither read nor write. The young duke, who had written one of the prize-winning verses in the *Guirlande de Julie,* found her dull. He had struggled bravely against the hateful alliance but had been forced to yield. He promised Marthe that the marriage would never be consummated, that he would manage to get an annulment, and asked her to wait for him.

Richelieu settled a fortune on his niece and the wedding was as opulent as the cardinal's wealth and the prestige of the Bourbons could make it. There were enough wedding presents to fill a museum, as indeed they have . . . the château of Chantilly, where some of them are on display. The list of guests formed a roster of the great; nevertheless, it included, at the insistence of Enghien, the name of his friend, Marion Delorme. The festivities at the Hôtel de Condé lasted twenty-four hours, and a magnificent time was had by all except the bride and the bridegroom.

On his wedding night the young duke wrote a document in legal verbiage, protesting against his marriage, after which he became seriously ill.

The Spanish army threatened Champagne, and the king, on his deathbed, appointed the barely recovered young man to lead the royal troops. He was no novice at war, but he was only twenty-two when he took command. On the eve of the battle of Rocroy news arrived of the death of Louis XIII, and older and more prudent strategists were ready to surrender the fortress. This would have meant not only the invasion of Champagne but the eventual siege of Paris.

Enghien rallied his men before dawn and then, wearing a plumed hat instead of a helmet, he led three furious attacks and routed the surprised Spaniards. Samuel Pepys wrote of him: ". . . there is not a more furious man in the world; danger in fight never disturbs him, except just to make him civil."

The young duke had acted in defiance of Mazarin's orders, with no strategy and a ruthless disregard for the lives of his men. That summer he moved on from one victory to another and in the fall returned to Paris, a conquering hero, to the court, the populace and two unhappy women. He was acclaimed in the streets and fêted in the banquet halls. He had made the house of Condé more powerful than ever, but his wife had the bad taste to be bearing his child, and this was hard to explain to his beloved cousin. When the heir presumptive to the titles and the estates of the Condés and the Montmorencys, as well as the fortune of Richelieu, was held in the arms of Mazarin at the baptismal font, his father was at La Barre on his knees before Marthe, trying to explain and imploring her to elope.

For six years thereafter he endeavored to have his marriage annulled. He remained in love with Marthe, though he never held her in his arms, but at last he bade her farewell. She did not weep but reproached herself for having loved a married man, and got herself to a nunnery where she expiated her sin for twenty-three years, as sister Marthe de Jésus. As usual, an anonymous versifier seized his pen:

Ninon

Lorsque Vigean quitta la cour
Les jeux, les graces, les amours
Entrèrent dans le monastère;
Ce jour-là la beauté se voilà,
Et fit voeu d'être solitaire.

(When Vigean left the court, play and love and grace took
flight and a convent sought, where beauty, setting the
world at naught, carefully veiled her face.)

From Rocroy and Arras the tides of war began to turn in
favor of the French, and when Monsieur le duc d'Enghien and
his followers took up their winter quarters in Paris, they were
the idols of the capital. They went to Marion's house in droves,
and sounds of revelry issued forth by night and by day. There
was feasting and dancing, and Bussy-Rabutin invented the
"game of love" in which Violence was to come to the aid of
Beauty in distress. A number of the men, including Enghien himself, found Ninon's hospitality an agreeable change.

Because of his frustrated love for his cousin, the duke had
shown little interest in casual relationships with women, though
he could have had his choice. He made no pretense of being in
love with Ninon, but he liked her. She was more a match for
his wit than Marion.

As she lay in bed watching the great hero undress and listening to his tales of victories, she noted his hairy chest and legs,
and quoted a Latin proverb: "*Vir pilosus vel fortis, vel libidinosus*
—[The hirsute are either strong or libidinous]."

The next morning, as she watched him dress, she murmured
mischievously, "How very strong you must be, Monsieur le
duc!"

There was no mistaking her meaning. Nevertheless, Enghien
took it good-naturedly. He continued his visits, "bringing the
winds of the Fronde in his cloak," and in the days of his glory
he never passed her without stopping his equipage, alighting and
coming over to kiss her hand. Ninon, for her part, never used
this important relationship to gain the slightest benefit.

Saint-Evremond, who was Ninon's greatest confidant, indi-

cates in his *Elégie à Mademoiselle de Lanclos* that the affair
with Condé lasted some time:

> Ce jeune duc qui gagnait des batailles,
> Qui sut couvrir de tant de funérailles
> Les champs fameux de Nordlingue et Rocroy,
> Qui sut remplir nos ennemis d'effroi,
> Las de fournir les sujets à l'Histoire,
> Voulant jouir quelquefois de sa gloire,
> De fier et grand, rendu civil et doux,
> Ce même duc allait souper chez vous,
> Comme un héros jamais ne se repose,
> Après souper il faisait autre chose,
> Et, sans savoir, s'il poussait des soupirs,
> Je sais, au moins, qu'il aimait ses plaisirs.

(This young duke who won battles, who knew how to
cover with so much ruin the famous fields of Nördlingen
and Rocroy, who knew how to fill our enemies with fear,
tired of furnishing subject matter for history, wanting at
times to enjoy the glory of a proud and great man, made
polite and sweet, this same duke went to dine with you,
and as a hero never takes a rest, after dinner he did something else; and if, without realizing it, he emitted sighs, I
know at least that he enjoyed his pleasures.)

Chapter XVII

FOR a Parisian, exile was a fate worse than imprisonment. The Bastille, so mysterious and gruesome in historical fiction, was actually, if the prisoner happened to be a gentleman, something of a club, where he occupied a comfortable apartment with his own furniture. If he were poor and put in one of the towers, he was still better lodged and fed than when at liberty.

François Ravaisson, who devoted twenty years to the study of the records and who published seventeen volumes of *Les Archives de la Bastille*, says that the courtyards resembled those of a college rather than a prison, being continuously filled with prisoners and their friends who indulged in all kinds of games. He maintains that the quality of the food would have excited the envy of many a bourgeois. There was breakfast and supper, and at midday a dinner consisting of soup, entree, a second meat and a dessert, accompanied by two bottles of burgundy or champagne. A third bottle was supplied each prisoner to take care of his thirst between meals. On holidays the allowance was raised to six bottles per man, and some of the prisoners even maintained their private cellars. They could order tobacco and other luxuries from the merchants who had set up shops for the purpose on the other side of the moat. Communication with the outside world, though forbidden, was actually accomplished quite easily. Of course there were dungeons for solitary confinement, but they were not used as much as we have been led to believe.

If Henry de Lanclos had been put in the Bastille he would have lived well, played his lute and composed his melodies at the expense of the state. Instead, he spent ten years roaming the provinces, yearning for Paris, earning a precarious living teaching the lute, and in his spare time composing and carousing. He spent some time at Grenoble, a foyer of libertinism. A minor poet has depicted him there in the company of a councilor of *parlement* eating the highly spiced regional dishes, washing them down with the "course" wines of the district, and singing indecent songs. Quite likely. There is also a report that he entered the service of Paul de Gondi, the future cardinal de Retz.

Occasionally Henry had tried to communicate with his wife, but it was a dangerous undertaking with the police of the Châtelet ever on the lookout, and it is doubtful if any of his messages got through. He had been condemned in absentia, and no royal pardon had been issued. However, after the death of the widow of his victim, there was no longer anyone to prosecute, and a few years after the deaths of Louis XIII and Richelieu the longing to return to the Marais proved strong enough for him to take the risk.

Henry found his wife dead and his daughter grown to maturity and in business for herself. He did not have far to inquire for her address. She welcomed him joyfully, but they both realized that for him to take up his residence with her would mean not only to risk his liberty but to interfere with hers.

He was in his late fifties and hungry for the companionship of people with interests similar to his own. His reputation as a musician had somewhat increased and he was listed by a leading musicologist, Père Mersenne, in *Harmonie universelle*, as a performer of the first rank.

It wasn't long before he found his proper milieu. He joined a group of musicians whose patron was Sieur Anne de Chambré, a gentleman in the service of Monsieur le Prince, as the duc d'Enghien was called since the death of his father. Chambré's home contained a room built as a classic temple in which the finest amateurs of music gathered to perform, where the mythology of ancient Greece was a cult, and music its form of worship. Mademoiselle de Chambré, herelf a fine musician, acted as hostess. The circle included the painter Eustache Le Sueur, the etchers Abraham Bosse and Robert Nanteuil, and Henry's old friend Denis Gaultier.[1]

The fame of the Gaultier family had spread throughout Europe. Jacques, a cousin of Denis, had been exiled to England for a murder of honor. There he had become the chief lutanist to Charles I. Ennemond, Gaultier le Vieux, a septuagenarian, had retired to the place of his birth, where he lived the life of a country squire surrounded by his progeny.

One day Henry de Lanclos decided to visit him. He rode toward the valley of the Dauphiné and spent the night at an inn, going next morning to the little town of Villette Serpaise. He surprised the old man, ruddy with health and purple from the grapes he had been sorting and sampling. They embraced warmly and after introductions to the family sat down under the trees to a dinner of fish and roast partridge, of home made cheese and fruits of the surrounding orchards, all washed down by Ennemond's best vintage. Henry patted each grandchild on the head and answered a hundred questions about his wanderings.

After dinner, when the two men were left alone, Gaultier talked of his youth and of the time he had played in the service of Marie de Medici. When Henry told of the Chambré circle it reminded the old man of the *Camarata* which had met in Florence in his youth to create a musical form modeled on Greek drama. They talked of Monteverdi's revolutionary harmonic combinations; they discussed the Italian opera which Mazarin had introduced at the Académie Royale de Musique. Inevitably the conversation turned to the good old days when they had played in the courtyards of the Marais to pick up a few *sous*.

"Do you ever play now?" asked Henry.

"I should say not," said Gaultier. "I employ my time in the garden and the vineyard and in bottling the vintage. My daughter-in-law says music is a frivolous waste of time. Besides, one of the children is always sleeping. Moreover, I have rheumatism in my fingers. Furthermore, I have completely forgotten how."

[1] "French composer of many effective pieces for lute." Oscar Thompson's *Cyclopedia of Music and Musicians*.

It grew chilly and they went indoors to sit before the fire. On a shelf in a dark corner the firelight revealed some musical instruments and Henry went over to examine them. He found a recorder, two lutes and a rebec, all in deplorable condition. They had been used by the children as toys. Henry examined them and, taking a string from one, applied it to another. Soon he had a lute and a rebec in good condition. Picking out a few chords on the former, he began first to improvise and then to play some of his own compositions. Gaultier listened with folded arms and bent head. Then Henry struck up a *courante* they used to play together. It was too much for the old man, who picked up the rebec and joined in. Soon they were playing duets as they had in the old days. One melody followed the other in a veritable orgy, and they never stopped until daylight came through the little window.

At breakfast the men were silent as they dipped their bread in bowls of wine. Whatever the Gaultier family thought, they were too polite to say before a stranger. The two men embraced and Henry turned his horse's head north, his saddlebags filled with bottles of the finest *cru*. He turned to wave a last farewell and caught the old man wiping his eyes. If later old Gaultier was punished by his daughter-in-law, he undoubtedly felt that it was worth it.

That year the Thirty Years' War came to an end with the Treaty of Westphalia. It reduced the emperor of the Holy Roman Empire to little more than the other German princes. France and her allies gained considerable advantages. Louis gained the three bishoprics of Metz, Toul and Verdun as well as Alsace, though the accession of the last was couched in such dubious terms that it became a pretext for further war.

The same year, 1648, the first war of the Fronde broke out, spreading from Paris to the provinces. Henry de Lanclos was called to action in Normandy under the banner of the duc de Longueville, the husband of Condé's beautiful sister Geneviève. In 1649, Henry was wounded by the comte d'Harcourt in the village of La Bouille, near Rouen. Ninon was at his deathbed.

He had nothing to bequeath her but advice. His last words were:

"*Soyez moins scrupuleuse sur le nombre que sur le choix de vos plaisirs* [Be less fastidious about the number of your pleasures than about their choice]."

Three years after his death, in 1652, Denis Gaultier brought out *La Rhétorique des dieux*, a magnificent vellum-bound volume, handwritten, and decorated by the artists of the Chambré group. The original, conserved in Berlin, was reprinted in Paris in 1932. It was a selection of his own compositions and contains *Tombeau de M. de Lanclos*, *La Consolation aux amis*, and *La Résolution des amis du sieur de Lanclos sur sa mort*. A commentary indited by Chambré says that "Gaultier, divine man, had been the best friend of the defunct, that he had expressed so graphically through the power of his art the grief caused by the loss of Lanclos, that all the hearers of these funeral chants had undergone the agony of a Passion."

There also remains for musicologists a volume called *Suites faciles pour une flute ou violon et une basse continue, de la composition de MM. Defau, Lanclos, Pinel, Lully, Bryninghs, Lefèbre et autres habiles maîtres*, with marked instructions for beginners. In another volume of the same series Henry de Lanclos is represented by two suites, one for lute, violin and flute with figured bass, and the second for treble and bass.

Henry de Lanclos's defects were those of his age and his class. He was not a borrower, but was willing to sing for his supper and play for his dinner. His marriage of convenience, as opposed to a *marriage d'inclination*, was in full accord with the mores of his century. So established was the institution of the arranged marriage that a regular scale of marriage portions was in operation. Two thousand to six thousand *livres* could buy one's daughter a sergeant, a petty commissioned officer or a merchant; twelve to twenty thousand a notary or *greffier* (court clerk or town clerk); thirty-five to forty-five a treasurer of France; forty-five to seventy-five a councilor; seventy-five to one hundred and fifty, a councilor of *parlement* or a minor judge; and two hundred thousand a "president or judge of the first rank, as well as a marquis or a duke." There is a letter on record in which a father writes to his son, "I beg you on my knees not to marry the woman of your choice."

Henry did not marry the woman of his choice. Had he done so, Ninon would not have been Ninon, and we should never have heard of him.

Chapter XVIII

THERE was a spell of dreary weather and Ninon became restless. Every afternoon from four o'clock on her little drawing room was crowded.

There were nobles, philosophers and poets, many of them debauched and dirty. There were soldiers who had not yet wiped off the mud and sweat of battle. Old men tried to hide their expansive bellies behind elaborately embroidered waistcoats, and sucked pastilles to disguise their fetid breaths. She could scarcely walk around the room without having to step over some silly boy who quoted verse and tried to peep up her skirts as she passed.

Libertinism, which had been driven underground by a wave of religious zeal, now came forth again. Men of the cloth and freethinkers argued eternal questions. Boisrobert and Saint-Pavin discussed Epicurus with Saint-Evremond, and the young duc d'Enghien boasted of his victories. Ninon was getting tired of them all. Her relations with Aubijoux had become more or less routine, and Coulon was on his way out. She could no longer bear his inebriety. The chevalier de Méré was distinctly above the rest. She had taken the opportunity to learn what she could from him, but she found him pedantic in love as well as in conversation.

One morning a fresh wind blew the clouds away and the sun came out of its winter retreat. She felt as if she had awakened from a long sleep. She ordered her sedan chair and told her *valet de chambre* that she would not be at home that afternoon. Her young maid, helping her to dress, recognized the mood of her mistress.

"Mademoiselle desires to wear her new green velour today?"

"You're very young, Delphine," Ninon replied. "One wears a

new frock to try to rekindle a dying love. For a new lover any dress is new."

She chose the gown in which she liked herself best, an ivory, watered silk with clusters of pink rosebuds. As Delphine brushed and arranged her long brown curls, she found herself humming a song of Malherbe:

Quand un nouveau feu s'allume . . .

She had no one in mind. Desire, without a specific object. She draped a white lace mantilla over her hair, tucked a lace handkerchief into her bosom, drew on her soft, ivory gloves from Grasse.

Her porters were waiting at the door. She instructed them to take her to the Cours by way of the rue Sainte-Honoré. Then she settled back against the yellow tufted satin, so gay and so becoming to her fresh complexion. She found the gentle swaying of the chair both soothing and stimulating.

The Cours-la-Reine was crowded. Carriages and sedan chairs passed up and down the middle, while equestrians rode at one side; people strolled under the trees, absorbed in conversation yet with an eye for who was with whom, and what they had on. The duc d'Enghien, surrounded by his followers, rode over and dismounted to kiss Ninon's hand and exchange a few words.

The Cours-la-Reine, built by Marie de Medici, runs alongside the Seine between what are now the Place de la Concorde and the Place de l'Alma.[1] Ninon ordered her men to rest her chair with its back to the river, so that she could watch the procession. In no time she found herself holding court. She knew she was looking her best, but for whom? For that handsome young actor who entertained her with gossip of the theatre and with compliments? Even as he talked, paying homage with his lips, his eyes kept straying to one of her porters, the one with the fine legs. Old Mondor of the Pont-Neuf passed in splendor, his sedan adorned with real gold, despite the edict against such extravagance.

Scarron, looking ill, had himself transported to her side to tell

[1] From the Pont des Invalides on to the Place de l'Alma it is now called the *Cours-Albert-Premier*.

her the latest gossip about the queen and Mazarin. An equipage passed with a young woman sitting between two gentlemen, one of whom Ninon recognized as the comte de Bussy-Rabutin. With him were his cousin, Marie de Rabutin-Chantal, and her husband, the marquis de Sévigné. They had recently been married.

"Her cousin seems more in love with her than her husband," observed Ninon.

"She is said to be very clever," remarked Scarron. "She has interesting eyes, one blue and one brown.

"Paris is changing," continued the poet, "it's not like the old days."

"I think it's wonderful as it is," said Ninon.

"Bassompierre said Paris was so full you could walk from end to end on the roofs of the coaches," said someone.

"Do you know what Bassompierre said to the queen?" asked Scarron, and without waiting for a reply he continued, "Her Majesty told him that now that he was out of the Bastille he would be taking a goodly crowd of whores to court. 'I'll wager, madame,' he replied, 'that you'll be taking more of them than I will.' "

Gramont's carriage passed and Ninon noticed the maréchal signaling a young horseman to join him. As the latter dismounted and walked his horse to the equipage, which had stopped, Ninon observed that he was tall and graceful, with fair hair and an earnest face, a new face which she had not seen in the Marais. Scarron, following her glance, remarked:

"That is Philippe de Montault-Benac, duc de Navailles. He was page to His Defunct Eminence. Now he commands a regiment of light cavalry for His Current Eminence. If he behaves, he'll get a maréchal's baton."

Ninon scarcely heard the end of the sentence. The chevalier had remounted, and she ordered her porters to follow him. As she rode, she scribbled a note on her tablet and sent it by her lackey. Soon the young duke was walking his horse at her side. He showed a mild surprise at being singled out by so attractive a young woman. As he was a stranger to the Marais, he didn't know who she was. His manners were gracious, and as he laughed readily at her sallies, she credited him with wit.

When they reached the *porte-cochère* of her home, she invited him in and gave her valet instructions that she was at home to no one the rest of the evening.

The damask draperies were drawn in the small reception room, and the candles lit. A wood fire was burning in the grate. They sat before the hearth, Navailles talking of his campaigns in Italy and in Flanders. She showed him some of her prized books, and if their hands touched accidentally, she quickly withdrew hers. She felt like a young girl on the threshold of first love. The bell at the gate tinkled and impatient knocking sounded through the house, but the door was not opened.

She invited the duke to stay to dinner. The meal was delicious, the wines exactly right. She ate heartily but, as was her custom, drank little. "Ninon," her friends said, "does not need to drink. She is intoxicated with the first spoonful of soup."

After dinner she sat at the clavecin and played toccatas. The soft light from the instrument's candles shed a halo of copper around her bent head. In the pauses, the crackling of the fire and Navailles's breathing could be heard. Suddenly, in a change of mood, she picked up her lute and, sitting at the feet of her guest, let her fingers caress the strings idly. She was impatient, but she wanted to prolong the delicious anticipation. The longer the delay, the greater the fulfillment. She began to play the insidious dance rhythms of Spain, accelerating her tempo. Her whole body moved and her low-cut bodice, seemingly by accident, slipped off one white shoulder.

It was nearly midnight when Navailles rose to go. They stood a moment, awkwardly, and then he took her in his arms and kissed her. No protruding belly got in their way. His breath was sweet. "You'll stay the night," she whispered.

She led him to her chamber, telling him to undress, that she would not be long. Then she went to her dressing room and rang for Delphine, her heart beating. She did not take for granted the attraction of nudity, unadorned. "That," she said, "is all right for a statue. A woman should have something for a man to take off." She bathed in fresh, cool, scented water and put on a night-gown of sheerest white linen, with point de Malines rippling at the wrists. Delphine arranged her hair under a soft lace night-cap. Over her shoulders she threw a white wool dressing gown lined with rustling rose-pink taffeta.

As she crossed the threshold of her chamber she was arrested by a strange noise. It sounded curiously like a snore. She approached the bed, and her candle flickered on a sleeping cavalier with mouth wide open. The intake of breath was gurgling and sono-rous, but the whistling note of the exhalation was more than she could bear. Fury mingled with disappointment, and her impulse was to awaken him and ask him to leave.

However, she soon thought better of it. The poor fellow had drunk too much. No doubt he was tired from a long day of rid-ing. In a way, she thought, it was her own fault. She had dallied too long. She gathered up his clothes and his sword and tiptoed out to spend the night in another room. As she got into bed she giggled at the story with which she would regale the company next day.

At dawn Navailles was awakened by the slamming of a door. Jumping up, he saw in the dim light a youth brandishing a sword.

"Monsieur," he cried, "I am a man of honor. I am ready to give you satisfaction." Then he looked for his clothes. It is difficult to be a man of honor without one's pants.

Ninon burst into laughter, greatly enjoying his embarrassment. He apologized, making what excuses he could. Ninon, taking no chances this time of too long a prologue, pulled off doubtlet and hose and, flinging them into a corner, jumped into bed.

The poor man did his best, but the more he tried the less he succeeded. He may have been one of those creatures who prefer to do their own wooing. When Ninon told the story to her friends, she added that she believed that blonds were less virile than brunets.

But the subsequent history of the duc de Navailles tends to show that he was somewhat infected with respectability. He mar-ried and his wife became dame of honor to the young queen,

Marie-Thérèse. He felt it his duty to inform Her Majesty that His Majesty was carrying on with Louise de la Vallière. Moreover, it was the duchesse de Navailles who discovered the secret door to the quarters occupied by the maids of honor, and who took it upon herself to have it walled up, thus complicating the king's nocturnal ramblings. For these betrayals the family Navailles was exiled for a short time. The duke became governor of Le Havre, and commanded armies, but he did not receive his marshal's baton until 1675. He wrote *Memoirs of the Principal Events from 1638 to 1683*, but his night with Ninon was not included.

Chapter XIX

In 1648 the King's Attorney presented seven fiscal edicts, six of which were designed to increase taxation. *Parlement* demanded that the King's Prerogative be exercised within the limits of human rather than divine power; it drew up articles of reform demanding, among other things, freedom from arbitrary arrest and imprisonment, and a limitation of the Crown's power of taxation. The Advocate General, Omer Talon, made a speech, indicting the regime, which rang around Europe:

> For ten years the country has been in ruins, the peasants reduced to sleeping on straw, their furniture sold to pay their taxes. To maintain luxury in Paris, millions of innocent persons are forced to live on bread made of bran and oats, with no hope or protection except in their weakness; owning nothing but their souls, because no means has been devised to sell these at auction.

The aristocrats, fearing the growing power of Mazarin, united in the Cabale des Importants. They united their cause with that of *parlement* and of the oppressed middle class. All claimed loyalty to the boy king and to the queen mother, provided she would renounce her minister-lover, who was filling not only the royal coffers but his own.

Negotiations were carried on between the representatives of *parlement* and the regent, Monsieur generally acting as spokesman for his sister-in-law. In May the King's Attorney presented an edict forbidding the assembling of the chambers of *parlement*. That body sent a deputation to the Palais Royal to protest, and a strange and frightening thing occurred. The deputation was followed by ten thousand or more growling men and women of the people. The queen, threatened, capitulated, but later she retracted her promise, and *parlement* drew up twenty-seven articles of reform. In July they took action on two of them, the first revoking all *intendants* whose commissions were not verified, and the second ordering the *procureur général* to inform against any bad administration of finances. This was the first would-be assumption of legislative authority by the judicial body, and a stormy meeting was held in the Palais du Luxembourg, where the delegates of the four sovereign courts met the duc d'Orléans and Mazarin. After days of argument the cardinal conceded that the reforms should be instituted, but saved face by insisting that the phrase "By order of His Majesty, the King," be affixed. Three days later he revoked all intendancies except those in frontier provinces.

Tension mounted and the government determined to use force. Two councilors of *parlement*, one the honest and popular Broussel, who had served since the days of Henri IV, were arrested and thrown into the Bastille. The whole city sprang to arms, riots broke out and the Day of the Barricades began. The Palais Royal was surrounded and the royal Guards fired upon. The queen was forced to release the prisoners. The failure of the government diminished its authority, but Condé had won a victory at Lens. Anne counted on the royal troops released by the Treaty of Westphalia, as well as on the militia, to subdue "the riffraff infested with the public good."

On the night of September 13 the court had quietly quit the capital and taken up residence at Rueil. *Parlement* demanded the return of the king, and also that no subjects, "of whatever quality or condition, shall be held prisoner longer than twenty-four hours without being interrogated . . . and given over to their natural judges."

The royal family returned to Paris, but not for long. On the night of Epiphany . . . *la Fête des Rois* . . . the queen had the traditional cake baked, containing a gold coin. While Louis and Philippe ate it she told them the story of the Magi, and when her favorite son bit into the coin, she put the gold paper crown on his head, upon which young Louis justifiably protested. She then put them to bed, imploring them not to fight.

That evening Orléans, Mazarin and Condé were dining with the maréchal de Gramont. Before dawn they all met at the entrance of the Cours-la-Reine and, followed by the sleepy courtiers, the cavalcade proceeded to the Palace of Saint-Germain-en-Laye. There they rested on improvised mattresses and straw, as it was the custom for the royal furniture to make the peregrinations from palace to palace with its owners. In the morning Paris awoke to find that the royal family had again lit out.

Parlement impeached Mazarin and ordered the men of Paris to take up arms. The court moved on to Poitiers, where they were under the protection of Turenne and his troops, and Condé, under the royal standard, began the siege.

The civil strife named the War of the Fronde, after the slingshot that boys played with, followed. The Bastille was gently besieged by the government forces as sumptuously dressed ladies brought their chairs to watch. It has been called an *opéra bouffe* war. The amount of gunpowder used was less than the face powder, and more ink was spilled by the pamphleteers than blood by the combatants. Condé, with few troops, confined his activities to intercepting supplies to the city and occupying bakeries and cattle markets. Most of the *précieuses* were on the side of the *frondeurs* and they wanted it to be a nice war, chivalrous and heroic, not brutal and savage. In a short time the fortress surrendered, to the sound of trumpets and drums.

The most beautiful *frondeuse*, and the most ardent, was Condé's sister, the duchesse de Longueville. She moved into the Hôtel de Ville, receiving the battle heroes in her chambers where "the air was alive with the talk of war and love, to the obbligato of violins." This lovely princess of the blood, scion of the Bourbons and the Montmorencys, was espousing the cause of the people. At fourteen Anne-Geneviève had been so religious that she had refused to attend a ball at the wicked court. Her mama had insisted, and on the advice of the good nuns she had obeyed, but had worn under her satin bodice a *cilice*, or hair shirt, so that every pleasurable wiggle would bring its admonitory scratching. *On dit* that the poor girl came home all scratched up. It wasn't long, however, before she abandoned her piety and soon she became a favorite in the salons and the rage at court.

Paul de Gondi, not yet the cardinal de Retz, wrote:

> The smallpox had left Madame de Longueville all the radiance of her beauty, and that of Madame de Bouillon, somewhat impaired, was still brilliant. Imagine, I beg you, these two ladies on the steps of the Hôtel de Ville, their appearance all the more lovely because it seemed unstudied, although it was not. Each held one of her children in her arms, as beautiful as their mothers. The Place de Grève was crammed with people, all the men shouting with delight, and all the women shedding tears of tender emotion.

Madame de Longueville was indeed the prima donna of the Fronde. Her husband was leading the campaign in Normandy, her elder brother, Condé, was in charge of the besieging forces, her other brother, Conti, supported the Frondeurs; her lover, La Rochefoucauld, was fighting in the streets of Paris, and it was no secret that she was bearing his child. She insisted that the baby be born at the Hôtel de Ville, for he was to be "a child of the people." As soon as she was able, she held the infant, who had been christened Charles-Paris d'Orléans, up for the shouting populace to see.

Since in the Fronde families were divided against themselves, and since the combatants often changed sides for trivial reasons, Ninon was not taken in by the grandiloquent aspects of the war. She was not among those present at the Hôtel de Ville, for she had not acquired the fashionable habit of attending battles or executions. She was at home to members of both factions, if they were her friends, and her salon, now the most lively and interesting one in Paris, was inevitably the scene of political discussion, which she kept from becoming acrimonious with exceeding tact. When adversaries met under her roof, they often became friends and it was said that "the friends of Ninon become friends of each other." She forbade slandering of those absent. "We should never speak ill of our enemies," she remarked, "they are the only people who do not deceive us."

Chapter XX

THE hero of the day was Pierre de Villars, a gentleman in the service of the prince de Conti. His handsome face and military bearing won him the name Villars-Oroondate, after the hero of Calprenède's *Cassandre* (in ten volumes), which everybody was reading. He was the darling of the ladies, and he was Ninon's lover.

Public gatherings were becoming dangerous and a woman could not go out alone, as bands of ribald and offensive youths roamed the streets. On the arm of Villars-Oroondate, however, Ninon felt safe, and the material hardships of the siege did not trouble her. She was excited and happy, enjoying a reasonable financial security, admiration, friendship and a lover who was not only physically to her taste but of whom she could be proud.

And then, suddenly, he was ordered by Conti to join his regiment, which was stationed at Lyon. Ninon offered to accompany him but he assured her that a woman would hamper a soldier's movements. She pleaded that she would not, that she just wished to be near him, but he was firm.

After his departure Ninon felt depressed. She could not become interested in any other man, and all the hardships that had seemed unimportant now became burdensome. She decided to give fate a little push.

She dressed as a cavalier, a sword at her side and a pistol in her belt. She wore a doublet over an embroidered *pourpoint*, pantaloons and high boots. Her long hair covered her lace ruff, and she penciled in the suggestion of a mustache. Gauntlets and a dashing Spanish hat completed the disguise.

Too impatient to await the passenger coach, which did not run that day, she went to the Hôtel de Sens and caught the mail coach, making herself as comfortable as she could among the mailbags. It was the custom for people to make their wills before leaving on a journey but Ninon never thought of danger. She risked not only discovery and arrest but attack by highwaymen. She was grateful that she knew how to handle a sword. One difficulty which she had not anticipated was that a young girl at an inn at which they stopped made it all too evident that she would be willing to grant the young cavalier her favors.

The journey took five days. As soon as she arrived she sought her lover's regiment. It is not known whether Villars had been ordered to move on or whether he repudiated her. It was a bitter disappointment.

Lyon was smoky and its gloomy fortifications were oppressive. The population seemed to her haughty and dull. She spent two nights in a dreary inn with no comforts and then, for the second time in her life, took refuge in a convent.

Whether she prayed when she sat in the quiet chapel with bowed head we do not know, but, as before, the music and the peace calmed her. However, it wasn't long before her tranquillity was rudely disturbed.

Alphonse du Plessis, cardinal de Richelieu, older brother of the great statesman, was bishop of Lyon. He had been a problem brother and Armand had given him the diocese to keep him out of mischief. It had proved, however, a playground for his eccentricities. He alternated between playing the role of God in a red satin robe, dispensing blessings, and that of Céladon in shepherd's rags, a beribboned crook taking the place of his crosier. On one occasion, despite his habit of a Carthusian monk, he was severely beaten by an irate husband.

On one of his rare visits to the convent he noticed Ninon and made inquiries about her. He came every day thereafter, and tried his various lines of approach, the major one being that it was a pity for a young and beautiful woman to waste her life. Time was precious, youth fleeting. One could repent later. He was aging, pompous and slightly mad, and his attempts at gallantry were both ludicrous and pathetic. Ninon would have none of him, but he became so persistent that peace vanished. The convent was no longer a refuge.

Not wishing to return to the inn, she advertised by the town crier, to the accompaniment of trumpet, that a lady was in need of a residence where she could live in safety and seclusion.

Marc-Antoine Pérachon, a wealthy man of no profession, heard the call. When he met Ninon he was enormously impressed by her charm and sophistication and he offered her a gift of one of his houses, worth eight thousand crowns. She was a jewel, he said, that needed a proper setting. She asked what the conditions were and Monsieur Pérachon said that all he would ask was permission to pay her a short visit each day and quietly enjoy her beauty from a distance.

Whatever Ninon thought, she accepted and she kept her share of the agreement. Not only was she polite, she was entertaining. Sometimes she even served her benefactor with light refreshment, as her instinct for hospitality was indomitable. It wasn't long, however, before Monsieur Pérachon began to feel he had been made something of a fool, and nothing infuriates a fool more than being made a fool of.

Ninon recognized the gleam in his eye but appeared not to notice. He began crudely to try to caress her and was delicately repulsed. Ninon was not at all addicted to the "correct rules of cruelty"; he simply did not appeal to her and she told him so. He flew into a rage and they had what is called "words."

Ninon thereupon returned the house to him after throwing him out of it. Tallemant writes: "She restored his generosities to him, for she was not self-seeking."

Nostalgia for Paris completely overwhelmed her. She wanted desperately to be among her own friends, to live amid her own possessions. In more conventional garb, and by stagecoach, she returned, and there was rejoicing in the Marais, although a few malicious gossips maintained that she had gone away to be secretly treated for *quelque incommodité*.

Her funds were low, and it was necessary to replenish them. The first applicant to present himself was César de Bourbon, duc de Vendôme, a man in his sixties, a natural, though legitimized, son of Henri IV and Gabrielle d'Estrées. He had plotted against Marie de Medici, prosecuted the war against the Huguenots and been jailed for a conspiracy against Richelieu. He had been a member of the *Cabale des Importants* and his younger son, the duc de Beaufort, was known as *le roy des Halles* (the king of the Markets) because he espoused the cause of the people. Vendôme later made peace with Mazarin, however, and permitted his older son, the duc de Mercoeur, to marry Laure Mancini, one of the cardinal's nieces.

Vendôme assumed that because of his rank the conquest of a courtesan would be easy. To his surprise, Ninon rejected him. He raised his offer, but she still refused, despite her great need for money. The duke pleaded his illustrious birth, and she replied, "When men boast of their ancestry, it is because they have little else to boast of."

He expressed his humiliation and outrage in four lines:

> Indigne de mes feux, indigne de mes larmes,
> Je renonce sans peine à tes faibles appas;
> Mon amour te prêtait des charmes,
> Ingrate, que tu n'avais pas.

(Unworthy of my passion, unworthy of my tears, I find it easy to renounce your feeble attractions; my love lent you charms, ingrate, that you never possessed.)

Ninon asked the duke's valet to wait and scribbled the reply:

> Insensible à tes feux, insensible à tes larmes,
> Je te vois renoncer à mes faibles appas;
> Mais, si l'amour prête des charmes,
> Pourquoi n'en empruntais-tu pas?

(Indifferent to your passion, indifferent to your tears, I see you renounce my feeble attractions; but if love lends charms why did you not borrow some?)

Vendôme sulked awhile, but Ninon's attraction overcame his pride. He asked to be permitted to see her on any terms, and soon he became her friend and confidant.

Chapter XXI

THE blockade of the city proved a failure. The bourgeois troops had protested that "the colonels and captains of Paris had not been appointed for the purpose of exposing themselves and the burghers of the said town to sorties in which they might well risk their lives." The archduke Leopold, governor of the Spanish Netherlands, told *parlement* that Mazarin had offered Spain peace at any price, that he might be free to deal with the rebellion at home. Philip IV, regarding this as treachery, had refused negotiations. *Parlement* asked the regent to withdraw the royal troops. The Court replied by attacking *parlement* for having received an embassy from an enemy country. In March 1649, Leopold crossed the frontier in the service of *parlement*, he said, in order to negotiate a peace between the two crowns. Under pressure of what looked suspiciously like a foreign invasion, and the mounting discontent of the burghers, who suffered inroads on their silverware after each search for "spies," the Peace of Rueil was signed, between the government and the Frondeurs.

The troops were discharged and there was rejoicing and dancing in the same streets that had been barricaded with paving-stones and hogsheads filled with earth and horse manure. On April 5 a thanksgiving service was held at Notre-Dame. *Parlement* voted a deputation to thank His Most Gracious Majesty and his mother for giving peace to their subjects, and petitioned them to return to Paris. The royal family entered the city to enthusiastic acclaim, which even included Mazarin. A great ball was held at the Hôtel de Ville. Frondeurs embraced royalists, and brothers became friends again. Condé, regarding himself as the savior of France, became arrogant. The people were left to pick up the pieces.

But, like many treaties, the Peace of Rueil led to the next war. A flood of anonymous attacks against the government, and especially the cardinal, and his relations with the queen-regent, kept pouring off the presses. The headquarters for their secret distribution was a bookstall near the Samaritaine fountain on the Pont-Neuf. A printer who was caught publishing a scurrilous attack was arrested and condemned to death. On his way to the gibbet he was rescued by the populace. Although hostilities had ceased, the spirit of rebellion was smoldering. Marion Delorme's house was under the observation of Mazarin's spies, as it had been of Richelieu's.

One day, with his henchman, Ninon's former lover, Jarzé, came to the Tuileries gardens, considered the sacred terrain of Vendôme's son, the duc de Beaufort, and his followers. They strutted around like naughty, defiant boys and then returned to court boasting that they had "defied the enemy in his stronghold."

It was shortly after that that the duc de Vendôme took Ninon and a few of her friends to dinner at a fashionable restaurant adjoining the Tuileries, Renard's Garden, known as the rendezvous of aristocratic Frondeurs.

As they entered, they saw a table in the center of the main hall occupied by a boisterous group of royalists. Jarzé sat at the head, a napkin tied around his neck. They were all the worse for drink, stuffing themselves with food, and shouting jokes and stories across the table.

Vendôme had reserved a corner table for his guests, but conversation was difficult amid the clatter.

"They say the queen is secretly married to her lover," he remarked; "he never took his final vows. At any rate, she's not sleeping with that lout over there. They say Paul de Gondi's been trying his luck too, but he hasn't a chance."

"Poor Anne," said Ninon. "I should hate to be a queen. She never got much attention from her husband, and now every keyhole in her suite has an eye glued to it."

Just then Jarzé spotted Ninon. He rose and bowed to her, tankard in hand.

"A toast!" he shouted. "I drink to *la belle* Ninon, the second best . . ." The ribald word froze on his lips and his eyes turned to the door. His enemy, the duc de Beaufort, sword unsheathed, had stepped in a few paces ahead of his men.

"Your son," said Ninon to Vendôme, "is either defending Her Majesty's virtue or my pre-eminence."

"The queen," said Vendôme, "had a fancy for my son at one time."

The young *Roy des Halles* advanced into the room. His voice was the only sound to be heard.

"Monsieur René du Plessis de la Roche-Pichemer, marquis de Jarzé, I trust you have brought your violins."

Jarzé, without his protector, Condé, was a sorry figure. He began to stutter, and Beaufort continued, "Because I am going to make you dance."

With that, he pulled the end of the tablecloth and dumped all the dishes and carafes of wine onto the banqueters. A skirmish followed in which the royalists were badly routed. The hero's father and his guests finished their dinner in a private dining room on the floor above.

Chapter XXII

LE MARQUIS DE SÉVIGNÉ is remembered by the world as the husband of the marquise. A handsome, impoverished Breton, related to the Retz family, he seems hardly a match for the wealthy and extremely clever Marie de Rabutin-Chantal, a Coulanges on her mother's side, and related to many of the first families of the country.

Madame la Marquise was interested in everything; Monsieur le Marquis was interested only in women. He enjoyed spending his wife's money on them, although he was far from generous with it. When Vendôme introduced him to Ninon, he had been married about five years. His daughter, then three, was to become the beautiful, snobbish Madame de Grignan, known to us as the recipient of her mother's letters. His son Charles was nursing. He was destined to become Ninon's lover.

Henri de Sévigné had no compunction about flaunting his loves, and when he fell in love with Ninon she became his constant companion. They were seen at the theatre, at the finest restaurants and on the Cours. He was a daily visitor and so much in love that he couldn't refrain from talking about it. He even confided in his wife's first cousin, the comte de Bussy-Rabutin, who was sighing in vain for the favors of the marquise.

The count tells about it all in his *Memoirs*:

Being related to Madame de Sévigné, I frequented her house as if it were my own and had many opportunities of noting the sorrow her husband caused her. So often she complained of the mental suffering she experienced owing to his faithlessness, and the ridicule which his caprice brought upon

107

him. I was fortunately of some comfort to her, but after a time, influenced by the marquis's folly, I fell in love with her myself. This state of things was brought about rather by opportunity than real love. One day Chenevil [Sévigné] told me that he had spent a very pleasant night, pleasant not only to himself, but to the lady in whose company he had been.

"You may gather from this," he said, "that I was not with your cousin; my companion was Ninon."

"I am sorry for you," I replied, "for my cousin is worth a thousand Ninons, and I feel sure that were she not your wife, she would be your mistress."

"That is very likely," said he.

I went straight to Madame de Sévigné and repeated this conversation.

"That kind of boasting is a poor compliment to me," she said, blushing with indignation.

"Do not let your husband guess you know this," I urged. "The consequences would be unpleasant."

"Really, you must be mad to talk thus, or you evidently think I am not in my right mind."

"Not at all, dear lady, you would be foolish not to pay him back in his own coin, sooner than to tell him what you know. Revenge yourself, fair Cousin, and I shall go shares; after all, your interests are as dear to me as my own."

"Steady, steady, Count," she said, "I am not so vexed as you think."

The next day I met Sévigné on the Cours and he took a seat in my carriage.

"I suppose," he said, "that you repeated our conversation to your cousin; she intimated as much to me."

"Not at all," I answered, "but your wife is a clever woman and as she has ample cause to discourse on jealousy, she naturally enough hits on the truth at times."

Sévigné was easily deceived and returned to the subject of his happiness; having enlarged upon the advantages accruing to a lover, he said he was going to be faithful to the end, that he was as much in love with Ninon as any man could be, and

that he was going to her house that very evening, as Vassé
was to entertain them, while he and Ninon made fun of
Vassé, their temporary host.

Henry-François, marquis de Vassé, the man Ninon and Sévigné
ridiculed, was extremely rich. He was vain and not too intelligent,
and he had poor digestion. As seems so often the case with those
who have a bad breath, he insisted upon breathing into the faces
of those with whom he conversed. When Ninon and Sévigné
paid him a visit, the conversation turned to diseases of the stomach.

"I never worry about anything like that," said Vassé, "I am
never bothered by my stomach."

"I can quite believe you," said Ninon, "you leave that to your
friends."

Some time later Bussy-Rabutin became a lieutenant general,
but he was soon dismissed for taking the wrong end of a dispute
with Turenne. For a flippant verse about the king he was thrown
into the Bastille, and upon his release was made a member of the
Academy. He was, however, requested to retire to his estate. In
the country he did what every gentleman did under the circumstances, wrote a book. He called it *L'Histoire amoureuse des
Gaules*, the ancient Gauls being thin disguises for contemporary
Frenchmen. He had no compunction about revealing secrets of
state. He thought very highly of his work, and wrote: "My letters
excel those of Madame de Sévigné."

Henri de Sévigné continued to be deeply in love with Ninon.
Nevertheless, when he opened, and not by mistake, a love letter
from Bussy-Rabutin to the marquise, he expelled the count from
the house with all the indignation of the deceiver deceived.

After three months Ninon grew tired of his devotion and ended
the liaison as quickly as possible. She had received from him in
three months only one inexpensive ring.

Sévigné consoled himself with a Madame Gondron, and the
chevalier d'Albret, brother of Moissens, challenged him to a duel
on her account. The marquis was wounded and died two days
later.

At twenty-five, the marquise de Sévigné was left a widow, for which posterity is grateful, for otherwise she might never have written some fifteen hundred letters which give us an intimate picture of the times, a more vivid evocation of a great century than any deliberate historian could have produced.

Chapter XXIII

THE beautiful body of Marion Delorme, which had delighted painters and lovers, was no longer shapely, owing to her frequent pregnancies, some of which had been aborted with drugs or blunt septic instruments plied by midwives who thereby risked their liberty, even their lives. Her clientele had diminished and she and her mother had moved from the Place Royale to an apartment on the rue de Thorigny.

One morning a peremptory knock sounded on the door. It was the secret police of Mazarin with a *lettre de cachet* which contained an order for her imprisonment for complicity in the Fronde. They found her lying on her bier, a maiden's crown on her head. By taking too strong a dose of antimony to abort a pregnancy, Marion had just escaped her fortieth birthday. Her illness had lasted three days, during which she had confessed eight times. After each absolution she had recalled other sins.

She had been a good daughter, supporting her mother, brothers and sister, and leaving provisions for them all. She left behind jewels and twenty thousand *livres'* worth of clothes.

During the century that followed, literature and legend arose about her. One writer maintained that she did not die at this time but escaped, living to consummate three marriages, one of them with a pirate who captured her on the high seas. Victor Hugo makes her the heroine of a play, Alfred de Vigny puts her in his novel *Cinq-Mars*, and Dumas uses her house on the Place Royale as the home of Milady, in *The Three Musketeers*.

Refuting all legends is a death certificate dated 1650.

Many of Marion's followers now crowded into Ninon's little drawing room. Among them were the "three brothers in

111

Sodomy": Saint-Pavin, a hunchback, an atheist who drew his living from the Church; Des Barreaux, Marion's original seducer; and the handsome and distinguished abbé Boisrobert. Because of his brilliant conversation he had been a favorite of Richelieu.

At first the talk of these men was circumspect, but inevitably their favorite topic cropped up, and when Boisrobert protested that it was unseemly to talk of such matters before a lady, Ninon replied that she was too much of a gentleman to mind. Then she commented on the fact that the priest seemed addicted to lackeys.

"Doesn't it prove monotonous?" she asked.

"On the contrary," Boisrobert replied, "it is the diversity in liveries that provides the spice."

Another visitor was Elbène, "Lord Chief Gossip of the Marais," an unworthy son of a distinguished courtier of Henri IV. He was attending the Academy Montmor, where a brand of convenient Epicureanism was taught, and where gentlemen learned to check their consciences with their hats. Alexandre d'Elbène frequented the best *ruelles* and the worst taverns, and was famous for his reluctance to pay his debts. This in no way affected his social standing, for then, as now, it was only the poor who felt the obligation to pay promptly.

As religion was not just a Sunday pastime but often a matter of life and death, it was a constant topic of conversation. The first question to put to a new arrival was: "Of what faith are you?" Many used libertinism as a cloak for debauchery, while others hid their excesses under ecclesiastical vestments.

Ninon never had been devout and her convictions were expressed by her friend, the poet Blot:

> Qu'importe que tu sois papiste,
> Calviniste ou luthérien,
> Mahométan, anabaptiste
> Ou de la secte de ton chien?
> Bois, f——, et n'offense personne:
> Ta religion est fort bonne.

(What does it matter if you are a Papist, Calvinist or

Lutheran, Mohammedan, Anabaptist or of the sect of your dog? Drink, f———, and offend no one: Your religion is very good.)

The marquis de Vassé, having turned his attention and his bad breath toward the marquise de Sévigné and been rebuffed, now renewed his plea to Ninon. She maintained she yielded out of curiosity to learn at first hand why so many of his mistresses had ended their days in convents, and she concluded that a life of repentance was little enough to pay for such a blunder. Vassé was extremely rich and Tallemant des Réaux wrote: "He did not cease to pay for it when his term was over."

Ninon was just past thirty, middle age, considering the average life span of her time. She still looked like a girl of eighteen and had by no means reached the apogee of her attraction for men. Despite a verse to the contrary, she did occasionally say "no."

Charles Faucon du Riz, seigneur de Charleval, a perfumed and beribboned dandy, was the darling of the dames, but it was Ninon he wanted. She liked him but "not that way." She turned him down with "You must await my caprice." He waited the rest of his life, though not in celibacy. His letters were frequently headed "At the siege of Madame ———" or "From the arms of Mademoiselle de ———" giving the full name. Ninon grew very fond of Charleval, and their friendship lasted forty years, until his death.

Antoine de Rambouillet, sieur de la Sablière, a brother-in-law of Tallemant des Réaux, having had his day of about three months, brought Ninon a plea from a Gascon friend who was burning with passion for the lady he had never seen. He threatened in verse that if he could not see her Tuesday he would kill himself on Wednesday. The choice of the day of his end was undoubtedly dictated by the necessity of the rhyme. Ninon invited him to a soiree, found him distasteful and made little effort to conceal the fact. There were, however, no suicides on her account.

Standing out in relief against the cynics and the pretty boys was Saint-Evremond, who had recognized Ninon's quality from the time they first met. He was now forty and a wen was beginning to grow between his eyes. His bitter mouth was capable of an enchanting smile, and no one could deliver a devastating comment with more grace. Whether he uttered a light witticism or a profound piece of wisdom, he was always interesting.

He had studied law, been a disciple of Gassendi, had fought valiantly under Condé and had been made an honorary field marshal. He was an atheist, so convincing that he had converted a number of his friends to his lack of faith, including the Great Condé. He had the highest respect for his own appetites and completely unorthodox ethics. Nevertheless, in three years of his military life he had been instrumental in saving some fifty thousand lives.

Chapter XXIV

COULON and Aubijoux were not getting along and the count was eager to get rid of his partner. As the councilor's inebriety increased he demanded less for his money, but Ninon found herself unable even to bear his presence. Aubijoux, in the sporadically paid service of Monsieur, could afford only half a mistress, so Ninon had to look around.

Her eyes lighted on Michel-Jérome Moreau, who was so much in love with her that he could neither eat nor sleep . . . except apparently enough to sustain life. He had been traipsing at her heels and the days on which she had refused to see him he sent long, impassioned letters which his valet thoroughly enjoyed while waiting on her doorstep. He was the son of a brilliant councilor of *parlement*, himself well educated, and a *libertin*. He had a fortune in his own right and he took on his share of the investment with enthusiasm. He was all of eighteen. Ninon did not find him attractive, which in the case of a "payer" was fortunate as she always found it difficult to accept money from one who gave her pleasure.

To facilitate getting rid of Coulon, or to enlarge her quarters, or perhaps because her landlord refused necessary repairs, Ninon decided to move. The comte d'Aubijoux found a small house in the Faubourg Saint-Germain where a new development was in progress. It was conveniently near the Palais d'Orléans [1] where he was quartered. The air was sweet and fresh, the streets quiet, and the mud comparatively clean. Ninon, with her books and her bibelots, her furniture and pots and baskets of clothes, journeyed across the Seine to her new home.

[1] The palace, built by Mari de Medici, now houses the Senate.

The parish of Saint-Sulpice was not unknown to her. As a child she had gone to the Fair of Saint-Germain, and later had visited Nicolas Vauquelin, sieur des Yveteux, in his "Paradise." The former tutor to Louis XIII had been dismissed for atheism. Under the influence of *L'Astrée* he had taken up what he considered a pagan existence. His garden was the Hesperides and the nymphs who guarded the golden apples had to be young and willing as well as accomplished musicians. Des Yveteux, despite his age, gamboled about clothed as a shepherd or a satyr, or one of the Greek gods. But he was no fool. The music was exquisite, the food not only delicious but healthful, and his murals and statuary were in the best taste. Ninon had spent an occasional day in the antic hay playing her lute with the ensemble.

She had also come to the *faubourg* to visit Scarron when he was taking his "tripe cure." Having tried every palliative known to his time, poor Scarron had gone to the Hôpital de la Charité on the rue des Saints-Pères to try the latest medical treatment. The patient sat immersed to his neck in the stomach lining of oxen. As this had to be fresh and warm to be effective, it was obtained daily from the slaughterhouses behind Les Halles and rushed in great copper kettles across the river. Scarron had been willing to try any therapy, even "to soak my dry parchment in a bath that is held salutary." He had taken up residence near the hospital, but not, of course, before inditing an *Adieu aux Marais et à la Place Royale* and burlesque farewells to each of his friends, including Ninon.

In spite of the Palais d'Orléans with its magnificent gardens, the Hôtel de Condé, and other vast properties, the section as a whole was sparsely built. It was actually the advent of Ninon that made it become fashionable and the expression "Faubourg Saint-Germain" was used for two succeeding centuries to denote the aristocracy.

When Ninon took up her residence there, Scarron was installed within walking distance at Saint-Michel. Being temporarily affluent, he had quit his sister's home and rented a large apartment in the Hôtel de Troyes on the rue d'Enfer. It was luxuriously furnished with a great deal of yellow damask, and Céleste, a former mistress who had retired on breach-of-promise money, kept house for him.

He had a special chair built with a second set of arms on which he could rest a table or a desk, and he kept at hand a hooked stick with which to draw objects nearer or to scratch himself. Each night two servants carried him to bed, and in the morning they installed him in his chair. In the afternoon he received friends, and the more pain he felt the more he joked. He liked reading extracts from his work and eliciting opinions. He was delighted when Ninon became his neighbor and a frequent visitor, for he valued her criticism.

The Saint-Michel quarter housed many convents where members of the nobility made retreats. It was also the meeting place of Frondeurs and the site of their clandestine press. Scarron had become an ardent Frondeur, somewhat influenced by the fact that Mazarin had ignored his request for a subsidy. His apartment became the meeting place of the leaders, Condé, Longueville, Retz and the pamphleteers, poets and spies. He began his *Mazarinades* against "the scoundrel, hated in Paris and Rome," circulating a poem advising the cardinal to flee lest:

> On te coupera, pauvre Jules,
> L'un et l'autre testicule:
> Et lors, ô cardinal pelé,
> Cardinal détesticulé,
> N'étant plus ni femme, ni homme,
> Comment paraîtras-tu dans Rome?

(One will cut from thee, poor Jules, first one and then the other testicle: and then, o peeled cardinal, castrated cardinal, being neither woman nor man, how will you appear in Rome?)

Having been compelled to play sycophant to a king, a queen-regent and two cardinal-ministers, Scarron was relieving his resentment in vituperation.

There were times when he earned a great deal, but his extravagant tastes, his pitiful physical condition, his generosity and an interminable lawsuit with his stepmother over his inheritance had combined to keep him in perpetual difficulties. Despite his handicaps, he never stopped working and in his short life he turned out essays, poems, brochures, novels and plays, in all, over sixty volumes.

If Aubijoux had expected to have more of Ninon's time when she moved out to the suburbs, he soon discovered his mistake. She had left the Marais, but the whole Marais came trailing after her. The tranquillity of the *faubourg* was at an end. Every afternoon processions of carriages, sedan chairs, equestrians and messengers crossed the Pont-Neuf and the Pont-Barbier. For blocks around hoofbeats, carriage wheels, voices and music rent the night. Long after the neighbors had extinguished their candles Ninon's cottage was blazing with lights. To her friends as well as to her lovers, she had become a necessity.

To this company she added local talent. A president of *parlement*, Michel Tambonneau, who occupied an ostentatious *hôtel* on the rue de l'Université, when not occupied with his judicial duties or his clandestine meetings with the Frondeurs followed the crowd to Ninon's. One of his favorite topics was the virtue of his wife. Delighted with Ninon's playing on the lute, he longed to have his dear spouse hear it, but this presented a delicate situation. He pondered over it for several days and then came to Ninon with the solution. He was not a president of *parlement* for nothing. He suggested that a tapestry be hung between Madame Tambonneau and the courtesan during the performance.

"Which do you think will give her greater immunity," Ninon asked, "a Flemish tapestry or a Gobelins?"

Chapter XXV

LADIES of the evening have been known to burn candles to whatever saint they believed might bring them business, and daughters of joy who repent can receive forgiveness. Marion Delorme had enticed bodies, but endeavored to save souls; she had acknowledged her sins and was therefore *persona grata* with the Divine Deputies.

La Compagnie du Saint-Sacrement had been originally formed to combat an increasing skepticism and to exercise charity. It "avenged the honor of God" by persecuting Huguenots, Jansenists and *libertins*. Well organized and ubiquitous, it attracted the support of people in high places who used it for their own purposes. Soon the victims of this organization were not only heretics but miscreants and people in someone's way. The Brethren were employed as secret police and it became their duty to spy on individuals to collect evidence. Protestants and atheists were put on an index, and life for them was made intolerable by a variety of petty annoyances which showed great ingenuity. Not only conduct but "evil thinking" was punished, sometimes by trickery and sometimes by violence.

The leader of this organization was the priest of Saint-Sulpice, the Reverend Jean-Jacques Olier, and there was rejoicing in the parish over the appearance of one beautiful but unrepentant sinner. It was not her profession that shocked the gentlemen of the cloth so much as her agnosticism.

Father Olier set his spies to work, but they were not very subtle spies, and it wasn't long before Ninon realized that she was being watched. Not only did it fail to frighten her, it amused her, and she continued to keep the noisy tenor of her way.

Spring made its annual appearance. The chestnut trees covered the walks with blossoms that looked like a blanket of snow, and the hawthorne and the lilac bloomed, and beneath a bush or behind a tree a Brother might be found lurking. As the days grew longer and the weather milder, the windows of the cottage were left open to admit the sweet and fragrant air. The air that was wafted out was redolent of other things.

There was a sound of revelry and people were heard to laugh, despite the fact that it was Lent, and it transpired, olfactorily, that meat was being served. No doubt the poor Brother's mouth watered as the aroma of succulent goose stewed in red wine and garlic, or of a joint turning on the spit, reached his hiding place. It was only too obvious what was going on, but to bring a charge there had to be evidence.

Tradesmen were questioned, but they had all been treated well by Mademoiselle de Lanclos, so they lost their memories.

And then one day fate played into the Reverend Father Olier's hands. As one of his men happened to be passing (and repassing to and fro) under the window of the room in which Ninon and her guests were dining he heard a man singing; being fond of music, he stopped to listen.

> Puisque l'adorable Ninon
> Trouve bon qu'on chante en carême,
> Je ne lui dirai jamais "non."
> Plut à Dieu qu'elle en fît de même.

(Since the adorable Ninon wishes me to sing in Lent, I cannot say no to her. I wish to God she wouldn't either.)

The singing of secular songs was forbidden during Lent. Here were grounds for action. But how prove it? If only there were a witness! Just then something struck the Brother's *calotte* and bounced off. He bent to pick it up. The thighbone of a roast chicken, and only half eaten. If the poor man cleaned Exhibit A before delivering it to his superior, who can blame him?

Olier took the evidence to the bailiff. This functionary found himself in a dilemma. His office called for justice for the outraged clergy, while in his heart he had a weakness for Ninon.

120

After a sleepless night he solved the problem by having her surreptitiously warned that he might be compelled to reprimand her. There was a hearing and the duc de Candale and the marquis de Mortémar undertook her defense. Their brief was salted with a little bribery. The case was dismissed.

But the danger was not passed. Slander was weaving its tissue of half-truths, and Madame Cornuel, famous for her mordant tongue, stage-whispered that Ninon was making cassocks for the abbé Boisrobert from her discarded petticoats.

Olier appealed to the religious elements at court, persuading them to send a delegation to the queen. When Anne suggested sending the culprit to a home for repentant girls Bautru, a court buffoon, undertook her defense.

"But, ma'am," he said, "she is neither *une fille* nor *repentie*."

Finally Her Majesty sent an officer with an order for Ninon to withdraw to a convent of her own choice. Ninon replied:

"Since the queen is gracious enough to leave the choice of a convent to me, I pray you tell Her Majesty that I select *Les Grands Cordeliers*."

The *Grands Cordeliers* was a monastery of the order of Saint-Francis. It had degenerated into a notoriously undisciplined and licentious institution of monks.

When Anne received the message she laughed and said, "Fie, the imp, let her do what she likes," and as she had other problems on her mind, including the flight of her cardinal-husband, the matter was dropped.

Ninon had escaped, but she realized that she must be more circumspect. To give her gatherings a less dangerous aspect she invited some young poets to mingle with the freethinkers. But the poor jingles they spouted soon offended her taste, and when they began to cast sheep's eyes at her she threw them out, saying she was afraid they would try to make love in Latin.

An announcement appeared in the *Gazette*. It said that Mademoiselle Ninon de Lanclos was going to America. She had a friend on the press who had inserted it to confuse her enemies.

She also thought it politic to attend an occasional mass, and one Sunday, at the fashionable Saint-Roche where Boisrobert preached, she found herself next to a well-dressed woman who obviously wanted to strike up an acquaintance. After the service this woman asked a friend, the Treasurer of Diverse Royal Pleasures, who the charming and elegant stranger was, and was told it was a Madame Argencourt, a Bretonne of good family, who had come to Paris to prosecute a lawsuit.

The following week Ninon found herself next to the same woman.

"Madame," she said, "I understand from Monsieur Dupin that you are a Bretonne here for a legal process. My husband is Jacques Paget, *Maître des Requêtes au Parlement*. Perhaps he can be of service to you. It would give me pleasure to assist so distinguished and pious a woman as you."

With a Breton brogue Ninon enlarged on the details of her suit. The abbé passed down the aisle and greeted her.

"Since you have lately arrived, how is it that you know Monsieur Boisrobert?" asked Madame Paget.

"He's my neighbor," replied Ninon. "I live in the suburbs."

"He is a bad character," said Madame Paget. "I hear he's mixed up with a notorious wench called Ninon."

"Don't believe everything you hear," said Ninon, "a quarter of it sometimes is false."

As Madame Paget was entering her carriage Boisrobert came up to her.

"I see you've been talking to my friend, Ninon de Lanclos. I call her 'my divine one.' "

Shortly thereafter Dupin, the Lord High Dispenser of Bounty for Royal Amusement, took Ninon to a garden party on the rue de Richelieu. There she met Dame Paget. But the wife of the *Maître des Requêtes* could hardly look down her nose at the notorious wench, because they were both guests of Monsieur Thevenin, the oculist, whose home was a well-known *maison de rendezvous*.

Boisrobert not only told the story in the *ruelles* but used it in his comedy *La Belle Plaideuse*.

Chapter XXVI

THE peace of Rueil had not brought peace. Incidents, reprisals, personal jealousies made new alignments for a second Fronde. Marriages were arranged for young people for the purpose of consolidating the positions of their parents. Even the great Turenne forsook his king, leading Spanish troops, and then for a liberal consideration rejoined the French royal forces.

Condé strutted around making enemies. He insulted Monsieur, Gondi, Beaufort, *parlement*, and even the duchesse de Chevreuse, Queen Anne's favorite. He stubbornly protected Jarzé and tried to force him on Anne, just to annoy Mazarin. Although he had entered into negotiations with Spain, the government dared not take action against a scion of the houses of Bourbon and Montmorency, at least not without the support of Monsieur, who was lieutenant general and had a considerable following. While this prince resented Condé, he was timid and indolent, and under the domination of his current flame, the abbé de la Rivière, who had been bribed by Condé to dissuade Monsieur from taking action. Mazarin, who found out everything, exposed the matter, and Monsieur, disillusioned with love, gave his consent to Condé's arrest.

Ninon's former lover, Moissens of the bullish approach, crashed into the council chamber and arrested his best friends, Condé, his brother Conti and their brother-in-law, the duc de Longueville. "*Les princes*," as they were referred to, were thrown into the prison of Vincennes where Paul de Gondi was also sojourning. The populace rejoiced and lit bonfires.

For his deed Moissens was rewarded with a baton, thereupon becoming the maréchal d'Albret. Lest they escape, *les princes* were removed to the prison at Le Havre where they remained for thirteen months, until Mazarin, on his way to self-imposed exile, personally released them.

The people of Orléans, fearing the approaching army, called upon their prince to defend them, but Monsieur, having a previous engagement, sent his daughter in his place. In March the Grande Mademoiselle, full-panoplied, with feathered helmet and a habit trimmed with gold military lace, took the road to Orléans, followed by ladies, light cavalry and raw recruits. It was said that her "*en avants*" put the regiment in good humor and out of step.

When she arrived at the gates of the city the governor was afraid to admit her and she cooled her horse's heels while the people climbed the ramparts to cheer her. Then she resorted to strategy. Dismissing her armed guards, she scrambled over some rubble and entered the walled city by a back gate. She thereby became the savior of Orléans and was carried around in triumph to the beating of drums. Until then her father had never liked her, but this victory incurred his hatred.

When she returned to Paris she was hailed as the Daughter of France. The army gave a banquet in her honor, and her palace, the Tuileries, for a time rivaled the Louvre in the splendor of its entertainment.

The royal family returned to Paris, followed some months later by His Eminence at the head of a small force. The appearance of the hated minister stirred the embers of the dying Fronde. The people were uncertain who their enemies were, so a mob attacked the Hôtel de Ville and five deputies were murdered.

In September of 1651 the Dauphin, having reached the age of thirteen, became Louis XIV in fact. Many who had fought the cardinal and the regent now rallied to the support of the king.

Condé gathered troops, including some Spanish regiments, and marched on Paris, which was barricaded with paving stones and hogsheads of dung. He met the royal troops under Turenne and a battle was fought outside the Porte Saint-Antoine. Here

La Rochefoucauld received a wound which caused him to return to his estate and devote himself to polishing maxims. Many others were badly hurt, including Jarzé. Condé fought like a demon with less than half the troops of his adversary, yet the Frondeurs were getting licked. It was the Grande Mademoiselle who saved the day. The artillery of the Bastille had been turned again toward the streets, in case of an uprising of the people; she gave the order to have the cannon switched around to face Turenne's army. This turned the tide, the gate was opened, and Mademoiselle de Montpensier and her cousin the prince de Condé, forgetting that they hated each other, fell into each other's arms, and when she told him of how many of his friends had been killed and wounded, he wept on her bosom.

Monsieur, her father, had fled. He did not return to Paris until he had secured pardon by betraying his fellow conspirators. Punishments were meted out, and the Grande Mademoiselle went into luxurious exile. The second Fronde was over, except at Bordeaux where patriotic peasants kept it going until vintage time, when they dared not neglect their ripened grapes.

The Fronde was over, but the countryside was devastated, the people starving. The armies of both sides had fed on the land through which they passed. Barracks did not exist and not only were the troops billeted with the peasants, but the hosts were obliged to contribute three to four *livres* a day for the nourishment of each man. To be used as a garrison was a calamity for any town. Its inhabitants were tortured for information about hoarded food supplies, men and women were thrashed with whips of thorns and children ruthlessly killed. Those who hid in caves or quarries were smoked out.

Parlement was defeated, the nobles were defeated, and so were the people, but the monarchy was consolidated. The young king was on his way to becoming the state.

The wars of the Fronde revealed an absence of patriotism in all classes. Ninon, who had little capacity for self-delusion, had taken no stand in a civil strife the issues of which were no clearer to her than they are to historians.

Chapter XXVII

To everyone's surprise Paul Scarron married. He said it was one of his best buffooneries.

He had been interested in the Société des Indes Equinoxiales which was planning to colonize the West Indies, then called *Les Iles*. He had heard stories of bent backs that had been straightened, stiffened joints that became flexible, and other conditions that had yielded to the magic of perpetual sunshine. He paid for his passage and began putting his affairs in order. Learning that the Aubigné family had spent some time in the West Indies, he invited them to call, in order to gain firsthand information.

Françoise d'Aubigné came with her mother and her aunt. Having outgrown her shabby frock, she was embarrassed before the brilliant company she found. She blushed and shed tears, but the host's kindness and tact soon put her at ease. She answered his questions so intelligently that he was delighted. He told her he was an admirer of her grandfather, and had read his *Histoire universelle* with great interest.

Agrippa d'Aubigné had been a writer, an ambassador, and was at one time the governor of La Rochelle, the stronghold of Protestantism. He had been a friend of Henri IV and when the latter changed to Catholicism he had noticed a scar beneath the king's mustache and had remarked:

"Sire, you have only renounced God with your lips, and it has sufficed for Him to pierce your lips, but if someday you renounce him in your heart, He will pierce that heart."

It was a prophecy that was recalled on the day that Ravaillac pierced the monarch's heart.

Agrippa d'Aubigné's oldest son, Constantin, married a rich widow and, surprising her *in flagrante delicto*, he dispatched her and her lover and fled. He embarked on a career of political double-crossing, contracted gambling debts and coined enough money to pay them honorably. And then, while sojourning in the prison at Niort, he married the daughter of the governor of the jail.

Françoise was born in 1636 within the precincts of the *conciergerie*. On Richelieu's death, Constantin was released and given the governorship of one of the small islands of the West Indies. He found the place uninhabitable so moved with his family to Martinique, where Françoise got her sunburn and her appellation, *la belle Indienne*.

When they returned to France her father disappeared and one of her brothers drowned himself. The poor child was shunted from one relative to another. For a time she lived with her father's sister, receiving kindness and a Protestant education, but she was soon taken away and placed with her mother's sister, who put her to housework and stable tasks, and tried, unsuccessfully, to convert her to Catholicism. After that Françoise was sent to the Ursulines where, as soon as she began to feel at home and contented, she was yanked out and put in a free convent. In time, and after a great deal of pressure, she was converted but, she made it clear, with reservations. Her mother, who never kissed her, gave her Plutarch's *Lives* to read, and for a short time she shared with her cousin instruction by the chevalier de Méré.

When Scarron learned of her unhappy life, he was so touched that he made a strange proposal:

"Mademoiselle, I realize how your protectrice takes advantage of your gentle nature and your defenseless position, yet I tremble to think what would become of you if this old woman's death should leave you still more unguarded. Your beauty and grace procure you many admirers, but you are not too young to understand that their admiration for a penniless young lady is not likely to lead to matrimony. I see only two alternatives: to accept a husband or to enter a convent. If you decide on the latter I shall pay your expenses; if you do not wish to become a nun, and if, in spite of my face, figure and helplessness, you will consent to marry me, to be my companion and bear my name, I shall do everything possible to make you happy, and I guarantee in advance that if you weep in my house it will only be on the day of my death."

Françoise accepted but asked that the wedding be postponed until she was sixteen. When the marriage contract was being drawn the notary asked Scarron what dowry the bride would bring.

"A pair of roguish eyes, a beautiful torso, a fine pair of hands and a capital of four pounds."

"And you, monsieur," asked the notary, "what do you bring her?"

"Immortality," replied Scarron.

Queen Anne said, "What on earth is Scarron going to do with Mademoiselle d'Aubigné?" But the queen was wrong. Françoise proved a comfort and a help. Scarron dictated his work to her and she received his guests with charm and dignity. When the conversation became too Rabelaisian she blushed and people started to watch their tongues. Her apparent modesty protected her from the advances of many of the guests. Scarron taught his wife Latin and Italian and guided her reading, helping to prepare her for the role she was ultimately to play. She developed a considerable wit and, being a clear thinker, could tell a story well.

Many years later Madame de Montespan, who had every reason to hate Françoise, wrote in her *Memoirs:*

It is said that I have a special talent for sustaining and enlivening a conversation; there is something in that, I admit, but to do her justice, Madame de Maintenon is without rival. She has quite a wealth of invention; the most arid subject becomes attractive in her hands; as for transitions, her skill is unequaled . . . if now and again some little touch of irony escapes her she knows how to temper it and instantly to nullify it by terms of praise at once natural and simple.

Scarron was most anxious to have Ninon like his wife, and Ninon did, in a way, but fundamentally the two women were very unlike.

Despite his increasing paralysis, Scarron worked for many hours each day, and with considerable success. His travesty of Virgil was translated into many languages; his *Roman comique* was widely read. It satirized the denizens of small towns and at the same time made a plea for more respect for people of the theatre. In *Le Typhon* he gave classical personages contemporary dialogue, a literary trick that is quite successful in our time. His *Jodelet ou le maître valet* was an immediate success and was continually on the repertory of Molière's troupe. Onto the Spanish pattern of intrigue and misunderstanding Scarron grafted characterization and satire. His Jodelet, named for the actor who played the part, was a rogue-valet with a penchant for pinching the behinds of plump ladies in waiting, a type which has persisted in France, in the Restoration plays of England and in opera.

Irritated by the humble attitude of authors who wrote fawning dedications to the high and mighty, he dedicated an edition of his poems to Dame Guillemette, his sister's lap dog, "the very honest and diverting little dog." He wrote that rich men had been observed to turn pale at the sight of a dedication which might cost them something but would give them eternal fame.

Scarron presented Ninon with a volume of his poems. As a frontispiece it had an engraving of himself drawn from the back, his profile rising from his rounded shoulders. He was surrounded by caricatured muses and satyrs. Since he went out so little, he had become an object of curiosity to the public, so he had written a description of himself in the foreword of the volume:

. . . some say that I am a cripple seated in a bowl, others that I have no thighs and that people place me on the table in a box where I chatter like a one-eyed magpie, and the rest say that my hat is held by a cord which passes through a pulley by which I raise and lower it to greet those who visit me. . . . You will complain undoubtedly, because every reader complains, and I complain like the rest of them when I am a reader, and you will criticize me because I show myself from behind. Indeed, it is not to turn my behind to the company but only because the convex of my back is better fitted to receive an inscription than the concave of my stomach, which is entirely hidden by my leaning head. . . . I had a well-shaped figure though small. My malady has shortened it by a good foot. My head is a little large for my body . . . teeth formerly square pearls are now the color of wood . . . and two are a little loose. . . . I am not unlike the letter Z. I have shortened arms as well as legs. Indeed I am an abstract of human misery.

Since I am getting on so well, I am going to tell you something of my temperament. The more so since this preface is written only to increase the size of the book at the request of the publisher who has been afraid of not getting back the expenses of printing.

Ninon was deeply touched. She knew better than anyone the bitter suffering of her friend, and she managed to spend a part of each day endeavoring to distract him.

Upon his marriage Scarron received a partial reimbursement of the money due him from his family, and he proceeded to use it for lavish dinners at the Hôtel de Troyes. The company was more brilliant than ever before, his young wife proving an added attraction. Ninon enjoyed these dinners. She was equally at home with the intellectuals and the nobility, many of whom she knew with their buskins off.

Mademoiselle de Scudéry came with her note-taking mind, and Françoise appeared in the next volume of *Clélie*. The Grande Mademoiselle came once or twice, but there were two people who never appeared, Cyrano de Bergerac, who hated Scarron, and Madame de Sévigné, who did not wish to encounter Ninon.

One evening, as the company was breaking up, Boisrobert arrived, bringing a young man with intelligent eyes and a petulant mouth. His chestnut curls fell forward as he bent over the hand of the hostess a little longer than was necessary. When at last he raised his head, his eye caught Ninon's and he asked to be presented. It was Boisrobert who took him over:

"Mademoiselle, permit me to present my dear friend, Louis de Mornay, marquis de Villarceaux. Mademoiselle Ninon de Lanclos."

Ninon was conscious of a *frisson* that she had not felt for a long time, possibly since she had known Coligny. They stood looking at each other so long that Scarron remarked, "What is this, the *coup de foudre?*" It was, indeed, love at first sight. Ninon wrote:

From the moment I found myself in the arms of Monsieur de Villarceaux I felt at home. I had attained the asylum I had long craved. He felt the same sentiment. Nature, it seemed, had designed us for each other.

Chapter XXVIII

THE marquis de Villarceaux was captain of the royal pack of seventy harriers and foxhounds. This was an esteemed post, providing four assistants. He was also lieutenant of the king's Light Cavalry as well as *capitaine-sous-lieutenant* of a company of men-at-arms of the Vexin under the duc d'Anjou. He was the eldest son of the cadet branch of a distinguished and wealthy family whose château was about twenty leagues from Paris. When not busy hunting game or women he wrote poetry and painted portraits . . . too well for the comfort of Madame Scarron.

With the physical attributes that appealed to Ninon, a quick mind and gracious manners, he seemed to combine all the qualities she most admired.

That the marquis had a wife and four children did not seem to matter; the family occupied the château in the Vexin while Louis had a *pied-à-terre* in the Palais Royal, which had just ceased to be the royal residence. The marquis and his wife were not on the best of terms.

Friends told Ninon stories about the past of her lover, but she was hardly in a position to throw stones. When he was twenty, after seducing his fiancée he had refused to marry her. In pique, or perhaps in trouble, Marie Girard had married a pompous lieutenant general who, for the delectation of his bride, hung his portrait in full array over the conjugal bed. Villarceaux then married one of the queen's maids of honor, was faithful to her all through the honeymoon, after which he sought out the woman he had jilted and as her husband was away made her his mistress. The eyes of the lieutenant general looked down from the portrait reproachfully, and Villarceaux maintained that this added piquancy to the performance. But Marie was getting even with him. While she was deceiving her husband with Villarceaux, she was deceiving Villarceaux with her sister's husband, and obviously deceiving her sister at the same time. By some crossing of wires the two lovers met, and instead of fighting a duel, they agreed that whichever could show more evidence of the lady's ardor could keep her. This necessitated producing locks of hair, ribbons and letters, and Villarceaux won by a considerable preponderance of evidence, whereupon he lost interest and turned to the maréchale de la Ferté, whose letters he showed to a few dozen intimate friends. It was said that he was very democratic as he made love to mistress and maid with impartiality.

But Ninon did not concern herself with his past. The present and the future were hers and, knowing that his passion equalled hers, she felt no jealousy. Having for some time devoted her superabundant energies to the forays of her homosexual and impotent friends, Louis de Mornay's virility acted like a love potion. She made no attempt to dissemble her own eagerness with coquetry. All her cynicism dropped from her. She forgot the sneering remarks she had made about *l'amour*.

Of a naturally gay temperament, she was now exuberant. Her eyes sparkled and her step was a dance. She delighted in her lover's presence and during his absence thought up all sorts of things to tell him, to do for him, to give him. She was bored by her poets and philosophers, lost interest in the *libertins* and soon closed her doors to the whole lot. Finding it distasteful to have relations with her payers, she even refused to see Aubijoux and Moreau. She had no capital and she cut off her source of income.

Villarceaux was delighted and flattered, and not afraid of the responsibility. He, too, forsook all others. They went about together starry-eyed, oblivious of the rest of the world.

When summer approached, Ninon and Louis, like most lovers, made the discovery that nature was beautiful. Louis longed to take her to the country, but his wife and children were in residence at the château, so he took her to his friend Charles de

Valliquierville, who occupied a small property on his estate in the Vexin.

Valliquierville had been one of the prime instigators of Gaston's plot against Richelieu and had had to take refuge in England when Monsieur turned informer. Upon the cardinal's death he had returned to France only to transfer his plotting ability to the conspiracy against the new cardinal in the Fronde. He was sincere in his convictions and one of the few Frondeurs motivated by pure patriotism. He had become disillusioned with politics and at the age of fifty had become a recluse. He was a vegetarian and "would not taste anything which had had life." He was regarded as an eccentric; La Rochefoucauld called it affectation.

His house was comfortable and well stocked with books. He was happy to receive the lovers and maintained his own regime without forcing it on them.

Ninon found him a stimulating companion, a scholar and a disciple of Montaigne. He was just the right ingredient to leaven the wild ecstasy of love. She found herself happy and fulfilled. To prolong this blessed state they stayed far into the autumn, until the discomforts of winter in the country forced them back to Paris.

Because of his position at court, and because of his wife, Villarceaux could not live openly with Ninon in Paris. He found a dwelling for her at the corner of the rue de Richelieu and the rue Neuve-Saint-Augustin, conveniently near his rooms at the Palais Royal. He spent every moment he could with her, and every moment that he could not he was tortured by suspicion and jealousy. He wondered whether a woman who had led the life of a courtesan could be faithful. He taxed her with this and she replied: "A woman who has loved only one man doesn't know the meaning of love." A reply to make him ponder the more.

He questioned everyone about her movements; he paid little boys to hide under her bed and when they reported that she had slept alone he refused to believe them, thinking that she in turn had bribed them to hold their tongues.

The house opposite was owned by Boisrobert, who was in financial difficulties. He offered it for sale with the stipulation that he be permitted to maintain a lodging in it for the rest of his life. Villarceaux bought the house for sixteen thousand *livres* and moved in, because from the upper windows he could look into Ninon's apartment. The time he didn't spend with his mistress he spent peeping at her.

He discovered nothing. Ninon, who had no scruples about the number of her affairs when it was her own business, took her loyalty to true love as a matter of course. Had she desired another man she would have yielded to him without hesitation. Her fidelity was not one of the will but of the flesh.

One night Louis sat at his post watching the flickering candle-light in Ninon's room. He had seen no one enter the house, but then love could always find a back stair. Ninon had seemed particularly gay that afternoon. Was there a reason? Why should her candle burn so late? Perhaps she was writing a letter, terms of endearment to someone . . . to whom? As the chimes of Saint-Roche struck the hours his misery increased. He decided to send his valet to inquire if she was well, knowing, of course, that she was. The man returned with a word that she was in excellent health. Was she alone? What a foolish question, she could have hidden a man easily. Or was his valet lying? He decided to see for himself.

Dressing hastily, he jammed on what he thought was a hat, crossed the street, let himself in noiselessly and mounted the maddeningly creaking stair. As he paused before the door of Ninon's apartment he formulated the words with which he would greet his rival. Then he burst the door open and rushed in with sword drawn. Ninon was in bed propped up by pillows. On each side of her burned a candelabrum, and on her raised knees was an open book. When she saw him she laughed her rippling, low laugh. Instead of his hat he had on his head a silver ewer. He had jammed it on so hard that she had to call her valet de chambre to dislodge it.

Being laughed at was more than Villarceaux could bear. Instead of apologizing he began to question and accuse her. Resentfully, she refused to answer and he stalked out. Injustice rankled in her heart. It would serve him right if she took another lover.

The next day she learned . . . he saw to it that she learned . . . that he was bedridden with a high fever. She sent word that she would nurse him, but he remained sulky and refused. She wrote him protestations of innocence to which he did not reply. Then she took a really serious step.

Her maid washed her lovely bronze hair, sprinkled it with scent and wound the tresses around her finger in curls. Ninon then handed her a scissors and told her to cut them off. When they lay in a shining heap on the dressing table, Delphine burst into tears. Ninon ran her fingers through her short crop, and then covered it with a lace nightcap. She wrapped the curls in a large kerchief and without a note of any kind sent them over to the marquis. "The fever left him immediately," writes Tallemant des Réaux, "learning which Ninon went to him, lay down in his bed and they remained abed together for eight whole days."

The story spread from the parish of Saint-Roche to the Marais. From there one of the wife-informers carried it to the Vexin. The marquise de Villarceaux had been very reasonable. She knew a great deal about her husband's peccadilloes. For a man to have women was one thing, but to have one woman was quite another.

Shortly thereafter Ninon found herself pregnant, and this time she rejoiced. There was no speculation as to the child's paternity. When a healthy boy was born he was welcomed by both parents and christened Louis-François.

Nothing is known about the childhood of this boy. It was customary for the "upper classes" to put infants out to nurse in the country, and it is probable Ninon did this, but it is stated that later she interested herself in his education, and we have documentary proof that she looked after his material welfare all her life.

Tallemant des Réaux credits her with a second son by Villarceaux, but there is no more evidence of it than of the children by other men. If a second child was born, it must have died in infancy.

There is a story created by the duc de Luynes that a son of Ninon by Jarzé was brought up as the chevalier de Villiers, and kept in ignorance of his mother's identity. He met her when she was over fifty and fell in love with her. The more she tried to turn his thoughts away, the more amorous he became, until she was compelled to tell him that she was his mother. Whereupon he went out into the garden and shot himself, dying in her arms with the words "*Je t'adore*" on his lips. It is pure fabrication with a touch of plagiarism from Sophocles. Nevertheless, it has been repeated in drama and story. It is a legend hard to kill because people like it.

Saint-Simon, writing later, credits her with a son who was killed at the siege of Lille in 1667. He would have been thirteen at the time. If any of these offspring achieved the light of birth they did so very quietly, for no proof of their existence has ever been found.

Chapter XXIX

THE following summer brought with it a nostalgia for the Vexin. Valliquierville was away and his house closed, but as the marquise de Villarceaux was not in residence, Louis decided to take Ninon to his own château.

He was as excited as a boy when he showed her the terraced Italian gardens, the willows weeping into the running brook and the *grande allée* with its vista of elms and chestnut trees. The castle, dating from the fifteenth century, stands by a lake. One of its wings separates two round towers, one of which, surmounted by a dovecot, was called the Tower of the Condemned. Its ground floor had been a prison, and the first floor a chapel where the prisoners of the *seigneur* made their last confessions of poaching or evading the tax before being strung up from the battlements.

The other tower rises from the lake and is entered by a discreet door from the wing. It had been lavishly furnished by the marquis as a retreat from family life. A short stair leads to an antechamber which opens into a large circular room. At the time of Ninon's incumbency the walls were covered with allegorical paintings. Her bedchamber was paneled in chestnut with cartouches enclosing medallions painted by Louis. In the ceiling the arabesques formed the Mornay coat of arms.

Two movable panels in the wall opened with a secret spring. Behind them were bookshelves, and behind the shelves a door leading to a closet with enough ventilation for a concealed mistress to breathe.

Concealment of a lover from a spouse who returns unexpectedly is not only one of the mainstays of French farce, it has apparently been a considerable factor in daily life. In 1673 a pamphlet was circulated reading:

To the male population of Paris:

Messieurs, you are warned that in Paris now they are making, by piercing the wall of the neighboring house, a chimney with a spring panel through which a lover can slip without anyone suspecting his presence.

The marquise did not appear, and it is doubtful if Ninon would have hidden if she had, but Louis never failed to look in the closet and to run his sword under Ninon's bed at unexpected times.

Ninon took advantage of the beauties of the countryside to take long walks and to relax in the shade. Louis took her to visit his tenants, and wherever they went she made friends.

Among the fountains there was one called the Fountain of Youth with the customary legend that whoever dipped his hands in the waters would never grow old. Early one morning when Louis was out with his dogs he came upon Ninon splashing in the fountain. The marquis was a painter of no little skill, but it would have taken a Renoir to record the opalescent tints of her wet flesh in the rays of the rising sun. Today when the occupants of the château take visitors around it is the *Tour de Ninon* and the *Bassin de Ninon* that they point out.

In the quiet, fragrant evenings the lovers lingered on the terrace, listening to the birds, watching the changing sky, and postponing like gourmets who savor their food their abandonment to the ecstatic night.

And yet, as the summer wore on, satiety set in. The thrush and the nightingale became just birds. Without Valliquierville conversation lagged.

Suddenly Ninon decided she was tired of living in hiding in another woman's home. Louis became peevish. He complained that she only loved him physically but found him lacking intellectually. She admitted that perhaps he was right. When she received a letter from Françoise Scarron it was like a seed falling on prepared ground:

. . . All your friends are sighing for your return. Since your departure my court has increased, but it is a very feeble substitute for them; they converse, they play, they drink, they yawn. Come back, my *très aimable*, all Paris implores you. If Monsieur de Villarceaux knew all the rumors that Madame de Fiesque was spreading about him, he would be ashamed to detain you any longer.

Saint-Evremond wants to send Chastillon, Moissens and du Rancy in the capacity of knights-errant to abduct you from your old château.

Come back, beautiful Ninon, we shall gather graces and pleasures.

Shortly after, the courier arrived with a poem from Saint-Evremond, which began:

> Chère Phylis, qu'êtes-vous devenue?
> Cet enchanteur qui vous a retenue
> Depuis trois ans par un charm nouveau,
> Vous retient-il en quelque vieux château?

(Dear Philis, what has become of you? This enchanter who has held you for three years past by some new charm, is he keeping you shut up in some old castle?)

The poem continues with a résumé of Ninon's love affairs, about which she had hardly been reticent, and points out that their chief attraction had been their diversity; a peaceful and prolonged possession creates distaste, and one no longer feels anything; to indulge in old pleasures from which the charm has fled, the sentiments become outworn, is to be dead in the midst of life. The poem ends in a rhymed couplet:

> Etre inconstant aussi longtemps qu'on peut,
> Car un temps vient où ne l'est pas qui veut.

(Be inconstant as long as possible, for a time comes when one no longer has desires.)

Other demands had been filtering through from the outside world and now, as love languished, Ninon began to heed them.

Some time before she had instituted a lawsuit for money due and won the verdict. A warrant had been issued, but her lawyer had not collected. She decided her interests demanded her return to Paris, so early in September she again took up residence in the apartment on the rue de Richelieu.

She and Villarceaux remained friends and granted each other the freedom which each would have taken without permission. Ninon was as happy to regain her liberty as she had been to relinquish it. As soon as word got around that she was back, she was surrounded by friends old and new, and Louis had to take his place among them. What remained of his love was mostly jealousy. He particularly resented Moissens, now the maréchal d'Albret, who took for granted he could take up his relationship with Ninon where they had left off. To the surprise of this gentleman of royal blood she told him she was not interested in warmed-over love.

Old Valliquierville maintained his disinterested concern for Ninon's welfare. They spent many hours together in discussion, analyzing the premises on which various religious creeds were founded. They even drew up a set of articles, a credo for "lack of faith." Ninon wrote:

If a man needs religion to conduct himself properly in this world, it is a sign that he has either a limited mind or a corrupt heart.

One day the chevalier de Méré turned up and Ninon asked him what had brought him after all the years.

"To tell the truth," he replied, "my mistress spoke so ill of you that it gave me a longing to see you again."

One day he brought his friend Blaise Pascal, who was coming out of his "*mondaine* period" during which Méré had introduced him to the *ruelles*. It was during this phase that Pascal wrote his *Discourse on the Passions of Love*. But now he was turning more and more to religion. His sister Jacqueline was a nun at the famous Jansenist convent of Port-Royal. Ninon, curious about everything, questioned him about the sect and its leader, and also about the calculating machine which the mathematician had invented at the age of sixteen. He promised to come and demonstrate it for her.

Villarceaux felt out in the cold. He found consolation here and there, for as is so often the case he combined a roving eye with a possessive nature. He boasted that he was through with Ninon, but that she persisted in making love whether he wished to or not. The gossips carried it back to her but she took no notice, understanding the piqued pride of a discarded lover. She never said a word against him in retaliation, but her commentary sums up her opinion of her own *grande passion:*

The poets are fools to have endowed the son of Venus with a torch and a bow and arrow; the power of this God resides purely in his bandeau; the more one loves, the less he reflects; when he begins to reflect he no longer loves.

Chapter XXX

AWARE that she had but to reach out her hand to take a new lover, Ninon enjoyed sleeping alone. Paris delighted her: the theatres, the music, the restaurants and, above all, the conversation. It was at this time that *La Compagnie Générale du Saint-Sacrement* chose to strike.

Knowing how well liked she was, that she had influential friends, and that she had once escaped them, they carefully prepared their case. They dared not risk bringing it before a magistrate who might be one of Ninon's past, present or potential lovers or friends. This limited the field, so they made their plea to a woman, the old maréchale de Gramont, who had direct access to the queen's ear. Backed up by Madame Vendôme and Madame de Sénecé, the young king's governess, the maréchale presented a convincing case to Anne. The creature not only flaunted her profession at the very door of the royal palace, scoffed at all the sanctities, including marriage, but she actually maintained that women should have the same rights as men. Moreover, the most attractive courtiers were spending much of their time on the rue de Richelieu.

This time Anne was persuaded. Ninon was escorted by three gloating noblewomen to the Madelonettes on the rue des Fontaines in the parish of Saint-Nicolas-des-Champs. The convent had been founded for women who led "debauched and scandalous lives." The charge was:

> ... to have made with the assistance of a number of gentlemen of the aristocracy a great show and triumphant noise

in her house, the scene of debauchery being carried to the highest degree ever witnessed.

Ninon was conducted to a dark and dreary cell and her three escorts departed happily. She was seated on her cot, somewhat bewildered by the sudden turn of events, when the Mother Superior came in smiling. Taking Ninon by the hand, she led her to a comfortable and cheerful apartment. "It isn't necessary," she said, "that the road to heaven be *too* rough."

Villarceaux did everything he could to obtain her release. Her friends in the Marais met secretly in protest. Letters were written and strings were pulled, but several weeks passed and nothing happened. Ninon, as she had done before at the Carmelites, made the best of the situation, reading, walking and making friends with the sweet nuns. She wrote to Boisrobert, praising their treatment and adding: "I think that, following your example, I shall begin to love my own sex."

One day one of the nuns noticed a stranger standing opposite the convent, looking at the building intently. The next day there were two strangers. At twilight cloaked and masked gentlemen came. They seemed to be measuring the height and thickness of the walls. It was all too obvious that some sort of attack or escape was being planned. The old nuns were terrified and the young ones thrilled. Someone carried the news to the queen.

As Anne had little confidence in the Watch, and with good reason, it become necessary to take precautions. One day the prisoner was removed under an escort of musketeers to a Benedictine convent at Lagny in the Seine-et-Oise.

Visitors were permitted, and as the court was then at Compiègne many of the courtiers found Lagny an excellent objective for their afternoon rides. The Marais, too, sent its quota of distinguished gentlemen. In a short time the sleepy little village began to wake up and an era of prosperity set in. L'Epée Royale, the modest inn, was crowded to the roof and the proprietor, to his astonishment, became a rich man.

Boisrobert came for a few days, and when he left, the chambermaid said to the next occupant of the room: "Will Monsieur require only one bed for himself and his lackey, like Monsieur l'Abbé?"

One afternoon the quiet of the convent was rent by more voices than usual, by horses' hoofs and by carriage wheels, and the sisters who peeped out saw that they were the wheels of one of the royal coaches. Who could it be this time, coming to see Mademoiselle de Lanclos?

Ninon sat quietly reading in her room and did not look up until her door opened and the chevalier d'Albret ushered in an odd little person, somewhat more woman than man. The wig, slightly off center, was in disarray; a scarlet *pourpoint* covered a fairly white linen blouse; a short skirt revealed high riding boots. The whole effect was of one who had dressed to run out of a burning house. There was a sword at her side, a holster in her belt, and a riding crop in her hand. A lackey followed with gifts which he placed on the table before backing out.

There was no need to introduce herself. She was the most widely discussed woman in Europe.

Christina, queen of Sweden, only child of the great Gustavus Adolphus, had abdicated because, as Voltaire later wrote, "she preferred talking to savants to reigning over a people who only knew armies."

Her father had died on the battefield and her mother, who had wanted a boy, revenged her widowhood on the child. From her earliest days Christina had done her best to remedy the defect. An unhappy, untidy girl, she rode astride, pursued masculine sports, read the classics in Greek and Latin, and mastered six living languages.

On ascending the throne she devoted herself to the business of government and made every effort to establish peace in her war-torn country. Her great love, however, was French culture.

To the collection of books which her father had confiscated in Germany she added many volumes, purchased by her agents throughout Europe. During the Fronde she had bought a whole library from Mazarin . . . and read it. She collected the finest Italian and Flemish paintings, and she also collected scientists and philosophers. She carried on a correspondence with Scarron, who admired her erudition and hoped for a subsidy. He received only a small gift. When she read *Le Grand Cyrus* she thought she recognized herself in one of the characters. She was flattered and sent Madeleine de Scudéry a donation.

Claude de Saumaise, the French classical scholar, came, but her greatest triumph was when Descartes accepted her invitation to live in her palace. She was so eager to imbibe his erudition that she insisted on his meeting her in the library at five every morning. Unaccustomed to the bitter climate, the poor man caught cold and died within a year of his arrival, turning her triumph into bitter remorse.

It was hoped that she would marry her cousin, Prince Charles Gustavus, and live happy ever after as Good Queen Christina and her loving consort, but she had no desire to marry or bear children.

At the abdication ceremony at Uppsala when not one of the nobles would remove her crown, she took the matter literally in her own hands and removed it herself. The Riksdag then granted her a pension and some lands. Charles Gustavus became King Charles X and remained her suitor, but she paid no attention. She was already preparing for her Grand Tour.

Lord Whitlocke, the British ambassador, came to bid her farewell and presented her, on behalf of Cromwell, with a dog and a cheese soaked in port wine. When he asked why she was leaving she replied, "For love of myself."

Charles Gustavus presented her with fifty thousand *riksdaler* and a jeweled hairpin. She regarded this gift a long time and then ordered her *valet de chambre* . . . she never had a woman serve her . . . to cut off her hair.

"Hurry, Clairiet," she said as he hesitated. "Cut it off. Do you think, having given away a kingdom, I mind losing my hair?"

She took with her books, eight thousand manuscripts, canvases of Titian, Veronese, Caravaggio, Raphael; tapestries, rugs and china; a hundred bales of silver, gold and bronze ware, and a few clothes.

She traveled with her retinue and her possessions to Denmark, Antwerp, Brussels and Innsbruck. In Brussels she officially embraced Catholicism. Her father had given his life to the cause of Protestantism, but she had long had a leaning toward the more colorful and dramatic religion of the Latin countries.

When she landed at Marseille she was met by the duc de Guise as the king's emissary. Mazarin had arranged to have her honored, entertained and stuffed with French food and wines on the way to Paris. This, he figured, would exhaust her and keep her out of political mischief. His hospitality was wasted. Christina touched no alcohol and ate merely to appease her hunger. She prefered eating alone to dining in company.

Everyone was curious about this "Wonder of the North," and when a letter arrived from the duc de Guise it was read to the court by the duchesse de Chevreuse, and recorded in the *Memoirs* of Madame de Motteville:

I shall try to amuse you, while very bored myself, by sending you a portrait of the queen I am attending. She is not tall, but of full figure, with large haunches. Her arm is beautiful and her hand white and well formed, though rather masculine. One shoulder is a little too high, a defect which she cleverly conceals by the peculiarity of her dress, her gait and her movements, so that one could not lay a wager on it. Her face is large but not unpleasant, her features are also large and pronounced . . . her complexion, though slightly marked with smallpox, is clear and good. She wears a fantastic headdress . . . her bodice, laced behind obliquely, is made almost like our doublets; and her shift shows all around above her skirt which she wears half unfastened on one side. She is very much powdered and pomaded, and hardly ever wears gloves. Her boots are like a man's and so are her voice and almost all her features . . . she is civil and agreeable and speaks eight languages, French as if she were born in Paris.

She knows more than our Academy and Sorbonne put together and understands painting as well as everything else, and knows more of the intrigues of our court than the courtiers themselves. In short she is a very extraordinary person. I shall accompany her to the court by way of Paris, so you can judge for yourself.

The triumphal march through Paris took seven hours. At Chantilly, Mazarin met the ex-queen and dined with her while the king and his brother watched incognito, disguising himself being one of Louis's favorite sports. When she finally arrived at court she looked her worst. Everyone was shocked. Madame de Motteville records:

> In no way did she resemble a woman; she had not even the necessary modesty; she let men wait on her in her most private hours; she affected to be a man in all her actions; she laughed immoderately when anything pleased her; she put her legs up on seats as high as the one she was sitting on and showed them too freely.

The ignorant stared and the wise listened; Mazarin was wary and Queen Anne disliked her. Louis took a fancy to her because she said to him in the hearing of his mother, "If I were in your place, sire, I should marry the woman I love." She referred to Maria Mancini, the misunderstood, ugly duckling of the Mancini brood, with whom Louis was romantically in love.

La Grande Mademoiselle was so eager to meet her that she went early one morning to a house where Christina had spent the night and . . . again quoting Madame de Motteville . . . "found her with two hideously ugly women who wallowed in her bed."

It was inevitable that Ninon should have heard all about Christina, but it was surprising how much Christina knew about Ninon. Four years before, in fact, at the Swedish-Polish peace conference at Lübeck, she had complained about affairs of state depriving her of her freedom. "Praise as you will," she had said, "the brilliant prerogatives of royalty; if one cannot do as one wishes without being exposed to the censure of mankind, I would sooner be Ninon than Christina."

Soon the two women were conversing as if they had known each other for years.

"What a passion all the French women have to kiss me," said Christina. "Is it because I look like a man?"

She was no longer blindly enamored of France. She said she found the people gushing, affected and frequently insincere. With the exception of Corneille, Turenne and Pascal, she had met only vain and stupid men, "a people of pretty dolls."

The young comtesse de la Suze, daughter of Ninon's first real love, Gaspard de Coligny, who had a sentimental attachment for Christina, had also been a convert to Catholicism.

"I told her that she was converted so as to be sure she would not meet her husband either in this world or the next," said the queen, and burst into loud laughter at her own wit.

Ninon asked her if she had seen Scarron and how his health was.

"His health is bad, nevertheless he is the gayest man in Paris, and no wonder, he has the most beautiful and lovable of wives."

All the time she talked she paced up and down, emphasizing her remarks with her whip and interspersing them with good round curse words.

She questioned Ninon about herself, asking her why she had never married. Then she added that she felt such a repulsion toward the conjugal relationship that she "would rather choose death than a husband."

Ninon told her all about the *Compagnie du Saint-Sacrement* and she was duly indignant. "Why don't you come with me to Rome?" she suggested. But Ninon apparently preferred imprisonment in France. She liked Christina, but she knew only too well what it meant to be subject to the whims of royalty, and future events proved how right she was.

Christina took an affectionate leave and went on her way to the Italian border where she was held up because of the plague in Italy. She wrote to Mazarin that without Mademoiselle de Lanclos "the court lacked its greatest ornament," and to the king she wrote suggesting that Ninon be liberated *"pour le divertissement qu'elle pourrait y prendre."*

A few days after, to the chagrin of the *Compagnie du Saint-Sacrement*, His Majesty's order came for Ninon's release.

Madame de Motteville wrote: "Ninon was the only one of all the women she met in France for whom Christina showed any mark of esteem."

Chapter XXXI

THE rue des Tournelles runs north from the rue Saint-Antoine where the statue of Beaumarchais now stands. On one side the short rue de la Bastille connects it with the Place de la Bastille, and a little farther, on the other side, is an entrance to the Place des Vosges, the Place Royale of Ninon's time. Continuing, one crosses the rue du Pas-de-la-Mule which happens to be one of the streets now set aside by the police for the promenading of prostitutes. The next cross street is called Minimes after the church where Ninon sang her naughty song. When she left Lagny, Ninon returned to the Marais and rented a dwelling on the rue des Tournelles.

The *concierge* of any house from 28 to 74 will maintain that she lived in his building. One even points out her boudoir, unaware that no such room existed in her time. As the houses are somewhat alike, and there were no numbers and no registration of houses in the seventeenth century, chroniclers differ as to which one she actually occupied. Emile Magne, a most careful documentarian, fixes it at the present Number 36. This house is now a garage and contains no staircase. Its upper stories are reached by the staircase of Number 34. Both houses are the same structure, the same heights in front and rear buildings which are contiguous. It seems therefore quite probable that they were the same house in Ninon's time. The whole quarter is still redolent of its famous occupant. The girls who stroll on high heels, swinging their handbags and their hips, or stand in doorways when it rains, know a good deal about Ninon de Lanclos. She is, in a way, their patron saint.

Ninon had enjoyed her idyl and had no regrets. Now she was

back in the Marais with a child and no income. Aubijoux had
died, and Villarceaux was in difficulties, having been dismissed
from his duties with the duc d'Anjou. It was old Valliquierville
who came to her assistance.

Some time before, he had loaned Villarceaux forty-eight hundred *livres* and he held a note calling for payment of annual
interest of a little over two hundred and sixty-six *livres*. On
August 17, 1657, a contract was drawn before the notaries and
actuaries of the king by which this interest was

> given, ceded, acquitted, transferred and relinquished by ir-
> revocable donation between living parties and in good legal
> form . . . free of all hindrances and trouble . . . to Louis-
> François de Mornay, illegitimate son of Demoiselle Anne de
> Lanclos and Mre. Louis de Mornay, marquis de Villarceaux,
> and after him to his children born in wedlock. . . .

The document also provided that, should the said legatee and
his children die before the donor, the amount should be divided
equally between Valliquierville and Ninon "providing she were
not a nun, a novice or deceased." It further stated that if the
child survived the donor he was to receive the principal at the age
of twenty-five. Jean de Bellanguerville, the child's guardian, was
appointed trustee.

Satisfied that Louis-François was provided for, Ninon found a
home for him in the country and began to pick up the threads
of her way of life.

Financial difficulties had forced the Scarrons out of the Hôtel
de Troyes, and after living a year with Paul's sister, they had
rented part of a house in the rue Neuve-Saint-Louis and were
once again Ninon's neighbors. It was here that Scarron headed
his letters *Maison de l'impécuniosité*. When things looked their
blackest he gave a sumptuous dinner to his literary friends.
Ninon, in rustling silk, shading from the green of spring foliage
to a suggestion of violet, assisted Françoise to receive.

The considerate guests not only brought their own food and
wines, but some of them brought their servants as well, for the
Scarrons employed only a valet, a housemaid and a cook.

At dinner Ninon found herself next to Mignard, who, having returned from Rome, was getting the recognition that eventually made him official court portrait painter. Scarron read aloud a poem he had composed to the "greatest artist of the century," inviting him to share his Maine capon and partridge and compare them with the viands of Rome. He ended with a delicate suggestion that the artist paint the portrait of Françoise.

Mignard complained to Ninon that he was distressed because his daughter had a poor memory.

"On the contrary, monsieur, you should consider yourself fortunate, for in that case she won't quote."

Politics could not be kept out of the discussions. Mazarin had made an alliance with Cromwell and had promised to cede Dunkirk to the English. The name of the Great Condé came up: he had been leading the Spanish troops and been condemned *in absentia* for high treason. Monsieur had returned from exile, and of course his brother had forgiven him.

Jean Segrais was there. Being the Grande Mademoiselle's Secretary in Charge of Philanthropies, he had brought many gifts from her. During one of the silences that so often fall on dinner tables Segrais's voice rang out. "A man of your attainments," he said to the host, "should have at least one child." All eyes turned to the poor deformed Scarron.

"Would you like to perform that service for me?" he asked. Segrais was silent and Scarron continued: "I have Mangin here who will accomplish this office at the proper time." He turned to his *valet de chambre* who was acting as waiter. "Will you not beget a child for my wife?" he asked.

"Why yes, monsieur, if it please God," replied the boy. The answer certainly pleased the company. Scarron's humor must often have made his wife's flesh creep.

On the days that the poet did not have guests he had himself carried by porters to the rue des Tournelles where he met the same people whom he entertained at home.

In Ninon's house a new kind of salon was forming. There were many more women than in former days. Her own sex no longer regarded her as a menace. They had learned that they

could depend on her for comfort and advice. She talked freely
about her own love affairs, but never about those which were
confided to her. Not only did she give advice, but she sometimes
supplemented it with money when she felt it would help a woman
to assert her independence. The women she gathered were known
as *les précieuses galantes*, and the men called themselves the
"Birds of the Tournelles," a pun invented by Charleval, who was
still "awaiting her caprice," and who wrote:

> Je ne suis plus oiseau des champs,
> Mais de ces oiseaux des Tournelles
> Qui parlent d'amour en tout temps
> Et qui plaignent les tourterelles
> De ne se baiser qu'au printemps.

(I am no longer a bird of the fields, but one of the birds of
the Tournelles [or turrets] who speak of love at all times and
who pity the turtle doves who only make love in the spring.)

One of the Pretenders to the Bedchamber was Claude-Emman-
uel Chapelle, who had inherited a fortune at the age of sixteen
when he was legitimized. At twenty he had spent some time in
a correctionary school. He had then become one of Gassendi's
disciples and had written a few plays which had never achieved
performance. Ninon saw that beneath his bluff and his brag-
gadocio he had a first-class mind. He paid court to her, pleading
in verse that his spirit languished all day, that he admired her
lute and her grace, he was full of chagrin and of love, and what
would she do in his place? She made clear what she wished; it
was to have him come to her home sober. He swore that if she
yielded to him he would reform, but if she rejected him he would
not go to bed sober for a month. Ninon knew better than to put
faith in a drunkard's promises of reform. Chapelle then changed
his tactics to vindictiveness:

> Il ne faut pas qu'on s'étonne
> Si souvent elle raisonne
> De la sublime vertu
> Dont Platon fut revêtu:

Car à bien compter son âge,
Elle peut avoir vécu
Avec ce grand personnage.

(No one should be surprised if she often reasons with the sublime virtue with which Plato was clothed, for considering her age, she might have lived with that great personage.)

Ninon could enjoy a laugh at her own expense, and she continued her friendly relations with Chapelle.

Chapter XXXII

ONE of Ninon's weaknesses, or perhaps it was a virtue, was an inordinate curiosity. She had her own tastes and preferences, but she was willing to listen with attention to all eccentrics who turned up in her drawing room.

The duc de Vivonne, brother of La Montespan, was considered the best-read man at court, and he certainly was entertaining, but he was ruthless and *vicieux* and Ninon did not like him. She admitted him, however, to the periphery of her circle, because he was amusing, and brought her scandal from the court.

When Queen Christina perpetrated her horrible crime, it was Vivonne who brought the story.

Christina, not being able to get into Italy, had returned to France and been given hospitality at the palace of Fontainebleau. One gloomy dawn . . . she had always been an early riser . . . she had her equerry and favorite, Count Monaldeschi, murdered in the beautiful Galerie des Cerfs. She had accused him of treason but had given him no trial, not even a chance to defend himself. "*Crime passionnel*," everyone cried, but had that been the case she would more likely have stabbed him herself. She was not present in the Galerie, but Vivonne maintained that he caught her watching the bloody deed from behind a screen.[1]

His Majesty was outraged. This was worse than murder, it was a breach of hospitality. No matter how Christina tried to justify herself, and she did, telling Mazarin that she would do it over again, she lost forever the respect of the French.

Among the other oddities that Ninon collected at this time was

[1] This inspired a bas-relief a century later which was exhibited in Paris, which in turn caused an outbreak of plays about Christina.

Louis de Lesclache. He was an Aristotelian philosopher without a degree who had published a number of books in impressive tooled-leather bindings. Half of them were devoted to reducing Aristotle to synoptic tables, and the other half explained the tables.[2] He didn't try to prove his theses by logic, he demonstrated them by mathematics.

Since he was clean, dressed in quiet good taste and with impeccable manners, Ninon did not at first regard him as a crackpot. Moreover, he had been accepted in some of the fashionable *ruelles*. He ranted against all the contemporary writers, and though he professed to admire science, he damned every scientist.

"You'll learn more from me in a month," he said, "than all these dilettantes can teach you in a lifetime."

For a time she was taken in and she listened with polite attention, trying sincerely to understand what he was getting at. It wasn't long, however, before she realized that he wasn't getting at anything. She began making inquiries about him and Pascal told her that on one occasion, when he was demonstrating his counting machine, Monsieur Lesclache had "demonstrated" the immortality of the soul by mathematics.

One afternoon she invited a few of her intimates to listen to his discourse. They began to ridicule and to bait the man and Ninon, who felt sorry for him, could not restrain them. He made such a fool of himself, however, that there was little she could say in his defense. He left saying that it was no use, he would never be able to influence her again.

But that was not the end of the matter. The next day one of his disciples came to take his place. Félix de Juvenal belonged to an ancient and noble family, he had been one of the habitués of the Hôtel de Rambouillet and a contributor to the *Guirlande de Julie*. He had been engaged for many years in writing a twenty-volume history which has not yet been published. He condemned everything. He passed judgment on the morals of women, at the very moment that he was trying to assail them. He had little success, however, as he was unattractive. Ninon said he had a face "like a badly baked biscuit."

[2] These books are now collectors' items.

She tried, nevertheless, to listen with an open mind, and it seemed to her that he formulated sentences when alone, froze them, and when in company defrosted them bit by bit. If someone interrupted with a question he frowned, waited a moment, and then continued from where he had left off.

Her patience was soon exhausted. She made it clear to him that he was no longer welcome.

He threatened revenge and she began to wonder if he were one of the spies of the *Compagnie du Saint-Sacrement*. When he returned to his home he published, at his own expense, a pamphlet called *Portrait de la coquette*, in the form of a letter from Aristandre to his nephew Timagène, warning him against the tricks of women. While it mentioned no names, Ninon was obviously its target, and the whole movement of *les précieuses galantes* was attacked. It was malicious and heavy-handed, yet Ninon felt that to let it go by unnoticed was dangerous. She decided to answer it. Her reply took the form of a letter from Eléanore to her niece Philomène, warning her to beware of philosophers who settle life by definitions and tables. She called it *La coquette vengée*.[3] Her brochure passed from hand to hand, and although it was overwritten, as was the fashion of the day, the portraits of Juvenal and Lesclache were so unmistakable that they were laughed out of society.

Chapelle showed *La coquette vengée* to his friend Molière, who said that he would like to meet the author.

[3] See Appendix A for text of *La coquette vengée*.

Chapter XXXIII

THE plague raged; the Seine rose up and overflowed its banks, causing loss of life and property; burials were difficult. Thieves had their day and ghouls their night. In the provinces the misery was even greater than in Paris. Wolves prowled to within a day's travel of the city to snatch babies from their cradles. Turenne wrote, "One can pass through a hundred villages without meeting a man."

Sully, the minister of Henry IV, had said that "plowing and pasture were the twin breasts of France, the true mines and treasures of Peru." But the breasts had been dried up by war and taxation; agriculture was moribund and once more France lay "corrupting in its own fertility." The young king danced while masses were being said for Madame Mancini, sister of the cardinal and mother of his beloved Marie.

Mazarin became inflated with his importance. He received visitors while being shaved and at the same time playing with a bird, a monkey or a cat. He never invited anyone to sit in his presence. He loaned the king money at a high rate of interest, sold crown offices for his own benefit, and deflected army and navy appropriations into his own coffers.

Saint-Evremond was in the Bastille, ostensibly for fighting a duel. His friends, Ninon among them, pulled the available strings and obtained his release. Shortly thereafter he accompanied the cardinal to the Spanish border to negotiate a treaty, for after Turenne's victory at the battle of the Dunes, the enemy had sued for peace.

The Treaty of the Pyrénées made France the preponderant state of Europe, with the Rhenish League under her protection.

Mazarin had continued what Richelieu had begun. The treaty called for the marriage of Louis to his cousin, the Infanta Marie-Thérèse.

Saint-Evremond, dissatisfied with the negotiations, wrote to the marquis de Créqui, accusing Mazarin of having sacrificed the interests of France for his own. It was this letter that was to be the cause of his exile, and to this separation from Ninon we owe their correspondence.

In the theatre the comedy of manners was establishing itself. Saint-Evremond had parodied the meeting of the Académie Française, Chapelle had written a travesty on provincial *précieuses*, and the abbé de Pure, a novel and a play called *The Précieuse or the Mystery of the Alcove*, by which he had succeeded in getting himself kicked out of the alcoves.

Three comedies, all derived from a plot of the Spanish dramatist Rojas, were running simultaneously. One was by Thomas Corneille, one by Boisrobert, and the third, by Scarron, introduced the character of a student's valet whose opening lines were in Latin.

Molière's company had been touring the provinces under the patronage of the prince de Conti, Condé's brother, but the prince became a convert to Jansenism, which made him withdraw his patronage from the theatre. Molière made several trips to Paris to find a new Maecenas. On one occasion his troupe performed at the Louvre and His Majesty was so pleased that he decreed that they should become *La Troupe de Monsieur, frère du Roi*. They were established at the Petit-Bourbon, which formed part of the Louvre, where their performances alternated with those of the Italian comedians.

Plagiarism was a matter of course. Ideas taken from the Spanish were adapted to French, then lifted by the English. Sometimes a piece that had been translated from French into English would be stolen by another French writer who would translate it into a different version. Nobody cared whether Molière took an idea from life or from Scarron.

On November 18, 1659, Ninon went with Chapelle to the Petit-Bourbon where a distinguished audience was gathered: the

Condés and the Vendômes, the Albrets, the Longuevilles and the Gramonts. There was Madeleine de Scudéry and Madame de Grignan, the Grande Mademoiselle, the duc de Guise, the chevalier de Méré, the cardinal de Retz. Julie d'Angennes, now the comtesse de Montausier, was there as well as many of the habitués of the old Salon de Rambouillet and their satellites. The important play of the afternoon was Pierre Corneille's *Cinna*. The one-act comedy that closed the performance was new. It was entitled *Les Précieuses ridicules*. The author played the valet posing as a marquis. He was a magnificent comedian and the audience was convulsed with laughter when Cathos asks to hear an improvisation, and he recites a verse that he "improvised only yesterday at the house of a duchess of my acquaintance":

> Oh! Oh! Je n'y prenois pas garde:
> Tandis que, sans songer à mal, je vous regarde,
> Votre oeil en tapinois me dérobe mon coeur.
> Au voleur, au voleur, au voleur, au voleur!

(Oh, oh, quite careless of your charm, my heart without a thought of harm, is slyly filched by glances lief . . . stop thief, stop thief, stop thief, stop thief.[1])

The play was applauded and the audience went out laughing. But the following day there was a reaction. The heroines, Cathos and Madelon, were identified as Catherine de Rambouillet and Madeleine de Scudéry. The *précieuses* were wrathful. Molière insisted that any resemblance to anyone living or dead was purely accidental, and the controversy is still raging. The piece was withdrawn for two weeks and then put back into the repertory where it has amused every generation since.

Chapelle brought Molière to Ninon's house. They found at once that they had a great deal in common. Molière told Ninon that the courtiers were constantly pulling him aside to say: "I'll tell you the story of my life and you can write a play about it."

[1] Translation by H. C. Chatfield-Taylor.

Chapter XXXIV

AT the Petit-Bourbon the king in silver, crowned with roses, danced *L'Amour malade*, a ballet in ten parts. Courtiers, society and the foreign ambassadors formed the audience. Crowds collected in the morning outside the doors of the theatre, for if there was still room, a few of the people were invited in. They regarded it as a privilege to stand in the cold twelve hours to see their young king perform. Louis enjoyed nothing more than dressing up and being the star, no doubt some compensation for the poor and almost ragged childhood the cardinal had forced upon him.

In the early spring he traveled to the frontier to meet his bride, the Infanta Marie-Thérèse. At Bordeaux he disappeared from his entourage for a clandestine meeting with Marie Mancini. He wept as he presented her with a pearl necklace which he had purchased from his aunt, Henriette-Marie, the widow of the decapitated Charles I. It must have been a sacrifice, for the cardinal had allowed him very little money.

Marie Mancini's words have been immortalized in Racine's *Bérénice:*

"Sire, you are king, you love me and you let me go."

On June 9, 1660, the day after Charles II had returned to the English throne, the royal wedding took place at Saint-Jean-de-Luz. The couple set out for Paris, which they reached on August 26.

Triumphal arches were erected everywhere and the air was sweetened with the perfume of flowers. The cortege moved along the rue Saint-Antoine, across a part of the Pont-Neuf to the Place Dauphine, and then back to the right bank, to the City

Hall on the Place de Grève where temporary thrones had been erected.

From a balcony of the Hôtel Beauvais, Anne of Austria, sitting between Turenne and her ailing husband, watched her son ride by. She saw, perhaps with pity, her niece, now her daughter-in-law, pass slowly in her carriage, the wheels of which were encrusted in gold and adorned with jasmine and myrtle, the symbols of love and peace.

From a balcony near that of the queen mother, two women watched the new queen of France. The gold and precious stones of her robe were fused into a dazzling blob by the tears of Marie Mancini as Françoise Scarron pressed her hand in sympathy. In addition to his true love and his future wife, young Louis was eagerly watched by Olympe Mancini, his sensual love, Henriette of England, his future mistress, and Madame de Beauvais, who had been designated to give him his first lesson in the rites of love.

That evening Madame Scarron wrote a description of the scene to the marquise de Villarceaux, whose husband was not in the procession, being, at the time, detained in the Bastille:

> I shall not attempt to give you an account of the entrance of the king . . . neither I nor anyone would know how to make you appreciate all the magnificence; I do not believe it possible to find anyone handsomer; the queen should have gone to bed last night well content with the husband she has chosen.

Marie-Thérèse was small and chubby, plain and with fair hair and the perpetually startled eyes of the Hapsburgs. Like Marie de Medici, she never learned to speak good French. She made a good wife for Louis, never interfering with affairs of state or of the bedchamber, "merry the whole day long if he smiled at her." Montespan wrote:

> If it were not for the king, she would pass her life in dressing gown, nightcap and slippers . . . at court everything seems to weigh her down, especially her diamonds . . . her two greatest interests are her husband and chocolate.

The queen bore her husband six children, one of whom survived, and when, after twenty-three years of marriage, she died, he exclaimed, "This is the first sorrow she has caused me."

There is one story about Marie-Thérèse that is not in the schoolbooks. While the marquise de Montespan was the official mistress, an African prince presented the queen with a blackamoor, aged twelve, and thirty inches tall without his turban. He gamboled about the queen's apartments like a kitten and the lonely queen took a fancy to him, sometimes taking him on her lap and caressing him. All the ladies of the court pampered Osmin and presented him with gifts. Montespan gave him an aigrette of rubies and diamonds for his turban. It soon became the fashion for ladies of the court to have blackamoors to carry their trains. "But so absurd a fashion had to disappear after the mishap I am about to relate," wrote Montespan in her *Memoirs*.

The queen being pregnant, prayers were said for her. "My pregnancy is different this time," she said. "I have never felt like this before."

Montespan continues:

She was delivered of a fine, healthy girl, black from head to toe, after which she went to sleep. The child's features bore none of those marks peculiar to people of color.

It was obligatory for certain of the nobility to be in the room during a royal *accouchement*, so that no tricks could be played with babies. This, moreover, was a situation for which there was no statutory remedy. The physicians met in one room, the chaplains in another, and the princes of the blood began to wonder. The decision was unanimous, the queen having no vote. The child was sent away to be brought up by a Negro family, and the *Gazette* announced that the royal infant had died shortly after birth.[1] Poor little Osmin was packed off, and the fashion of blackamoors carrying trains was taboo.

[1] The child was raised as the daughter of the Negro family and when she grew up she entered a Benedictine nunnery at Moret. Her portrait can be seen in the Sainte-Geneviève library at the College of Henri IV.

"What did the poor queen say?" Ninon asked the duc de Vivonne.

"She explained that one day, early in her pregnancy, Osmin had hidden behind a wardrobe and suddenly jumped out to playfully give her a fright. My sister said that in this he was only too successful."

Cardinal Mazarin, having married off his king to the powerful house of the Spanish Hapsburgs, having married all seven of his nieces to members of the nobility, and himself to the queen, died. Hortense, his favorite niece, was heir to his acknowledged fortune, and her husband perpetuated his name, calling himself the duc de Mazarin. The millions in gold which were hidden away in various fortresses were revealed by Colbert to Louis, who confiscated them, thereupon becoming the richest monarch in Europe.

Immediately after the minister's death, the twenty-three-year-old king spent several hours alone. This was extraordinary. It was said that he was thinking. The next day, when the Council asked him to whom they should address themselves, he replied, "To me." It was the first step toward absolute monarchy.

He then proceeded to choose ministers from business and professional groups rather than from men of rank. His education had been very deficient, but one thing he had learned: that kings had a divine right. He was not named *Louis-Dieudonné* for nothing.

Chapter XXXV

THE fact that Villarceaux had been a friend of Scarron by no means prevented the marquis from trying to court the poet's wife. It is said that Françoise put up serious resistance. She was cautious, wanting above everything in the world "to be respected." It was some years later when she wrote, indelibly, to be quoted both for and against her, a sentence which is the keynote of her character: "There is nothing cleverer than irreproachable conduct."

Tallemant des Réaux wrote of her:

His wife is welcome everywhere; up to this time it is believed that she has not made the leap (*fait le saut*). . . . Villarceaux attaches himself there and the husband pleasantly mocks those who wish to suspect him.

One contemporary asserts that Françoise was seen in bed with the marquis, while another finds proof of her virtue in the fact that, though poor, she refused an offer of thirty thousand crowns. Saint-Simon claims that she spent summers with Villarceaux, and Ninon maintained that "it was not difficult for her to be virtuous as she was not too troubled by the temptations of the flesh." All this interest of whether she did or didn't was idle curiosity until it became pertinent to the history of France.

The likelihood is that toward the end of Scarron's life his wife "made the leap." At first he took the gossip lightly, but his attitude changed. In his helplessness and pain his jealousy and utter frustration must indeed have been bitter. In a poem and a letter to Ninon he wrote of his despair at the treachery of woman and his longing for death. That he did not always control his temper at this time is not surprising. Françoise complained to Ménage that he spoke harshly to her before their guests, and implored him to tell her husband that if he had anything embarrassing to say to her to please do so in private.

Scarron spent part of his last summer with his sister in the country, dictating to his valet, having "a thousand devils in my arms and legs." Fouquet had given him a small benefice but debts piled up, and when he returned to Paris in the fall there was no money for fuel and his clothes were too threadbare to permit him to go out. Ninon came to see him almost daily, bringing the delicacies he could not afford.

"I never imagined it would be so easy to mock at death," he told her, and added, "What a beautiful satire I could write on the hiccups."

Characteristically, he wrote what he called his *Testament burlesque* in verse. "The time has come," it begins, "for the *cul-de-jatte* who can move neither hand nor foot, and who has never taken a step, to walk to the end."

To his beloved wife he bequeaths permission to remarry because:

> In spite of myself I have forced her to make a fasting which should put her in good appetite; let her enjoy it then a little, and that her prudent wisdom not have recourse to a paralytic, but that she may enjoy the benefits which the sacred tie permit. However, if any other husband approach her, may she not reproach him with the virtues of the first husband to wound the second.

What a pity he could not have read a letter that Françoise wrote Ninon six years later:

> What do you think of the comparison someone has dared to make to me of Monsieur M———— to Monsieur Scarron? My God, what a difference! Without fortune, without pleasures, he [Scarron] attracted good company to his home . . . he had that charm which all the world knows, and what kindness of heart! . . . My husband had an excellent background; I corrected his licenses.

Scarron adds in his will that should God send him a posthumous child he will revoke his gifts to his wife. Then he makes bequests to his friends, a hogshead of wine to one, a cheese to another; pomades, madrigals, sonnets. To Boisrobert, four hundred pounds of lies, to the Corneille brothers five hundred pounds of solemnity. The next bequest reads: "To Molière, cuckoldom." Molière was not yet married, but the world knows how he later suffered from that complaint.

In October Scarron died. His body was carried on a litter between two horses and buried in the church of Saint-Gervais, to a dirge played by Charles Couperin.

Neglecting nothing, the poet had written his own epitaph, which still remains.[1]

Françoise Scarron was twenty-five when she was left a widow and destitute. Her home had to be relinquished and her possessions sold to pay the creditors. Her beauty had matured, she had gained poise and she received a number of proposals, some including marriage, but as Bussy-Rabutin wrote: "She chose her glorious and irreproachable poverty." The historian of the Great Century, Boulanger, on the other hand, says, "Her reputation was as good as could be expected in the case of a young widow in needy circumstances."

While awaiting a small pension from the queen mother, she lived on bounty from rich and influential friends, always performing services to repay them. She was well on her way to becoming a beloved and respected "nanny." Everyone was vastly

---

[1] Epitaph de Scarron, l'Eglise de Saint-Gervais:

> Celui qu'ici maintenant dort
> Fit plus de pitié que d'envie,
> Et souffrit mille fois la mort
> Avant que de perdre la vie.
>
> Passant, ne fais ici de bruit,
> Garde bien que tu ne l'éveille;
> Car voici la première nuit
> Que le pauvre Scarron sommeille.

(He who sleeps here now caused more pity than envy and suffered death a thousand times before losing life. Passer-by, make no noise here and take care you do not awaken him, for this is the first night that poor Scarron sleeps.)

amused when the soothsayer of the Albret family predicted for her a crown and a scepter.

Her rich friends provided her with odd jobs and their castoff clothing, but it was Ninon who took her into her home, asking nothing in return. She moved into the rue des Tournelles and remained six or eight months. The gossips stage-whispered that it was more than friendship. La Fare in *Memoirs of the Age of Louis XIV* wrote: "For whole months at a time Ninon and Françoise shared the same bed," a condition which he regarded as proof of intimate relations.

Some time later Montespan wrote in her *Memoirs:*

Mademoiselle de Lenclos is universally known in the world for the agreeableness of her superior wit and her charms of face and person. . . . At the death of the poet, Scarron, Mademoiselle d'Aubigné, once more in poverty, found in Mademoiselle de Lenclos a generous and persevering friend who at once offered her her house and table. Mademoiselle d'Aubigné passed eight or ten months in the intimate society of this philosophical woman.

But her conscience or her prudery not permitting her to tolerate longer a manner of life in which she seemed to detect license, she quit Ninon, advising her to renounce coquetry, while the other was advising her to abandon herself to it.

As for *l'affaire* Villarceaux, Montespan writes:

The pretended amours of Mademoiselle d'Aubigné and the marquis de Villarceaux, Ninon's friend, are an invention of malicious envy. I justified Madam Scarron on the matter before the king when I asked for her for the education of the princes, and having rendered her that justice from conviction rather than necessity, I shall certainly not charge her with it today.

The marquise de Montespan lived to regret her championship of Françoise Scarron.

In "Ninon's Tower" at the Château de Villarceaux there is a

portrait of Françoise Scarron, nude, holding a slight drapery. The face is unmistakably the same as that of the well-known portrait made by Mignard years later. The artist is Louis de Mornay, marquis de Villarceaux. Her detractors regarded this as proof of her guilt while her defenders maintain that it is proof of her innocence. They claim that Villarceaux painted it from imagination in revenge for her having repulsed him.[2]

Many years later Saint-Evremond, wishing to clear up the matter for something he was writing, wrote from London to ask Ninon for the facts. She replied:

> Scarron was my friend; his wife gave me infinite pleasure by her conversation, and in the end I decided she was too *gauche* for love. As to details, I know nothing, I saw nothing, but I often lent my yellow room to her and Villarceaux.

How precise one must be with words! "I decided she was too *gauche* for love" has been used as an argument on both sides.

"She was virtuous by conviction as well as temperament," Ninon said, and many years after she wrote:

> We met every day but were not of one mind. Had she followed my advice she would not have attained the elevation where you now see her, but she would have been happier.

Ninon made the mistake of judging Françoise by herself.

---

[2] This portrait was bought at a sale at Versailles by the Regina Mater of Saint-Cyr, the academy for young ladies which Maintenon founded. It is said that the Mother Superior contemplated having the figure clothed with a coat of paint. This was never done, however, and eventually the portrait reached the château, which is not strange, as the Mother Superior was herself a Mornay.

Chapter XXXVI

FOUQUET, who had been Minister of Finance under Mazarin, had followed his master's example and lined his pockets with the country's gold. He was a brilliant financier who had become an advocate at the age of sixteen. He was a generous patron of the arts, a most agreeable gentleman, and, unlike the cardinal, had many devoted friends. However, he made two fatal blunders. He outshone his king in splendor, and he was exceedingly polite to one of the royal mistresses.

His estate, Vaux-le-Vicomte, at Mélun, showed an opulence and a good taste beside which the royal palaces were mediocre. His octagonal château and its park were the work of three men: Le Vau, the architect, Le Brun, the decorator, and Le Nôtre, the landscape gardener. The paintings and statuary, the tapestries, the mosaic floors, the parks, cascades and fountains, the terraces and grottoes were breath-taking.

When it was completed he invited the king and queen, the mistresses and a court of some six thousand persons to spend a few days with him.

The rooms were immaculate and comfortably warmed, and the food was supervised by his distinguished *maître d'hôtel*, Vatel. The service was of solid gold, the napery of fine linen and rare lace. The entertainment was as prodigal as the setting. There were baths, swings, cards and billiards; in the pavilions erected for the occasion fans, handkerchiefs, perfumes and sweets were given away, and on each guest's dressing table was a well-filled purse for gambling. At night there were music, dancing and fireworks, and it was here that Molière and his troupe first performed *Les Fâcheux*, which had been written to order in a fortnight. Henriette d'Angleterre's star was sinking in the royal firmament and that of Louise de la Vallière was rising, and Fouquet thought it politic, as host, to pay some attention to the young girl, who had as yet no official standing.

Louis was affronted. On his departure he said, "Monsieur le Ministre, I can never dare receive you under my roof. You would be too poorly housed."

About a month later the king and his Minister of Finance took a business trip. One morning at Nantes, as they were working together, Louis seemed restless. He rose from time to time to look out of the window, and when finally he saw what he was looking for in the courtyard, he smilingly dismissed Fouquet. Then he watched from behind the curtain as d'Artagnan, the captain of his musketeers, took the astonished minister into custody.

A search was made of Fouquet's papers, and incriminating documents were found, including the letter of Saint-Evremond to Créqui about the Treaty of the Pyrénées. Fouquet's trial at the Arsenal lasted three years and was the sensation of France. He was questioned about gold, about the wax and the sugar taxes. His conduct was dignified and his answers brilliant. He constantly referred to Colbert as "my prosecutor."

Although his defections were undeniable, the judges were inclined to be lenient, so Colbert had them changed, and some maintained that he falsified some of the documents.

The verdict was guilty, and the sentence banishment, and confiscation of property by the Crown.

The king was not satisfied. He changed the sentence to life imprisonment. Fouquet spent the rest of his days at Pignerole, the fortress-prison. His devoted valet insisted on going with him. The portion of his fortune which had not been embezzled went to his wife and the rest into the royal coffers.[1] Considering that Fouquet was not the only official who lined his pockets with public funds, many thought the sentence was unjustly severe, somewhat motivated by royal pique.

Ninon had a lover at the time who was also a good friend. He

[1] The case bears some resemblance to that of Henry VIII and Cardinal Wolsey after the building of Hampton Court.

was a serious man who had her welfare at heart, and she really liked and admired him. Jean Hurault, sieur de Gourville, came from a lower stratum. He had originally been a menial in the family of La Rochefoucauld and had risen to the post of steward and friend of his master. His brilliant financial strategy had saved the family from ruin. Mazarin's attention had been called to him and he soon became involved with the cardinal and Fouquet.

When the incriminating letter of Saint-Evremond was found Gourville warned him that he was in danger of arrest, and Saint-Evremond fled Paris, going first to Normandy and thence to Holland. The following year Charles II of England welcomed him and gave him a pension. A new life began for him in London and he was to meet there the other woman of his life, Hortense Mancini, duchesse de Mazarin.

Soon Gourville realized that he too was in danger. Nobody who had been connected with Fouquet could breathe freely. He decided to take himself off while he could. He had forty thousand gold *écus* which he wanted to leave behind. He deposited twenty thousand with a friend, the Grand Almoner of Notre-Dame, and the other twenty thousand with Ninon. Then he disappeared.[2]

Toward the end of the year Ninon was threatened with the loss of her home. Nothing could have distressed her more. The owners found themselves obliged to sell, and the new owner might want to occupy it himself. She arranged for the purchase of the property in partnership with Gérard du Burg, "ordinary council of the king in his councils," a truculent Bordelais living in Paris. He was not an intimate friend, but an acquaintance who came to her *foyer* to meet celebrities. She found him ridiculous but somewhat amusing. It was agreed that Ninon should retain her occupation of the house, and if either of the partners died, the other was to take full possession of the premises.

She probably obtained the capital for her share from her current payer, Monsieur Léon Fourreau. Tallemant des Réaux writes:

[2] An *écu* was three *livres*, a *livre* slightly less than an English pound.

Fourreau, a stout fellow, the son of Madame Larcher, acted as her banker; he had but one talent and that was an admirable knowledge of the virtues of meat. She drew notes of credit on him: Monsieur Foureau will pay, etc. etc. It is believed that he hardly had anything out of it. She treated him as if he were a horse and once, when he showed her an abscess on his leg, she called it a "quittor" and excluded him from her alcove.

A wise precaution, for who knew what an abscess might come from?

The house had three stories in front and four in the rear section. The servants slept on the second story and the third story of the front edifice served as an attic. The deed of purchase describes it:

> . . . a house situated in Paris, rue des Tournelles, parish of Saint-Paul, occupied at present by Mademoiselle de l'Enclos, consisting of a round porte-cochère which forms the entrance of the above-mentioned house, a large courtyard, another medium-sized courtyard and a small courtyard in which there is a skylight [*jour?*] above the said cellar (1) room and kitchen, a passage to enter said house, and next to the staircase a toilet [*siège privé*].
>
> On the first floor a room, a dressing room and a small room (*cabinet*); on the second floor a room, a dressing room and a small room; on the third floor a room, with a gallery above, two attics, of which one is wainscotted. . . .

Feeling at last secure, Ninon proceeded to make alterations and to add to her furnishings, a task which she thoroughly enjoyed. Monsieur Fourreau continued to supply her with funds which, when invested, eventually gave her enough of an income to enable her to dismiss him.

Chapter XXXVII

HENRIETTE, the daughter of Charles I, had been smuggled out of England in boy's clothing. She terrified her nurse by telling the innkeepers' wives and the postilions that she was not really a boy but a princess with beautiful dresses. Although she and her mother, the sister of Louis XIII, had been welcomed at the French court, it wasn't long before they suffered neglect and hardship. A marriage between Henriette and young Louis would have united the two countries, but the king would have nothing to do with his cousin, whom he called "the little bones of the Holy Innocents."

When Gaston d'Orléans died, his nephew Philippe, duc d'Anjou, brother of Louis XIV, became the duc d'Orléans, de Valois and de Chartres, with the privilege of handing His Majesty his shirt. He became "Monsieur" and when he married his cousin Henriette she became "Madame." The Grande Mademoiselle said he did it only to be for once the center of the festivities.

"But," as Madame de la Fayette put it, "the miracle of inflaming the heart of the prince d'Orléans was not in the power of any woman." Monsieur's darling was the middle-aged supercilious dandy, the chevalier de Lorraine, painted, perfumed and peevish. This attachment left the young bride to her own resources, which proved to be not inconsiderable.

As His Majesty paid visits to his wife only for purposes of the state, he had time and energy for dalliance, and his roving eye began to perceive that his cousin and sister-in-law was no longer a skinny adolescent but a mature and beautiful woman, with intelligence and a lovable disposition, who was being neglected by her husband.

Louis organized boating parties and hunts, *fêtes-champêtres*, torchlight balls and moonlight drives, all for Madame. At Fontainebleau they performed *The Ballet of the Seasons*. Henriette played Diana, while the king, dressed as Spring, knelt to worship the goddess. There were whispers behind fans. Anne of Austria did not object to Louis having a mistress, but to choose Henriette not only humiliated her favorite son but might be regarded as incestuous. The court decided to be scandalized.

To throw dust into prying eyes, the couple arranged to have Madame's little maid of honor, Louise de la Baume Le Blanc, present at most of their meetings. By pretending that Louise was the attraction, the king was enabled to visit Henriette frequently. The maid of honor was a pious, virtuous girl of sixteen with no bosom; she was neither pretty nor quick-witted, and she had two handicaps: she was slightly lame and utterly sincere. It wasn't long before the *rendezvous à trois* became *à deux* but the two were His Majesty and Louise.

The transformation at Versailles had commenced. The trio, Le Vau, Le Brun and Le Nôtre, were engaged by the king to turn what had been merely the hunting lodge of his father into the magnificent palace it is today. For the fountains and the canal, water was drawn from Paris, which could scarcely spare it; in the theatre of the palace a moving stage was installed. A sumptuous festival was given, called *The Delights of the Enchanted Isles*, which lasted a week.

The new minister, Colbert, assumed the duties of a number of ministries. Of bourgeois origin, he was honest and a businessman. He imposed high tariffs on imports, built canals all over France, established a fleet, founded the Academy of Sciences. He reorganized the economy of the country. Companies were formed for trade with America and the Orient. He bought for the government the Gobelins tapestry works, so called because the owners in the fifteenth century had believed that the beautiful colors of their dyes were due to friendly goblins in their stream. Colbert encouraged the manufacture of silk, the use of needle work, and he established some of the great lacemaking industries. Ninon said, "One day France will lead the world in fashion." Colbert made tobacco a government monopoly, which it still remains. The king uttered a proclamation: "It is no disgrace to be in trade."

That autumn saw the death of the queen's father, Philip IV of Spain, and in the early spring the king's mother, Anne of Austria, died. The court went into lavish mourning, assuaged somewhat by theatre, music and ballet.

There was famine in the provinces. Dead children were found in the fields, their mouths stuffed with grass. In the cities, however, the tide was turning. Tradesmen had more money than professionals. Women, girls and even children kept shop; industry and speculation increased, and merchants became sharper.

The queen and Louise awaited simultaneously the births of the king's children. On November 1, just before noon, His Majesty announced from a window of the palace that a dauphin had been born. The fountains ran with wine, Spanish dancers performed in the courtyard, prisoners were freed and alms distributed. Louise, who had been made the duchesse de la Vallière, bore her child with less fanfare.

At night the young king continued to climb about the roofs and to enter the chambers of the maids of honor, but he continued to love Louise a long time, until she left him to go into a convent. In the meantime he had started his relations with La Montespan.

"The business of being king," said His Majesty, "is great, noble and delightful."

Chapter XXXVIII

NINON had the usual reasons for believing herself pregnant, and two men claimed paternity of the forthcoming child. One was the duc d'Estrées, grandson of Henri IV and Gabrielle d'Estrées, a vice-admiral, and the other was the abbé Jean Coëffier d'Effiat, brother of the unfortunate Cinq-Mars. The abbé had bulging eyes and Ninon said that when she slept with him she was always a little nervous that they would drop out.

"We need a King Solomon," said the duke.

"We need some dice," said the abbé, producing the ivories which happened to be in the pocket of his cassock. They rolled a *passe-deux* and d'Estrées got the highest number.

"Never mind, my dear," said the priest, "when this one is finished, I'll make you another."

The infant, however, never was finished, and after a brief interlude with a handsome Italian two new lovers claimed Ninon's attention.

Claude, comte de Choiseul, was a marshal and Guillaume-Louis Pécour was a dancer, young and the idol of the opera. One was accorded afternoons, the other evenings. One day, curious about the identity of his co-lover, Choiseul arrived out of turn. Ninon's *valet de chambre* tried to get rid of him but he insisted on waiting. He paced the salon and after a time the door opened and Monsieur Pécour appeared, delicately drawing on his pearl-gray gloves and looking as if he had swallowed a canary. The count recognized him with surprise.

"Monsieur Pécour, indeed! I had no idea you were giving Mademoiselle de Lanclos dancing lessons."

"Mademoiselle de Lanclos is far too proficient in everything

177

she undertakes to require instruction, as Monsieur le Maréchal should know."

Choiseul searched his mind for a piece of repartee worthy of his rank. Finally he said, "Where the devil did you get that peculiar uniform you're wearing? What regiment do you serve?"

Pécour replied, "*Je commande, monsieur, un corps que vous avez servi depuis longtemps!*" [1]

Although Choiseul was dignified, handsome and reliable, Ninon found him dull and pompous, and soon she dismissed him with a line borrowed from Corneille:

"Seigneur, what virtues you have made me hate."

He accepted his dismissal as a lover, grateful that she let him remain a friend. Some years later he was decorated and he came to show her the gold cross on its azure ribbon. That year there had been a notoriously unworthy list of honors, and as the count strutted before the mirror Ninon said:

"Monsieur, if you don't stop admiring yourself I shall recite the names of your companions of the order to you."

A very jealous lover was Louis, comte de Nançay, marquis de la Chastre, quartermaster in the cavalry. During his short incumbency he was the only one. When duty called him to the Palatinate, he was desolate. He thought that if he made Ninon promise to await his return she might keep her word.

"Be sure, monsieur, I shall not forget you," was all she would say.

"Forget me? That is not enough. Promise that you will not deceive me."

"My dear Monsieur le Marquis, I never deceive anybody. Infidelity? That is pardonable, but never perfidy."

Which of course raised La Chastre's jealousy to the boiling point, and he would not let the matter drop. He demanded a promise in writing, and as he was going to war, she wanted him to have peace of mind and signed a pledge. He carried the paper next to his heart, except, of course, when showing it off to his friends.

Touched by his sentiment, Ninon remained faithful until the

[1] A play on the word *corps* which also means body.

next temptation. As was her way, she gave herself completely to the new lover, and when finally the love was consummated, she lay in his arms peacefully a moment and then burst out laughing. "Ah," she cried, "*le bon billet qu'a La Chastre!*"

Her partner, quite naturally, demanded an explanation and, when he heard it, was so flattered that he told the story to a few friends. The phrase "*un bon billet de La Chastre*" remained for a generation the synonym for any worthless document.

When the marquis returned from Germany he was greeted by kind friends with the story. He went to the rue des Tournelles in a rage. Ninon's defense was that she had signed the promise under duress. She ridiculed the whole matter and La Chastre rose and stalked out, or rather halfway out, because he found her still irresistible, and it all ended in a romp in bed.

When he finally left she ran out to the top of the stairs and called down:

"But remember, Marquis, we are still not reconciled."

Chapter XXXIX

AFTER the Fronde most of the nobles left their domains in the hands of deputies and took up residence at court where they led "a parade and antechamber existence." This enabled the king to keep an eye on them. From independent princes and landowners with a sense of responsibility to their tenants they were debauched into fawning flatterers, trying to undermine each other while basking in the rays of the sun king. They dined copiously, dressed magnificently, enjoyed the cream of theatrical and musical presentations, gambled, danced, hunted and dallied with each other's wives and mistresses. Despite this, life at the palace had its drawbacks. It was so cold a short distance from the hearths that the wine froze in the glasses; the courtiers were herded into small rooms in the upper stories, where the corridors were in a state of filth to which they themselves largely contributed. The royal spaniels and greyhounds were actually housed better, sleeping in kennels that were velvet-lined and decorated with bronze.

The passion for gambling became a frenzy. *Hoca, lansquenet, raquette, portique* and *trou-madame* were the fashion. Mazarin and Fouquet had been reckless, and Monsieur, Gaston d'Orléans, had lost half a million *livres* to the comte de Gramont, which necessitated his cheating his daughter, the Grande Mademoiselle, out of her inheritance. One Christmas Day Madame de Montespan lost seven hundred thousand *écus*.

The life of the court was repeated in diminishing degrees throughout the country. People played in each other's *hôtels*, in taverns and in coaches, games sometimes lasting for three days and nights. Cheating was known as "correcting fortune" and really distinguished families had special cards and loaded dice manufactured for them for the purpose. Crime was severely punished in the lower classes, but a person of rank could literally get away with murder. The police system was futile against influence and bribery, and witnesses to a crime, fearing that they would later be wiped out, usually suffered loss of memory. It was a corrupt age, a frivolous age, but the "age of arsenic" was yet to come.

Women drank, gambled and took snuff. When they had money of their own they frequently kept lovers, which is how many young officers got equipped for the army.

A day in the life of a woman of fashion began about noon when her maid drew back the curtains of her bed to hand her a cup of soup or chocolate. The base of her toilet preparations was an essence of veal broth and stewed sheep's fat.[1] She made her toilette with the assistance of her maid. Cheeks, lips, ears and shoulders were rouged; her eyebrows were darkened and the *mouches* put in place. The most important functionary in her life was the hairdresser. Famous coiffeurs were lavished with gifts and flattery and could command enormous fees. Madame sat at her dressing table giving instructions to her cook, her footman, her *valet de chambre;* she received love notes and listened to bits of gossip. Sometimes she would be entertained with an aria by a tenor whose status was above the valet's and below the hairdresser's. When merchants arrived with bolts of brocade or velvet, or with trays of glittering jewels, she did not hesitate to interrupt Monteverdi or Cavalli in order to make her selection.[2]

In the afternoon there was dinner, an affair of several hours. She might go to the theatre or ride in her sedan chair in the Cours-la-Reine, or stroll in the Place Royale. The evenings were given to dancing, gaming and *toujours l'amour.*

At Ninon's no gambling was permitted. There was music and what Carlyle called "the overflowing tide of French talk, ebbing

---

[1] This is not surprising as the latter is the main ingredient of our lanolin.
[2] An excellent representation of this, although it represents the early eighteenth century, is the first act of Hugo von Hofmannsthal's *Der Rosenkavalier.*

only toward the small hours of the morning." There were little dinners, and the love-making was done strictly in private. If a gentleman wished to enjoy himself in a clean, wholesome fashion, to dine without fear of being poisoned and to say what he believed without fear of blackmail, he could do no better than visit the house of the notorious courtesan of the Marais. But he would have to mind his manners.

The king usually began dinner with four soups. He then ran the gamut of the animal kingdom, garnished with the vegetable kingdom, ending up with a *digestif*, all without forks. At Ninon's table no guest ate himself into a stupor, and although the finest wines were served, nobody ever got more than merry.

Her household consisted of a cook, a kitchenmaid, a *valet de chambre* [3] and a personal maid. She treated them exceptionally well and they were devoted to her. There were no dining rooms as we know them today. Tables were set up in the room that happened to be comfortably heated and convenient at the time. The fashion was for gamy food, highly spiced, a custom convenient for poisoners, but Ninon's dishes were simple, served in a natural form. She was fond of introducing vegetables that were new, and she took a personal interest in their preparation. As her position became more established, her dinners became famous.

One afternoon the conversation turned to the subject of the cooking of various countries, and some of the guests related their experiences abroad. The comte de Gramont told of being at the court of Charles II while the so-called Merry Monarch was dining in state. The lackeys all served him on bended knee and the king explained to Gramont that this was a mark of respect which no other European monarch enjoyed.

"I thank Your Majesty for the explanation," Gramont quoted himself as replying. "I thought they were begging your pardon for serving you so bad a dinner."

Ninon no longer followed the fashion, she set it. She wore her hair parted in the middle with a bunch of short curls on each side, a style which became known as *coiffure à la Ninon*. Her

[3] Pierre Porron, known as La Pierre in various spellings.

words were repeated in the *ruelles* and often reached the court. Sometimes, when His Majesty had made a decision he would ask one of the courtiers, "What does Ninon say about it?" And once he exclaimed: "What extraordinary times these are when Ninon molds public opinion and directs the conscience of the king!"

It was a brocaded era of torturing stays and velvet masks; of the language of fans and ribbons and dropped handkerchiefs; of coquetry and affectation and of foolish, florid verse. It was Ninon who first raised her voice against the bonds of artificiality, and its sounds reached the ears of a few intrepid souls. Women had what privileges they could wangle, but no rights. They could be mistreated and set aside by their husbands with impunity. They didn't even have anything to say over their own children.

Les précieuses galantes who gathered around Ninon were women of education who wanted to improve their status and who waged a campaign against corruption and pedantry. Madame Coulanges wrote to Madame de Sévigné: "The women now run after Ninon as the men formerly did." Among her friends was Madame de la Fayette, who Boileau said was the most intelligent woman in France, and whose first novel, *La Princesse de Montpensier*, had appeared unsigned, as was the custom. Her husband had disappeared and she and La Rochefoucauld had entered into a relationship which endured until his death. His *Réflexions et maximes morales* had also appeared anonymously, although no one had any doubt about the authorship. The maxims had been batted about the salons for years, achieving their polish by rubbing against many minds. La Rochefoucauld was now Grand Master of His Majesty's Wardrobe, an office which entailed pulling up the king's breeches.

"When women are intelligent," he said to Ninon, "I prefer their conversation to that of men. There is a certain suavity in their talk which is lacking in our sex."

"You're in a position to know," said Ninon. She was referring to his three great loves, the duchesse de Chevreuse, the duchesse de Longueville, and now Madame de la Fayette, all brilliant and witty women.

Molière was in sympathy with the objectives of *les précieuses galantes* and he used some of the lines he heard at Ninon's in his *Ecole des femmes*. *Tartuffe* had been simmering in his mind. He had written three acts when he brought it to read to Ninon. She told him of her experiences with amorous clergymen who had tried to convert her. Among them was the abbé Pons, her neighbor, who excused his advances by quoting the temptations of St. Paul.

Emile Magne writes:

Some sort of collaboration undoubtedly existed between Ninon and the poet, and towards the end of 1663 or the beginning of 1664 Molière was planning a more direct crusade against the *Compagnie du Saint-Sacrement*. He submitted his general outline of *Tartuffe* for inspection.

The mouthpiece of the religious party at the time was an abusive writer, Antoine de Somais, who published bitter attacks against Molière, and compiled a dictionary of the *précieuses* and the *précieuses galantes*. He listed names, addresses and indiscretions. Of Ninon he said:

She is a very thoughtful woman who gives way to a degree of melancholy of which people who only see her in company would not believe her capable, since in public she always appears charming and full of vivacity, which makes her sought after. With regard to beauty, although she is so well versed in the art of attracting love, it must still be granted that her mind is more attractive than her face, and that many people would escape her thralls if they did no more than look at her.

And he adds that the comte de Guiche sought her company for that alone and "not for intrigue, although the frequency of his visits leaves room for doubt."

Ninon was not disturbed by anything that was said or written about her, and she continued her campaign for the causes in which she believed. "How unfortunate women are," she wrote, "their own sex is their greatest enemy. Husbands tyrannize them, lovers deceive and often dishonor them. They have many admirers and often not a true friend. Is it surprising that they find it necessary to resort to dissimulation and caprice?"

Chapter XL

Ninon decided to earn money some other way.

She had passed her forty-second birthday. Her attraction, if anything, had increased, and she looked no more than twenty-five. Nevertheless, she took her hand mirror over to the window every day, to watch for the little lines around the mouth and the eyes that must sooner or later make their appearance.

"If God had to give a woman wrinkles," she said, "he might at least have put them on the soles of her feet." Realistic enough to know that she could not compete with the freshness of youth, she conducted her life according to her age. As her romantic activities diminished her artistic and intellectual interests increased.

To augment her income she decided to teach the subject she knew best, so she established at her home a School of Gallantry. Women of the aristocracy who wanted their sons taught gracious manners applied for their admission, and it was considered an honor to be allowed to matriculate. It was said that a Lanclos pupil could be immediately recognized in society.

Having a vast experience of human nature on various levels, she was well qualified. She tempered the bold and encouraged the shy, and her tolerance and understanding made young people tell her things they would confide in no one else. In the course of her pedagogy a number of her precepts traveled by word of mouth and eventually achieved the light of print. If some of them sound today like ash-tray mottoes, we must remember that the aphorisms of one generation become the clichés of the next.

To one young man who confided a dawning love, and was fearful lest he make the wrong move, she said:

Only by showing your respect by your assiduous attentions, infinite kindness and unwavering deference can you hope to to share the great love that your beloved has for her own beauty. Talk to her continually about herself, and seldom about yourself. You can take for granted that she is a hundred times more interested in the charms of her own person than in the whole gamut of your emotions.

To another with an urge to confess:

Never tell a loved one of an infidelity: you would be badly rewarded for your trouble. Although one dislikes being deceived, one likes even less to be undeceived.

To a young man who prided himself on his trenchant wit:

There are times when friendship is endangered by a too brilliant piece of repartee.

Among other precepts:

Love is a pleasure which involves only one duty; friendship is a sacred sentiment which calls for constant sacrifice.

Love is a duel in which the woman could always come off victorious if she chose.

True attachment begins where love ends.

If you happen to be the one who ceases to love first, let the woman have the advantage of making the break and seeming cruel.

A woman who is through with a man will relinquish him for anything but another woman.

When sin knocks at the door of indigence with a purse of gold, he rarely is refused admittance.

We should lay in a store of food, but never of pleasures; these should be gathered day by day.

A woman should not take a lover without the consent of her heart, nor a husband without the consent of her reason.

Man's passion is brief; the more ardent the more brief.

It is really amusing that they have made a law of modesty for women, who esteem nothing in men so much as impudence.

I have noticed that the men of intellect have less resistance in the bedchamber than the imbeciles.

What is more ridiculous than a deceived husband who confides his troubles?

The bed is a field of battle where the victors often pay dearly.

I have observed that men lie even more than women.

Happy lovers are those who love without talking about it.

There are moments when women prefer to be treated a little brusquely, rather than too carefully. More hearts have been lost by men's clumsiness than have been saved by women's virtue.

Young women came to Ninon to learn the secret of her attraction, and when one of them asked how large a woman's breast should be, she replied: "Large enough to fill the hand of an honest man.[1]

As a rule, Ninon taught by precept only, but then she was never one to follow rules. It was inevitable that some of her pupils should demand demonstration. One of these was Philippe de Courcillon, marquis de Dangeau. He was head of a regiment, "helped his luck" at cards and spent a good deal of his time writing verse. He became a chronicler of court life and his *Memoirs* are often quoted by historians.[2]

Another teacher's pet at this time was the nineteen-year-old Armand de Gramont, comte de Guiche, whom Madame de la

---

[1] *Honnête homme*, for which we have no exact translation in the sense that it was used in the seventeenth and eighteenth centuries.

[2] He married first the sister of the maréchal d'Estrées, and then a countess of the Palatinate, both very wealthy. He succeeded to the place of Georges de Scudéry in the Académie.

Fayette called a "handsome, well-built, intrepid and gallant courtier, full of grandeur and dignity." He was, however, often short of cash. On several occasions Ninon loaned him money which he neglected to return. As she always regarded a loan as a potential gift, she paid little attention to his negligence. However, one night, thinking she was asleep, he arose quietly and helped himself from her coffer. The next morning when he left he said, "*Au revoir*," and she replied, "*Adieu*." He asked why and she told him he would find the reason in his purse. He blushed and stammered excuses, but she never admitted him to her house again.

Saint-Pavin teased her about her school, and went around singing to the air of "*La Violette*":

> "Tous les blondins vont chez moi à l'école,
>> Pour faire leur salut.
> Je veux sauver Duras, Dangeau, Briole,
>> Et c'est là mon seul but.
>
> Honi soit qui mal y pense,
>> Je suis pénitente, moi,
>> Je suis pénitente."

("All the young sparks come to me to school for their salvation. I want to save Duras, Dangeau, Briole, and this is my sole object. Evil to him who evil thinks. I am a penitent, I am a penitent.")

Chapter XLI

THE duc de Navailles, the gentleman who fell asleep in Ninon's bed, had suggested the marquise de Montespan as lady in waiting to the young queen. The marquis, with their children, had gone to his château in the Pyrénées and expected his wife to join him, but the beautiful and spirited Athénaïs preferred Versailles to the provinces, and the king to her husband. She wrote excuses for several years, and eventually the marquis gave up hope and went into deep mourning, draped the horses in black, and invited his friends to attend funeral services. He declared that Madame de Montespan had died of an attack of coquetry complicated by ambition, and spoke of marrying again when his year of mourning was over.

The king was amused. He said, "Now that he has buried you, I hope he lets you rest in peace." Which was more than His Majesty did.

Louise de la Vallière had borne the king two children, been made a duchess and the official mistress, all with a sense of guilt and shame. Although the king never ceased to love her, the brilliant star of Montespan began to rise. Concerning Louise, she wrote in her *Memoirs:*

> Mere love-making, however pleasant, bored him at last if the charm of ready speech and ready wit were lacking. I do not profess to be a prodigy, but those who know me do me the justice to admit that, where I am, it is very difficult for boredom to find ever so small a footing.

Montespan maintained that she did her best to restore the king's love for poor little La Vallière, but "God alone can work miracles such as these." When after ten years she herself was succeeded by Mademoiselle Fontanges and Madame Scarron, it was not God to whom she appealed for the miracle, but the Devil.

History has not yet decided whether it was Montespan who poisoned Fontanges, but it is accepted that she lent herself to the performance of a Black Mass in order to hold the king's love.

In 1667, Colbert made an appointment which eventually brought the horrors to light and which laid the foundations for what is today one of the great criminal investigation departments of Europe, the Sûreté. He designated Gabriel-Nicolas de la Reynie *lieutenant-prefet* of the Paris police.

That year Ninon was involved in lawsuits. Monsieur Elbène, her old friend, was in more serious trouble than usual. The edifice of gay living which he had built with other people's money had tumbled. Some of it had been Ninon's money. He had given her mortgages as security for her loans, and when she had endeavored to sell them to protect her own interests, she found that some of them had been granted to other people as well as to her. It was a question of establishing priority and in one instance she lost. Nevertheless, she continued to help Elbène with money, knowing it would never be returned.

Saint-Evremond, too, had advanced "the Great Cunctator," as he named him, a sum of twenty-three hundred *livres*. Upon Elbène's marriage Saint-Evremond had asked for the return of this money and there was an acrimonious correspondence between the old friends. Ninon, knowing Saint-Evremond's need, undertook to pay a hundred *pistoles* of this debt, but as he did not receive it at once, Saint-Evremond wrote to their intermediary:

If you see Mademoiselle de Lanclos I beg you to assure her that no one is her more humble servant than I am, although I have heard nothing further about the 100 *pistoles* than if there had never been any *pistoles* in the world. Her good faith is great, but my absence is long, and after eight years there is nothing easier than not to remember people when the memory costs 100 *pistoles*.

Ninon was hurt. She had sent the money with an explanation of the delay and added:

If you consider the matter carefully you will see that you ought not rail at one who is your banker. Love me well enough, however, to bear my censure.

She induced Saint-Evremond somewhat to reduce the amount of the indebtedness of Elbène, to which he consented, and though he apologized, the correspondence was dropped for some time.

Versailles continued to grow in splendor, Mansart adding his genius to the architecture, and the portraits of Mignard making it a veritable museum of fine art. It was a fairy palace for its thousands of occupants. There was a round of pleasure such as the occidental world had never known, and the mainspring of it all was the God-given sun king who might very well have said, "I am the State."

The great men of letters and art had free access to His Majesty and the courtiers adored him. The greatest punishment he could inflict was to send them back to their own homes. The duc de Richelieu said to Françoise Scarron, "I would rather die than spend two months without seeing him," and Vardes on his return from exile said, "Sire, far from your presence a man is not only unhappy, he is ridiculous!"

It was said that His Majesty never passed a chambermaid without raising his hat, and it was whispered that sometimes it wasn't only his hat that he raised.

He had time for war and time for the arts, time for love and for affairs of state. He had time to listen, and his fingers were on the pulse of the nation. Never was an absolute monarch so velvet-gloved and so adored. He needed no bodyguards.

One morning early His Majesty strolled through the great halls before the courtiers were about. He liked to watch the carpenters and glaziers, the upholsterers and painters at work, and to chat with them.

In the Galerie des Glaces he noticed a workman standing tiptoe on top of a ladder, reaching up to unhook the enormous crystal and silver chandelier from the ceiling. The king feared the little fellow would break his neck.

"Be careful," said His Majesty, "let me hold the ladder."

"Sire," said the workman, "a thousand pardons, but if you will do so I shall be much obliged. On account of this great ambassador who is expected all my companions have lost their heads and left me alone."

The king held the ladder while the man unhooked the chandelier. He then stepped down carefully, resting his hand on the king's shoulder. He thanked the king graciously and then left the hall, the lusters tinkling as he walked.

That night everyone in the palace was discussing the boldness of a thief who had in broad daylight stolen one of the chandeliers. The Lord High Provost was informed of the matter and he assured the king that the man could not escape; they would get him in no time.

"We must request the Lord High Provost," said Louis, "to let the matter rest. As you well know, in cases of theft accomplices are liable to punishment as well, and it was I who held the ladder for the thief."

A change came over the king. He was beginning to think in terms of country and glory, which meant war and conquest. In 1667, incited by Colbert, he declared war on Spain and invaded the Spanish Netherlands. Turenne walked into Flanders and took one fortress after another "in the name of Marie-Thérèse." Condé took the Franche-Comté, although the Anglo-Dutch-Swedish alliance later forced Louis prudently to sign the Treaty of Aix-la-Chapelle, restoring the Franche-Comté to Spain. In the fall the armies returned for celebrations of victory.

Louis wanted the aid of Charles II, and in 1670 he sent Henriette on a secret mission to her brother, who hoped to re-establish the Roman Church in England and to turn that country into an absolute monarchy, like France. The project was known only to a few and Madame conducted it with diplomacy, returning with the Treaty of Dover.

The next day, feeling ill, she drank some chicory water, and within a few hours died, convinced that she had been poisoned by her husband's lover, the chevalier de Lorraine, who had given the order for the drink. The marquise de Montespan hurried to Saint-Cloud, and when she later described Henriette's suffering to the king, he said:

"If this crime is my brother's handiwork, his head shall fall on the scaffold." The scaffold was reserved for the aristocracy. The common people were accorded the gallows.

A quarrel ensued between the brothers and the chevalier de Lorraine was arrested. The danger of the age was not only in being poisoned but in being readily accused of poisoning. At the funeral Bossuet delivered one of his most eloquent perorations:

Oh, disastrous night, oh, dreadful night, when there resounded, all of a sudden, like a clap of thunder, this astonishing news: "Madame is dying! Madame is dead!"

The king wanted Monsieur to marry their cousin, the Grande Mademoiselle, but both parties disliked each other sufficiently to disregard a royal request. Philippe married a German princess, Elizabeth Charlotte, daughter of the Elector Palatine. When she arrived at the French court everyone thought there must be some mistake. She was homely, fat, pock-marked. Saint-Simon said she had the face and manners of a Swiss Guard. She could not talk, curtsy, ride, dance or play cards. For the first three days she opened her mouth only once . . . to swallow a single olive.

Nevertheless "Lizalotte" turned out to be a breath of air in the stiffling, crowded, fetid atmosphere. She had a fresh point of view and was not afraid to say and write what she meant. The interesting and frank *Letters of Madame* almost rank today with the letters of the marquise de Sévigné.

Chapter XLII

IT was a crisp autumn morning and Ninon sat at her open window, listening to the street cries, each chanted in its traditional cadence.

"*Vieux habits, vieux galons,*" shouted the old-clothes merchant, looking up at the windows as he passed.

"*Voilà le plaisir des dames, pomme, prune, amande,*" sang a girl with tarts. A crowd of urchins at the corner surrounded a vendor, held captive by the smell of roasting chestnuts.

"*Tout chauds, tout brûlants,*" sang the man as he measured out little cornucopias.

Just below the window a blind musician played a popular tune on a very bad violin. He knew that Mademoiselle de Lanclos was never too busy to throw him a few coins wrapped in a little piece of paper.

An elegantly dressed man turned the corner. Ninon knew his walk well. It was Gourville, coming to call on her at last.

During his absence he had been hanged in effigy, but the political winds had changed and he was no longer a shady speculator but a financial genius. He had been back some time but had not come to call.

She received him in her intimate salon, greeting him warmly. They talked of the old days. He told her of his travels and of his new position. He was now financial adviser to the Condé family and living at Chantilly. He told Ninon of something that had happened at the palace. The prince had taken over Vatel, who had been Fouquet's *maître d'hôtel* before the minister went to prison. The Condés gave a banquet at which the king and queen were guests. Many more people had come than had been

194

expected and at two of the twenty-seven tables there was a shortage of meat. Vatel was upset, feeling that his honor was at stake. "I cannot bear disgrace," he had said. Gourville told His Highness, who graciously assured Vatel that everything was in order.

The fireworks, which had cost sixteen thousand francs, would not go off. At four in the morning Vatel made the rounds of the kitchens and found that only two of the purveyors of fish had arrived. He became distracted and woke Gourville.

"Sir," Vatel had said, "I cannot outlive this humiliation." Gourville tried to reassure him, but he went into his room and, setting the hilt of his sword against the door, ran into it. Just as he was breathing his last the rest of the fish arrived.

Ninon was deeply touched. "There are too few people nowadays," she said, "who have a real pride in their work."

Gourville admired her new furniture and assured her that she looked younger than ever. Yet, with all his friendliness, she felt a certain restraint on his part. She thought she knew the reason.

She had heard how, on his return to Paris, he had gone to the *Grand Pénitencier de Notre-Dame* for the return of the sixty thousand *livres* which he had deposited. The Almoner had raised his eyes to heaven and said that he had dispensed it in alms. Ninon waited for Gourville to ask for the money he had left with her, but he rose to leave without mentioning it.

"Gourville," she said, "I am afraid I have bad news for you."

"I've been expecting it," he replied.

"The worst possible news for any man," she continued. "I hope you are no longer in love with me, for I have lost my desire for you."

She rose and went to her coffer.

"But I have not lost my memory," she said, handing him his sixty thousand *livres*. "And you ought to be ashamed of yourself," she added, "not to know me better."

Gourville remained one of her most intimate friends as well as her financial adviser for the rest of his life. He amassed a fortune and secretly married a daughter of his first employer, La Rochefoucauld.

Ninon could hardly have had a better financial adviser. Her legal matters were now in the hands of an honest advocate, and François Arouet, father of the future Voltaire, was her notary. She bought an annuity, making over to the Hôpital des Incurables twenty-five thousand *livres*, for which she received two thousand a year. She drew a thousand *livres* from the town of Lyon and seventeen hundred from the *gabelle*, or salt tax. Two gentlemen who had borrowed sums from her with which to gamble were now paying her back yearly. She had always been thrifty, never acquisitive, and all she wanted was enough to maintain her home and enjoy her liberty; liberty as La Bruyère had defined it: the ability to employ one's time as one chose. Independence also meant to Ninon that she was in a position to help her friends when they were in difficulties.

Chapter XLIII

SAINT-EVREMOND had reason to be grateful for Ninon's generosity. During his exile in the Netherlands Ninon had more than once come to his assistance.

One of his letters to her, dated from The Hague in 1669, has been often quoted. It reads, in part:

> With all due respect to the old dreamer, Solon, who counted no man happy in view of death, I look upon you as you are now, in full enjoyment of life, as the happiest of all possible creatures.
>
> The highest and best in the land have laid their love at your feet, and you have loved often enough to have left nothing untasted, and were wise enough to stop in time to avoid the ill effects of a surfeit of passion. Your sex has never attained such a degree of felicity; there are few princesses who do not envy your lot while they realize the hardships of their condition; and who knows but that the convents hold some saintly women who would gladly exchange their peace of mind for the pleasant excitement which must have been experienced by you. None but love troubles have ever touched you, and you know better than many that, where love is concerned, all other joys are unworthy of the name.
>
> Now my next remark must appear brutal, were I not quoting your oft-repeated words! You have certainly left behind the heyday of your youth; yet beauty of form and face is still yours, while the heavy hand of time cannot impair your charm of manner nor lessen by one iota your lively wit.

Your very charms have a ratio of virtue; while a lover is pressing his suit, a friend may trust you with the fullest confidence. Your word is the surest bond a man can hold, and if you promise to pay a hundred *pistoles* on feudal rights, they can be depended upon as if they were already in hand:

With such virtues, it is hardly a wonder that ministers sit at your board! What surprises me is that you are not all-powerful in some vast kingdom where your people would be happier than those of Cyprus in the days of the good and great divinity.

Come with me, dear, and let us wander away to India, there to worship a deity together with the people I have described to you; there a man lives for centuries, and every moment of life is fraught with pleasure. You have, however, gained much, as far as this country goes, since you have discovered yourself to be three years younger than you imagined.[1] Alas, how you must deplore the condition of us poor atoms of humanity in our daily race toward the last inevitable goal. When you, on the other hand, feel your age gaining upon you by the mere power of retrospect, you simply cast off the weight of years as you would drop some extra garment in this cold weather.

My years go apace; yet realizing, as I must, certain signs of decay in my earlier vitality, I could comfort myself for its loss were I certain to retain, even in its present condition, the vigor I still possess.

If only we could be together in a dainty refined home of our own, bound by such wedlock as that of ———, many examples of which exist here as well as in Madrid. We should doubtless devote much time to the elevation of our minds, but were it merely for the sake of vindicating its honor, and of keeping pace with its more carnal companion, this mortal would also reap a share of human delights. Anyhow, I could then impart to you some Indian

[1] Possibly a mistake in the registration of her birth, which would account for some writers claiming she was ninety when she died.

ideals which, after all, might prove far pleasanter than the French realities.

In letters to d'Hervart, who handled his business matters, Saint-Evremond wrote:

. . . If you should see this lady [Ninon] assure her that she has no truer friend than myself in this world, and that when I wish to flatter my powers of discernment, I feel that I, better than any other, can gauge her worth. Moreover, I hold that those who pride themselves on realizing to the full her good qualities are infringing upon my rights.

and again:

. . . Leaving aside the serious dissertation, I shall pass on to talk about Mademoiselle de Lanclos. I beg you to congratulate her for me on the delightful nature of her occupation, namely that of choosing one lover from among the twenty on her list; but if you did this, she might mistake my sincerity for a form of spiteful wonder; in which she would be utterly wrong. France can claim no worthy gentleman, if his taste agree with mine, who does not deem it good fortune to become a recipient of that lady's favor. Her payment of my hundred *pistoles* is a miracle in the days in which we live; anyhow, nothing can alter the fact that it is a great source of joy to have the option of being inconstant and of changing lovers according to one's sweet will.

At twenty, constancy in a woman is counted a merit; at thirty, infidelity is a virtue; whereas, at forty, the woman who deceives her lover is as lucky as others who are themselves deceived.

Find out, please, from Mademoiselle de l'Enclos and from Monsieur d'Elbène, whether or not I am at liberty to draw.

After a lapse of some time Ninon received an unexpected letter from Saint-Evremond:

I have been trying for more than a year to obtain news from you from everybody, but nobody can give me any.

M. de la Bastille tells me that you are in good health, but adds that if you have no more lovers, you are satisfied to have a greater number of friends.

The falsity of the latter piece of news casts a doubt upon the verity of the former, because you are born to love as long as you live. Lovers and gamblers have something in common: who has loved will love.

If I had been told you have become devout, I might have believed it, for that would be to pass from a human passion to the love of God, and give occupation to the soul. But not to love is a species of void which cannot be consistent with your heart.

He goes on, in prose and in verse, tells that there is a rumor of the comte de Gramont's death (which is untrue) and then remarks that the *Gazette de Hollande* says the duc de Lauzun is to be married, which he does not believe.

This, however, was true, the duc de Lauzun was to be married, and it inspired one of the letters of the marquise de Sévigné which is an outstanding example of suspense; it is addressed to Monsieur de Coulanges:

Paris, Monday, December 15, 1670

I am going to tell you a thing, the most astonishing, the most surprising, the most marvelous, the most miraculous, the most magnificent, the most confounding, the most unheard-of, the most singular, the most extraordinary, the most incredible, the most unforeseen, the greatest, the least, the rarest, the most common, the most public, the most private till today, the most enviable; in short, a thing of which there is but one example in the past age, and that not an exact one, either; a thing that we cannot believe in Paris; how then will it gain credit at Lyon? A thing which will make everybody cry, "Lord, have mercy on us!" A thing which causes the greatest joy to Madame de Rohan and Madame de Hauterive; a thing, *enfin*, which is to occur Sunday, yet perhaps will not be finished on Monday. I cannot bring myself to tell you;

guess what it is. I give you three guesses. Give up?[1] Well then, I find I must tell you. Monsieur de Lauzun is to be married next Sunday at the Louvre, to —— Pray, guess to whom! I give you four times to do it in. I give you ten, I give you a hundred. Says Madame de Coulanges, "It is really very hard to guess: perhaps it is Madame de la Vallière." Indeed, madame, it is not. "It is Mademoiselle de Retz, then."

No, nor she neither; you are extremely provincial. "Lord bless me," say you, "what stupid wretches we are! It is Mademoiselle de Colbert all the while." Nay, now you are still further from the mark. "Why then it must certainly be Mademoiselle de Créqui." You haven't it yet. Well, I find I must tell you at last. He is to be married next Sunday at the Louvre, with the king's leave, to Mademoiselle de ——, Mademoiselle ——, guess, pray guess her name: he is to be married to Mademoielle, the Grande Mademoiselle; Mademoiselle, daughter of the late Monsieur; Mademoiselle, granddaughter of Henri IV; Mademoiselle d'Eu, Mademoiselle de Dombes, Mademoiselle de Montpensier, Mademoiselle d'Orléans, Mademoiselle the king's cousin-germain, Mademoiselle destined for the throne, Mademoiselle, the only match in France that was worthy of Monsieur! ...

And all without benefit of Thesaurus. Ambitious and unscrupulous, Lauzun got his inside information by eavesdropping from under the bed of the king and Montespan. Louis refused permission for the marriage which took place nevertheless with the result that the bridegroom spent the first ten years of wedded life in prison at Pignerol.

[1] *Jeter la langue aux chiens* means "give up." Today the French throw their tongues to the cats instead of the dogs.

Chapter XLIV

LA ROCHEFOUCAULD came to dinner and brought his son, Charles-Paris d'Orléans, duc de Longueville, the one who had been born at the Hôtel de Ville during the Fronde. As in the case of his *Maxims*, the authorship of the young man was anonymous but everyone knew. Dangeau was there, and Tallemant des Réaux, to whom we are indebted for part of the conversation. They were talking about the war in Holland and the recklessness of French youth. Dangeau said he would do his duty and no more. Ninon remarked:

"I don't doubt, Monsieur le Marquis, that you will conduct yourself cautiously, but it is for young Longueville that I am anxious. I am afraid he will do something foolhardy." It was on this slim evidence that the young man has been credited with being Ninon's last lover.

Saint-Evremond teased Ninon about her being attracted to young men. He wrote that he could see her eyes "alight with the anticipation of a new conquest." To which she replied: "My charms are now solid and severe, and you know you must not jest with a personage."

Nevertheless, came the spring, and Ninon's fancy turned to thoughts of love. By this time the Sévigné baby had reached the age of twenty-three.

The marquise had never remarried. She had mellowed, as her letters show, and no longer held resentment against Ninon for having been her husband's mistress. They had met at a concert and she had shown a readiness to become friends. When, however, her son confided in her that he was in love with the courtesan, her attitude changed. The young marquis had competed with Racine for the favors of the leading actress of the day, Marie Desmours, known as La Champmeslé, and the end of his affair with her dovetailed with the beginning of his infatuation for Ninon. In a letter to her daughter, the beautiful Madame de Grignan, dated March 13, 1671, Madame de Sévigné wrote:

> . . . Your brother wears the chains of Ninon; I trust they may do him no harm. There are minds that shudder at such ties. This same Ninon corrupted the morals of his father. Let us commend him to God. A Christian, or at least one who wishes to be a Christian, cannot witness these irregularities without concern. . . .

and again:

> . . . Your brother is at Saint-Germain with Ninon and the actress Champmeslé; Despreaux is there too. We must really take matters in hand.

And on April 1:

> . . . I have been extremely diverted with our *Hurlu-berlu* headdresses; some of them looked as if you could have blown them off their wearers' shoulders. La Choiseul was a perfect sight. Ninon, who frequently makes apt remarks, said she was for all the world as like a *Printemps d'Hôtellerie* [1] as one drop of water to another. A most excellent simile.
>
> But that Ninon is a dangerous creature; if you only knew how she argues on religion, it would make you shudder. Her zeal to pervert the minds of young people is much the same as that of a certain gentleman of Saint-Germain whom we once saw at Livry.
>
> She says that your brother has all the simplicity of the dove, that he is just like his mother, and that Madame de Grignan has all the fire of the family and has more sense than to be so docile. A certain person would have taken

[1] The highly colored prints of women representing the seasons displayed in country inns.

your part and put her out of countenance on that score; but she bade him hold his tongue and said she knew more about the matter than he did. What a depravity of taste! Because she knows you to be handsome and witty, she must needs saddle you with the other qualifications without which, according to her rule, there is no being perfect.

I am greatly concerned for the harm she does my son in this matter, but please do not take any notice of it to him. Madame de la Fayette and I use all our endeavors to extricate him from so dangerous an attachment. Besides her, he has a little actress and all the players of the town on his hands, to whom he gives suppers; in short, he is completely infatuated.

Charles wrote his mother:

I have just returned from what I might call a delightful symphony; guess whom I met there? Mademoiselle de Lanclos, Madame de la Sablière, Madame de Salines . . .

In this brief caprice Ninon seems to have been somewhat emotionally involved. Tallemant des Réaux wrote that when the young marquis looked at another woman on the Cours she would say crossly, "You have a roving eye, monsieur," and once she struck him with her fan and then covered his face with kisses. This sounds thoroughly unlike Ninon, but it is human to be unlike oneself. The young marquis never seemed too enthusiastic and when she gave delicious little dinners for him he came reluctantly, with the air of a martyr. This acted as a stimulant to her jealousy and she demanded that he give her Champmeslé's letters, which he did. He told this to Mamma, who insisted that he demand them back. Madame de Sévigné wrote:

After all, be a transaction ever so questionable, there is always a course of honesty to pursue; he has had the decency to admit this and to agree with me. In fact he saw my arguments so clearly that he rushed off to Ninon's house and, partly by skillful persuasion and partly by force, recovered the correspondence, and thus saved the poor thing. I made him burn the lot.

Inevitably Ninon awoke to the absurdity of her position, and dismissed the young man. The whole affair had lasted a little over a month. On April 8 the marquise writes her daughter:

> . . . But a word or two concerning your brother: Ninon has dismissed him. She is weary of loving without being loved in return; she insisted on his returning her letters, which he has done accordingly. I was not a little pleased at the break. I gave him a hint of the duty he owed to God . . . he laid the blame on me and said that I had given him some of the ice that was in my composition, that he had no desire to resemble me in that particular, and that I had better have conferred it on my daughter . . . he said the most extravagant things in the world, and so did I; in short it was a scene worthy of Molière. . . . Ninon told him that he was a mere pumpkin fricasseed in snow. See what it is to keep good company! One learns such pretty expressions.

Charles was dismissed by La Champmeslé at about the same time as by Ninon. He found little sympathy at home. His mother wrote:

> Ninon has really left him. He was wretched when she cared for him, now he is in despair because she no longer loves him and treats him with disdain.

And on April 27:

> . . . You will have been entertained by your brother's adventures; just now he is reveling in comparative rest; he still sees Ninon every day, but only as a friend. The other day they went someplace where they met five or six of their friends who showed by their expressions what they thought, supposing him to be the happy man. She guessed their thoughts and said quietly:
>
> "Gentlemen, you are extremely wicked if you think there is anything doubtful between us. I assure you we are more

like brother and sister. Besides, Sévigné is . . ." and she went
on to the favorite comparison you have heard before.

It is true that he is iced all over. I shall take him with me
to Brittany where I hope to restore him to perfect health.

Ninon says your brother's nature is not capable of definition, and that neither he nor others have understood his
character.

Charles de Sévigné is another of the young men credited with
being Ninon's last lover.

When the brief affair was over Ninon was not sorry. She had
surprised herself by this autumnal burgeoning of emotion.
Some years later Madame de Sévigné, who kept in touch with
Ninon's affairs, "saw without dread her grandson, the marquis
de Grignan, pay his respects to Mademoiselle de Lanclos."

Chapter XLV

Of the newer salons, only that of Madeleine de Scudéry, "who possessed all the charms save physical beauty," carried on the tradition of the Rambouillet group. Her *Samedis* were less aristocratic and more literary. Women were beginning to publish their writings, and she herself had produced *Artamène, ou Le Grand Cyrus*, in ten volumes. It won a large and admiring public. Her next ten-volume novel, *Clélie*, aroused some mockery and misunderstanding. It preached passion-free love and included a *Carte du Tendre*, or map of tenderness, in the allegorical manner used in *Pilgrim's Progress* a quarter of a century later. In this *roman à clé*, or novel in which fictitious characters mask contemporary ones, her descriptions and analyses of her contemporaries are so accurate that they were all recognized. The character of Clarice has been identified as Ninon, and the description accords with other contemporary estimates of the courtesan:

Clarice . . . one of the most fascinating women of the world, whose wit and temperament have an individuality of their own. Clarice is well built and agreeably tall, her natural grace is very attractive. Her hair is the loveliest chestnut; her face is oval, her complexion fair; she has a sweet mouth with lips of brightest red; a little dimple in her chin suits to perfection; her black eyes flash fun and mischief, and her whole expression reveals intellect and wit. As to brains, Clarice seems to have been blessed with more than her share; moreover, she is versatile to a rarely equaled degree. She can be cheerful and amusing; accommodates herself to every passing mood and circumstance, gets on, in short, with all sorts and conditions of men, but especially with people of quality. She is not loath to talk, expresses herself with ease, is moved to frequent and contagiously merry laughter; she can enjoy a trifling joke and loves to chaff her friends.

But apart from all these aids to pleasure, this charming woman does not, for all that, lack the fire of reflection, nor the more serious qualities of intelligent thinkers. Her very nature gives her the desirable power of sympathy, which she never refuses to those in trouble.

Clarice can detach herself from the enjoyment of the moment when friendship demands it; she is faithful and evidently worthy of confidence. Her soul is above petty quarrels; she is generous and warmhearted. In short, Clarice has gained the hearts of the noblest of the land: men and women, indiscriminately different from one another in mind, in condition, in interests, in intelligence, in temperament, all agree in declaring Clarice charming; added to wit and kindness, she possesses untold qualities, all deserving of the highest esteem.

Ninon continued to write a little, not for publication but for self-expression and circulation among her intimates. Julie d'Angennes had started the fashion of pen portraits and the Grande Mademoiselle had revived it. Ninon wrote *Portrait d'un inconnu*, which is included in a collection of "the most agreeable prose pieces of the time." She also wrote verse, maxims and many letters. *Réponse à une lettre de l'autre monde*, addressed to Saint-Evremond, is attributed to her.

Madeleine de Scudéry tried to attract Ninon to her literary gatherings. Ninon admired her as a writer and pitied her as an unattractive spinster who had never really matured. She no longer ridiculed the *Carte du Tendre*, knowing what frustration had prompted it. Occasionally she visited the group on the rue des Ciseaux, but she lost patience with their solemnity. Their turgid rhetoric sounded twice as bad when it was shouted, as it had to be, for poor Mademoiselle de Scudéry was growing very deaf.

The number of salons continued to increase. The most notorious was that of Marie-Anne Mancini, duchesse de Bouillon, the youngest of the Mancini girls.

At fifteen she had presided over a literary-gallant circle. After her marriage she had lived for a time in the country where La Fontaine was a forest ranger and had made friends with him. She had been perspicacious enough to realize that his fables and not his *contes*, as he believed, were his real forte, and she had been instrumental in having them published and in bringing the author to Paris.

On the other hand, she had made a magnificent error in judgment. One of her protégé's had written a play called *Phèdre et Hippolite* which he managed to have produced about the same time as Racine's *Phèdre*. At the première of Racine's play the little duchess filled the house with her followers and there was an inspired talking, hissing and booing that killed it. However, it soon revived as we know, and the other one is forgotten.

Racine himself was no model of ethical conduct. Molière had produced his first tragedy, *La Thébaïde*, in 1664. The actor-manager had edited the script to make it more playable and paid the author what we would call "advance royalties." But the public did not like it. Molière next produced Racine's *Alexandre*, which had a huge success, and while it was running at the Palais Royal, Racine surreptitiously put it into rehearsal at the Hôtel de Bourgogne, where it opened without warning.

It was an unwritten law that an unpublished play was the property of the first troupe that presented it. Racine's excuse was that he was not satisfied with Molière's production. Molière then withheld royalties, dividing the money among his company. Racine made love to Molière's leading lady and induced her and her husband to join his company. The playwrights became enemies, splitting the world of letters into two factions. Ninon aligned herself on the side of Molière.

Madame de Bouillon was now occupying an exquisite little house on the Quai Malaquais, built by Mansart, decorated by

Le Brun, the flower beds laid out by Le Nôtre, à la Versailles. Here, while the duke was away hunting stag, she had a hunting ground of her own. Pretty, with beautiful legs and small feet, gay and capricious, she had a prurient curiosity to know and experience everything. She had a series of lovers, with the customary interludes in a convent, but she complained that she was treated by men with too much respect.

Benserade, the actor, the duc de Vendôme and his inebriate brother, the Grand Prior, Pradon, La Fare and the duc de Vivonne formed the nucleus of her group. She was pampered by everyone, yet she had one frustration. The naughty Ninon had politely refused all her invitations. A courtesan who had become a personage would add greatly to her gatherings. She sent her lackey repeatedly with invitations and eventually Ninon, not wishing to be rude, accepted one.

That afternoon the duchess rallied her most bizarre characters; she served her finest food and wines; she put herself out to be very wicked. She told of a visit she had made with her sister to the notorious fortuneteller, La Voisin, to learn how to cast a spell on Olympe's husband, the comte de Soissons. The conversation was deliberately daring, and soon there began what threatened to be an orgy. Ninon was always tolerant of the vices which she herself did not practice, but she had a distaste for communal love-making, and she took her departure. She walked along the quai for several blocks, taking deep breaths, to get it all out of her system, and she never went to see the duchesse de Bouillon again.

There was another house, however, where she enjoyed visiting and where she met the kind of people with whom she felt at home. Marguerite de la Sablière was the sister-in-law of Tallemant des Réaux and the estranged wife of Antoine de Rambouillet, one of Ninon's brief caprices. He had treated his wife ruthlessly, taken away not only her possessions but their children as well. Disillusioned and depressed, Marguerite had tried to forget her trouble in the pursuit of learning. She studied mathematics and the classics, she read philosophy with Bernier, one of the Gassendi disciples.

Ninon admired Madame de la Sablière and felt in greater rapport with her than she had with any other woman. She dined frequently at the rue des Petits-Champs where she encountered Molière, Mignard, La Fontaine, Boileau and others to her taste. Bernier wrote to Saint-Evremond at the time that he considered Mademoiselle de Lanclos "superior in intellect" to Madame de la Sablière.

The discussions lasted late into the night while Ninon's porters waited in the warm kitchen. One of the guests was the abbé des Roches, of whom Ninon wrote:

> He spends his life at Madame de la Sablière's listening to philosophical talk which he does not understand. His carriage is always at the door and is very convenient. It takes away the really intelligent people who have no carriages. He is philosophy's turnspit.

Boileau was engaged in an attack on the Faculty of Theology of the Sorbonne, which was threatening to proscribe Descartes and his works on the grounds of impiety. Ninon supported Boileau, but she realized that Molière's pen would be the most efficacious way of handling the matter. The group induced him to write a burlesque, mocking the Faculty, with the result that this august body actually abandoned their project.

The king said, "I like Boileau as a necessary scourge which one can pit against the bad taste of second-rate authors." And of Molière, when he presented him to Montespan, "Here you see the one man in France who has most wit, most talent and most modesty and good sense. I thank God for letting him be born in my reign, and I pray that He may preserve him for us for a long time."

Condé had shown marked favor to the playwright, the public adored him, his actors worshiped him and he had made money. Nevertheless, he was an unhappy man. He had married the actress Armande Béjart, young sister of Madeleine, who had been his leading lady and mistress for many years. It was bruited about that Armande was not Madeleine's sister but her daughter, and possibly, therefore, the daughter of Molière. Racine did not hesitate to promote this theory, and anonymous pamphlets on the subject were distributed by Molière's enemies. Two sons had died in infancy; his wife had deceived him, as Scarron had facetiously predicted in his will; he was weary of having to produce work on demand. Moreover, *parlement* had prohibited the performance of *Tartuffe* and the bishops of Paris forbade it to be "read, presented or listened to." Worst of all, his friend and collaborator, Lulli, had betrayed him. By demanding that every performance which included music should be under his control, Lulli became the music dictator of his time. The Palais Royal and the Hôtel de Bourgogne had to limit their music, and by prohibiting the services of the royal dancers he forced the directors of these theatres to use inferior talent. What hurt Molière most was that the king had supported Lulli in this controversy. Molière was tired and his health was failing. For a short time he had retired with Chapelle to the apartment of a friend in the village of Auteuil, but it did not help him. He returned to Paris, for his life was in the theatre.

One evening there was an intimate little supper *chez* La Sablière: Molière, Boileau, Bernier, Ninon and the hostess. Molière seemed particularly depressed. He was engaged at the time in writing *Le Malade imaginaire*, perhaps the most incisive of his attacks on the medical profession. He was worried that an invalid's bedchamber might prove dreary to the audience. He felt insecure, knowing that a comedian's reputation hung on his latest performance. They all tried to cheer him, but Boileau, best understanding a writer's needs, asked him to read aloud extracts from the work.

Molière described the set, explained the action and declaimed the dialogue, indicating each character by a change of voice. The laughter of his listeners was more encouraging than the highest praise.

The third act was not quite right. Third acts have been troublesome through the ages. It needed something, what we now call "the obligatory scene."

Bernier was a member of the Medical Faculty of Montpellier, the ceremony of which was particularly elaborate. He described it and someone suggested the idea of having the patient apply for a medical degree. They all began to improvise on that theme, and before the evening was over the Interlude of Act III was written. The questions in macaronic Latin, the admonitions to eat and to drink, to purge and to bleed, even if it kill the patient, are still vastly amusing to the audiences at the Comédie Française.

The play was a huge success, and Molière added another classic to the repertoire. At the fourth performance he was feeling ill and said to one of the young actors, "How much must a man suffer before he can die?"

This young man and Armande tried to dissuade him from taking part in the performance.

"What would you have me do?" he asked. "There are fifty poor workmen who have only their day's wages to support them; what would they do if I didn't go on?"

Molière got through the last act. While he was taking the oath he was seized with a convulsion. He had to be covered by the chorus of surgeons and apothecaries.

He was taken to his home on the nearby rue de Richelieu and died before his wife reached him. It was the year 1673 and he was fifty-one.

Tartuffe had been reinstated by the king, but the clergy had never forgiven its author. Moreover, actors were not entitled to extreme unction unless they formally renounced the theatre. The archbishop of Paris refused grace and the widow appealed to the king, who granted permission for interment on condition that the ceremony take place at midnight, with no pomp or solemn service. The coffin was covered with the pall of the Upholsterers Guild. An intendant referred to Armande as "the daughter of her husband and the wife of her father."

Montespan made an entry in her *Memoirs*:

. . . poor Molière broke a blood vessel in his chest while playing with too great fervor the title part of his *Malade imaginaire*. When they brought the news to the king he turned pale and, clasping his hands together, nearly burst

Lulli began his career at court as a *baladin*, composer and violinist in *Les Vingt-quatre Violons du Roy*. He soon persuaded Louis to let him form a new string orchestra which at first comprised seventeen players, then increased to twenty-one. Under his leadership it became infinitely superior to the old band. He became Instrumental Composer to the King and Music Master to the Royal Family. With these titles went an income of thirty thousand *livres*. Between 1658 and 1671 he had composed thirty ballets. His collaboration with Molière began with *Le Mariage forcé* and ended with *Le Bourgeois Gentilhomme*.

In 1671 the Italian Players inaugurated opera in the Italian style. They presented *Pomone* at the Jeu de Paume on the rue Mazarine, music by Robert Cambert and libretto by Pierre Perrin. It was an enormous success; nevertheless, the administration ran into bankruptcy: Cambert fled and Perrin was thrown into prison for debt. This was Lulli's big chance. He bought the rights, took out letters patent and established the second Académie de Musique et de Danse, on the rue de Vaugirard. At the death of Molière they moved to the theatre of the Palais Royal where Lulli remained director until his death.

He had composed the ballets for two operas by the Italian Cavalli, and was familiar with the Italian operatic style. His first production was a heroic pastoral, the second, in 1673, was really the first French opera, *Cadmus et Hermione*, his own composition with libretto by Quinault. He had obtained from Louis the exclusive right to organize operatic productions in Paris. He composed the operas, trained the chorus and the orchestra, directed the *mises en scènes* and conducted the performances.

He had become a French subject, and in 1662 had married the daughter of a court musician with a large dowry. The marriage contract, describing him as the "son of a Florentine gentleman," was signed by the king, the queen and the queen mother.

Knowing that Ninon was an amateur of music, Molière had brought Lulli to her home, where he took part in the kind of conversation that musicians never tire of . . . talk about music. He met there a German musician, Hebenstreit, who played for them the dulcimer, an instrument new to Paris. Ninon played her lute and Lulli tried his new airs on the clavecin. Emile Magne writes:

> Lulli feared her [Ninon's] criticism which was all-powerful in musical matters, and never forgot that a word from her would counteract all the purchased praise of the gazetteers.

"Feeling is the soul of song," she told him. "However little taste the listener may have, he will always prefer emotion to the most brilliant execution, because brilliance appeals to the ear alone, and not to the heart. A fine talent, a beautiful voice, or a finished technique commands admiration, but it is only the expression of sincerely felt emotion that will move others."

If we feel that this is self-evident, we must consider that she spoke at the height of the classic period, more than a century before the advent of romanticism in music.

She also deplored the fact that good composers wasted beautiful melodies on trivial words. She believed that words were an integral part of the song, thereby anticipating the great nineteenth-century composers of *Lieder* who went to Goethe, Schiller, Heine, Mörike for their inspiration.

Whether or not Lulli actually "feared her criticism" is hard to say, but he did come to her frequently to try out a motet or ask her to sing for him one of his arias.

Mademoiselle de Lanclos had reached an age where she was the confidante of both sexes, and as Lulli was a man of both sexes, he soon began to tell her his troubles.

He acted the part of a devoted husband, siring a child a year, and to avoid scandal was seen every Sunday driving to church with his wife and progeny.

When not composing, conducting, dancing, directing, visiting the *ruelles* or performing uxorial or courtly duties, he occupied his leisure with the young Italian *castrati* who had been imported by Mazarin to sing feminine parts. Some of the boys carried their roles as well as their costumes over into private life, and despite the fact that the practice of homosexuality was punishable by death, quite a number of gentlemen in high places were implicated in these scandals.

217

Lulli, however, had managed adroitly. His Majesty must have closed his eyes for the benefit of his ears. But he made one mistake. He singled out a boy for special attention, taking him into his home to be raised with his own children. Thereupon his mistress, a clavecinist of jealous disposition, informed Madame Lulli of what was going on. Lulli was in trouble. Ninon listened, but in this case there was very little she could suggest.

He never was Ninon's lover, although he wrote:

> Adorable Ninon,
> Vous avez trop d'esprit pour vouloir dire 'non';
> Le plaisir de pécher vaut mieux que le pardon.

(Adorable Ninon, you have too much understanding to want to say 'no'; the pleasure of sinning is worth more than the forgiveness.)

This was, however, merely a gesture of formal courtesy.

Chapter XLVII

SEVEN independent republics constituted the United Provinces, the most important maritime power, controlling European commerce. The Bank of Amsterdam ranked as first in the world and the University of Leyden was attracting great scholars from many countries. It was the time of Spinoza, Huygens, Grotius; of Rembrandt, Ruysdael, Hals, Cuyp and Jan Vermeer, a *grand siècle* for Holland too.

The Dutch had dared to stand up against the god of Versailles; their gazettes had even ridiculed him. A war of tariffs and boycotts culminated in an attack by the French. Fifteen thousand troops, the pick of the cavalry, were crossing the Rhine, fording it at a shallow spot. Condé was beside them in a copper boat. On the other side was a single regiment already being shelled by French artillery. The French troops passed safely across and the Dutch began to surrender peacefully when the young duc de Longueville, Condé's nephew and La Rochefoucauld's illegitimate son, "his head full of the fumes of wine, fired a pistol at his adversaries who were on their knees begging for their lives. He cried, 'No quarter for this rabble!' Whereupon the Dutch in desperation fired a volley which killed the young duke."

A year before, at her dinner party, Ninon had said: "But it is for young Longueville that I am anxious. I am afraid he will do something foolhardy."

As a result of this episode Condé received the only battle wound he ever had, a broken wrist.

Turenne had but to cross the Yssel to reach Amsterdam. The king crossed on a pontoon with the infantry. One victory after another, and then, when the French hesitated, Holland opened the sluices of the Zuider Zee. The waters surged in, spreading over fields, uniting with rivers to form a turbulent sea over the land. Fine country estates disappeared, herds of cattle were drowned, Amsterdam rose out of the waters like a fortress and could only be reached by boat. The salt left the soil barren for years to come, but the French invasion had been stopped.

While the war with Holland was going on abroad worse things were happening at home. The priests of Notre-Dame warned the judicial authorities that innumerable penitents were confessing dreadful crimes. "Women," Madame de Longueville said, "no longer cared for innocent pleasures." La Voisin, the abortionist and poisoner of the Marais, was arrested. It transpired that Madame de Montespan was ordering spells to be cast over the king, that she might hold his love. Louis dismissed these charges.

Poisoning was nothing new. It had existed since long before the Merovingian dynasty, but within reason. With the introduction of the two Medici women into the French royal line it took a great step forward, but it was in the latter half of the seventeenth century that it became a really fine art. Important people employed tasters, and La Vigoureux, the soothsayer, was heard to say: "Three more poisonings and my fortune is made." Cyrano de Bergerac wrote, "Those whom you condemn as sorcerers are simply poisoners."

Black Mass, with its obscene and scatological devil-worship, infanticide for ritual purposes, and mysterious deaths by poison became a national scandal in which the aristocracy and the clergy were involved. Montespan made secret nocturnal expeditions clothed only in a black mantle and a mask for the purpose of winning back by magic the love of the king.

Animal organs in a pathological state, putrefied, dried and sprinkled with arsenic, were believed to induce a similar condition in the corresponding organ of the human being who swallowed the brew. Even the viscera of suicides and hanged men, of people who had died from cancer, venereal diseases or the plague were in demand by the alchemists. The public executioner did quite a little business on the side by selling the by-products of his trade.

Gaudin Saint-Croix, the chemist, had died suddenly from the fumes of his own concoction in 1669. When his casket of drugs was opened by the police, it revealed documents that damned a number of well-known people, including his mistress, la marquise de Brinvilliers. "Medea was a saint compared to her," wrote Madame de Sévigné. It also contained letters of the respectable financier, Pénotier, who had selected a rich father-in-law who had the misfortune to die suddenly under suspicious circumstances.

La Brinvilliers fled the country, and as she wandered from place to place she kept a diary. One of La Reynie's men disguised as a priest gained her confidence. The diary revealed that the dozens of patients at the charity hospital to whom she had so kindly brought food, and who had died shortly thereafter, had been the guinea pigs for her lover's preparations, the understudies used in the rehearsal of the drama to come.

Brinvilliers confronted Pénotier and threatened that if she were condemned to execution many others would be put to The Question[1] and would share her fate. Madame de Sévigné wrote to her daughter:

Madame de Brinvilliers is not so comfortable as I am; she is in prison and endeavors to pass her time as pleasantly as she can; she desired yesterday to play at piquet because she was bored. Her confession has been found. It informs us that at the age of seventeen she ceased to be a virgin; that she had ever since gone on at the same rate;[2] that she had poisoned her father, her brother, one of her children

---

[1] *La Question:* interrogation and torture *ordinaire* and *extraordinaire*, abolished by Louis XVI.

[2] "Marguerite of Navarre," writes Jacques de la Garde, scandalized the court by the multiplicity of her lovers from the age of eleven. This official record was subsequently beaten by Marie-Madeleine de Dreux d'Aubray, marquise de Brinvilliers.

and herself, but the last was only to make trial of an antidote.

Madame de Brinvilliers after playing piquet decided to destroy herself.

Here Madame de Sévigné could not bear to finish because it was too horrible, but she requested Monsieur de Coulanges to continue the letter:

She thrust a stick, not into her eye, nor into her ear, nor into her mouth; I leave you to guess where; but she would certainly have died if timely assistance had not been rendered her.

Four months after her confession to some thirty murders, Marie-Marguerite, marquise de Brinvilliers, was tortured, tried, and in bare feet and a white chemise driven to the Hôtel de Ville on the Place de Grève and there beheaded. All the socialites, including the gentle Madame de Sévigné, came to witness the *amende honorable*.

After that there were too many interrogatories for the police to handle, so the king appointed a special commission of twelve jurists of high repute. Nicolas de la Reynie sat as judge as well as chief examining counsel. He sent a secret report daily to His Majesty. The *Chambre Ardente* sat for two years, and though the public clamored for news, not a word of the proceeding appeared in the press, although a second periodical had come out, *Le Mercure galant*,[3] which promised to inform the *honnêtes gens* of what was going on in the world. The news got around Paris by word of mouth and was spread throughout the provinces by letters and travelers. Daily the king received a secret report from La Reynie, and no doubt he learned a good deal about the activities of the Montespan. In view of the fact that she was the mother of six of his children, he permitted her to remain at court.

A warrant was issued for the little duchesse de Bouillon, who was accused of dealing in sorcery. Her visits with her sister

[3] Later the *Mercure de France*.

Olympe to La Voisin were revealed. The beautiful Bouillon was put on the stand and cross-questioned by La Reynie, who asked:

"Madame, have you ever seen the Devil?"

"I see him at this very moment," she replied, "and a very ugly man he is, disguised as a counsel of state."

Chapter XLVIII

WHEN Montespan was looking for a suitable governess for her children, the maréchal d'Albret presented Madame Scarron, who, as usual, made an excellent impression. With the approval of Louis, Françoise was engaged to rear and educate the royal bastards. For this purpose, the king took over one of his houses at Vaugirard, a little village on the road from Paris to Versailles.[1]

It was here, when he visited his children, that the king got to know the *gouvernante* as they walked and talked in the little garden.

When the children grew older, Françoise was brought to the palace as lady in waiting to the queen, and the king soon made her a marquise and gave her the estate of Maintenon, near Versailles.

As she became more important at the court, Ninon saw little of her old friend, although, according to Saint-Simon, the women occasionally met in secret. Ninon made no effort to use her illustrious "friend at court" for any personal advantage, a fact on which Madame de la Fayette commented.

We have, from Montespan's journal, the following:

Ninon, by the consent of all those who have come near her, is good nature itself. One of her relations or friends was a candidate for a vacant post as farmer-general, and he besought her to make some useful effort for him. "I have no one but Madame de Maintenon," she replied to this relation. And the

[1] This house, with two stories added, is now in use as an apartment house. It stands in what has been left of its garden on the Boulevard Montparnasse near the rue du Cherche-Midi. Its original stone pediment and baroque cherubs can be seen imbedded in the stone of the superstructure.

other said to her: "Madame de Maintenon? It is as though you had the king himself."

Mademoiselle de Lenclos, trimming her pen with her trusty knife, wrote to the lady in waiting an agreeable and polished letter, one of those letters careful without stiffness, that one writes, indulging oneself a little with the intention of getting oneself read.

Maintenon showed Ninon's letter to the king.

"This is an excellent opportunity," he said, "to see with my own eyes this extraordinary person of whom I've heard so much. I saw her one day at the opera just as she was getting into her carriage, but my incognito did not permit me to approach her. She seemed to me small but well made."

Françoise summoned Ninon to the palace, asking her to arrive in time for mass and to spend the day with her as the king would be absent at Marly.

During the service His Majesty examined Ninon from the seclusion of his golden box and then ostensibly departed for Marly.

The two women retired to Maintenon's apartments and the scene that followed was told by Ninon to a colonel who reported it to Montespan, who immediately recorded it in her *Memoirs*, as accurately, she maintains, as she could:

NINON DE LENCLOS: It is not my preservation which should surprise you, since from morning to night I breathe that voluptuous air of independence which refreshes the blood and puts in play its circulation. I am morally the same person that you came to visit in the rue des Tournelles. My dressing gown, as you well know, was my preferred garb. Today as then, Madame la Marquise, I should choose to place on my escutcheon the Latin device of the towns of San Marino and Lucca . . . *Libertas*. You have complimented me on my beauty, I congratulate you upon yours, and I am surprised that you have so kept and preserved it in the midst of the constraints and servitude that grandeur and greatness involve.

MADAME DE MAINTENON: At the beginning I argued as you do, and I believed I should never reach the end of the year without disgust. Little by little I imposed silence on my emotions and my regrets. A life of great activity and occupation, however, by separating us from ourselves, extinguished those exacting delicacies. I remembered my sufferings and fears and privations after the death of that poor man [Scarron], and as labor has been the yoke imposed by God on every human being, I submitted with good grace to the respectable work of an educator. Few teachers are attached to their pupils. I attached myself to mine with tenderness and delight. The king's children were amiable and pretty as few children are.

MADEMOISELLE DE LENCLOS: From the most handsome and amiable man in the world there could not come mediocre offspring. Is it true that Madame de Montespan is no longer your friend? That is a rumor which has credit in the capital. If it is true I regret it and I am sorry for you.

MADAME DE MAINTENON: Madame de Montespan, as all Paris knows, obtained my pension for me after the death of the queen mother. This service will always remain in my heart and my memory. I have thanked her a thousand times for it. When the young queen of Portugal charged herself with my fate, the marquise, who had known me at the Hôtel d'Albret, desired to retain me in France, where she destined me for the children of the king. I did what she desired. I took charge of his numerous children out of respect for my benefactor and attachment to herself. Today, when their first education is completed, and His Majesty has recompensed me with the gift of the Maintenon estate, the marquise pretends that my role is finished, that I was wrong to permit myself to be made lady in waiting, and that the recognition due to her imposes an obligation on me to obey her in everything, and to withdraw from this neighborhood.

NINON DE LENCLOS: An absolute retreat? That is too much.
But as for myself, I should be enchanted to see you quit
the court and return to society. Society is your element.
You know it by heart. You have shone there, you will
again. You would be surrounded by those delicate and
senuous minds that used to applaud with delight your
agreeable stories, your brilliant conversation. At court,
where etiquette selects our words, as it rules our atti-
tudes, you cannot be yourself; you cannot refrain from
coloring your discourse, not with the king, perhaps,
whose calm gaze reveals a man of integrity, but with
those eminences, those grandeurs, those loyal and serene
highnesses whose artificial and factitious perfumes already filled your chapel before the incense of the sacrifice had reached the altar.

At this point His Majesty stepped out of the closet where he
had been hiding and, bowing gracefully, said:

"I have long wished, mademoiselle, for this unique and agreeable opportunity, for which I am indebted to Madame de Maintenon. Be seated, I pray you, and permit My Highness, perfumed
though I be, to enjoy for a moment your witty conversation. So,
mademoiselle, the atmosphere here does not meet with your approval! And in order to enjoy Madame's society you try to disgust her with it, and to deprive Us of her."

"Sire," replied our heroine, "I have neither the power nor the
authority to render my intentions formidable. I trust my regrets
will be pardoned, and I know that if Madame left Versailles it
would cause the same grief here that her absence has caused us in
Paris."

"One has one's detractors in every locality," said His Majesty.
"If Madame de Maintenon has met with one at Versailles she
would not be free from them elsewhere, and you, at Paris, would
be without rampart or armor; but grant me this, I can well protect my friends. I think the town is ill-informed, and that Madame
de Montespan has no interest in separating Madame from her
children, who are also mine. You will greatly oblige me, made-

moiselle, if you will adopt this opinion and publish it in your society, which is always select, though it is so numerous."

After a little more talk the king introduced, of his own accord, the subject of Ninon's request, and as the place of farmer-general was vacant, he accorded it to Ninon's candidate, saying that it was the first time she had asked a favor. He urged that if she wished anything else she had but to request it of Madame de Maintenon.

"You must see, mademoiselle, that it is well to leave Madame in this place as an agent with me for you, and your particular ambassadress."

With that His Highness took his leave, this time using the front staircase.

Montespan, who was beginning to suspect trouble, went to the apartments of Maintenon to ask what Louis thought of Ninon. She records the reply:

His Majesty has for some time had a great desire to see her, as he has heard her spoken of since his youth as a person of great wit. He imagined her to have larger eyes and something a little more virile in her physiognomy. He was greatly, and I must say, agreeably surprised to find he had been mistaken. "One can see eyes of far greater size," His Majesty told me, "but not more brilliant, more animated or more amiable. Her mouth, admirably molded, is almost as small as Madame de Montespan's. Her pretty, almost round face has something Georgian about it, unless I am mistaken. She says and lets you understand everything she likes; she awaits your replies without interruption; her contradictions preserve urbanity; she is respectful without servility; her pleasant voice, although not of silver, is nonetheless the voice of a nymph. In conclusion, I am charmed with her."

Thus spake *le roi soleil.*

Chapter XLIX

FIFTY-SEVEN is late middle age in any century. Ninon began to take on weight which she controlled somewhat by abstemiousness and black silk corsets. She continued to take her daily bath and her underwear was of the sheerest white batiste, now called "*ninon*." Her petticoats and dresses were of brightly colored silks, violet, brown and green predominating. Her eyes, a little smaller, were still bright and her complexion as clear as ever. One of her friends asked her how she managed to keep her beauty so long and she replied:

"It is because I have never been addicted to wine, cards or women."

Saint-Evremond sent the duke of St. Albans, natural son of Charles II, to Ninon for advice. He wrote a note of introduction in which he commented on the young man's attractions. Ninon replied:

> What do you mean by thinking that the contemplation of a young man could give me pleasure now . . . my body, to tell the truth, is no longer worth considering, but my mind still contains some glimmering of life.

She was beset by more lawsuits than love suits, and the one that troubled her most concerned her house, for she was again in danger of losing it. When she had purchased it in partnership with Gérard du Burg the agreement had been that she was to continue in occupancy and maintain the upkeep of the premises until the death of either partner, when the other would take sole possession. Burg, being much younger than Ninon, assumed she would die first and looked forward to retiring to the rue des Tour-

229

nelles in his old age. However, he died in 1675 and his heirs laid claim to the property. There must have been some possibility of their winning the case because instead of putting in a defense Ninon resorted to strategy.

A man named Mondian, former steward to Anne of Austria, claimed that Mademoiselle de Lanclos owed him three thousand *livres*. She refused to pay and Mondian confiscated the house. The bailiffs posted notices and announced the seizure before the doors of the parish church of Saint-Paul. Ninon still refused to pay, and on March 21, 1678, the property was formally seized and put up for sale. It was purchased by a Monsieur Guy for the sum of eleven thousand six hundred *livres*, and it somehow appeared, when the weather had cleared, that the purchase had been made on behalf of one Demoiselle Anne de Lanclos.

Enjoying full possession of her home now, she made further improvements. At the back of the court was the kitchen, dark but very fully equipped. Before the fireplace stood a huge *crémaillère* [1] on which was suspended the soup pot. Copper and brass saucepans in various sizes reflected, like the preliminary sketches for a painting, the blazing fire itself. There were chafing dishes and dripping pans, roasters, coffeepots of every size and sweetmeat tins; a turnspit, skewers, bowls and knives and a mortar and pestle of white marble.

The stair from the kitchen led directly to her intimate apartment, which consisted of a closet, an antechamber and a bedroom. The closet walls were covered with Flemish tapestries. In the antechamber, which was sumptuously furnished, there was a couch with Indian silk flanked by two small tables inlaid with mother-of-pearl and ormolu. On one side of the marble mantel was a thermometer, on the other a barometer. A bookcase held her library, bound in calf or parchment. This room no doubt often witnessed the preliminary stages of love.

The bedroom was large, the walls and windows draped with striped and checked taffetas. There were several comfortable arm-

---

[1] An upright piece of toothed iron on which pots can be hung at different levels.

chairs, a number of tables and a Chinese fire screen. Over the mantel were two large mirrors and on the walls were portraits of her friends. The bed was of oak surmounted by a Duchesse canopy and enclosed in silk draperies. There was a Turkish carpet, and there were a number of low stools upholstered in satin and damask; there was a bureau with eighteen small drawers where she kept her letters and a desk where she kept her accounts, as well as a secretary of marquetry. Dusting must have been a major operation. It was in this room that she received those closest to her heart, often in dressing gown and slippers.

In this rear building was *la pièce d'assemblée* where she received every afternoon. It was paneled in wood with gilt moldings and lighted by candelabra of inlaid tortoise shell. The room, overcrowded with furniture, was reflected in the large pier glass over the chimney. There was a massive clock on the mantel by Théodore Denize, enclosed in a case of ebony and gold, and rare items of faïence on both sides.

Her smaller and more intimate salon faced the street. Here she kept her most prized bibelots, here she received her intimate friends and played her lute.

Ninon would shut herself in for days at a time, to read and write and think. These periods of solitude always replenished her and she would then welcome her friends with renewed enthusiasm.

In the winter she received from five to nine. Her gatherings were now more exclusive: the comtesse de Suze, the comtesse d'Orlonne, the comtesse de Fiesque, the duchesse de Sully, the marquise de la Ferté, Madame Choiseul, and Madame de Cornuel.

To our generation these names may connote nothing but streets, confectionery shops or characters in operettas, but they constituted the Social Register of Ninon's days.

The Great Condé, considerably mellowed, came in from Chantilly from time to time and occupied the *fauteuil* of honor next to the hearth. The marquis de Ruvigny, deputy governor of Reformed Churches, came to discuss politics with Arnauld de Pomponne, Secretary of State for Foreign Affairs. He had been one of the old Rambouillet circle and was now enjoying correspondence with Madame de Sévigné. Both men confided affairs of state to Ninon.

La Rochefoucauld came over from his *hôtel* on the rue de Seine where he was living with Madame de la Fayette—platonically, it was said by some. He was still handsome with dark brows, but he was lame with gout. Occasionally Madame de la Fayette came with him and Ninon said she was "like a countryside full of fruit and flowers." Her *Princesse de Clèves* was about to appear, unsigned. It is considered the first French novel with psychological implications. Her beautiful predecessor in the affections of the duke, while not wearing the hair shirt as she did at her first ball, had returned to religion and was now behind the doors of the Carmelites.

Ninon had a great respect for the English although she had never visited their country. She wrote: "I have always liked the English because with them the least [*moindre*] individual is a well-brought-up man."

The duke of Monmouth amused the company by telling a story of Nell Gwynne, who shared the favors of King Charles II with Louise de Kéroualle, duchess of Portsmouth. The actress was riding through Oxford when her sedan chair was stoned by a mob. Drawing the curtains aside, she leaned out, raised her hand and said:

"Gentlemen! Gentlemen, desist, I pray you. I am the Protestant whore."

Whereupon they not only desisted, they cheered.

Only Madame de Sévigné held herself aloof, but not too aloof to listen to the news-gatherers who came from the rue des Tournelles. One of the reporters was Gourville. The marquise supped with him in his new house on the Condé estate where, she wrote, "there were water-works, bowers, terraces, six hautboys in one corner, six violins in another and the most melodious flutes." La Rochefoucauld was there, so was Briole, Ninon's pupil, and Madame de Coulanges. Ninon's name was on everyone's tongue.

One evening when Ninon had a small group, her friend Huygens, the Dutch philosopher, brought Fontenelle, who had just published his *Disgressions sur les anciens et les modernes*. The discussion quite naturally turned to the relative values of the civilizations of ancient Greece and modern Europe. Agreeing with Fontenelle, Ninon took the side of her contemporaries.

"Monsieur," she said to one of her adversaries, "rather than not maintain your thesis you even assert that the vices of the ancients were as superior to ours as were their virtues!"

The discussion went on and on, her Denize clock striking the hours. Ninon could no longer suppress her yawns, but no one made a move to leave. Finally she rose and said sweetly:

"At what hour, messieurs, used the ancient Lacedaemonians go to bed?"

Chapter L

ONE afternoon Ninon was visiting the old duchesse de la Feuillade. Before her marriage the hostess had been a neophyte converted to Jansenism by Pascal, and was one of the unfortunate women who had been driven from the abbey of Port-Royal.[1] She told the story of the little band who had refused to sign the formula laid down by the Jesuits. Although Ninon had never been of their faith, never believed in divine grace, she had always admired their integrity and their bravery in the face of persecution.

During the discussion the chevalier de Méré was announced. He had grown old. He and Ninon were delighted to see each other, and that evening he wrote in his notes: "Women who have been gallant never become narrow-minded." A distinctly debatable statement. A few weeks later Ninon received a letter from him:

I vow, mademoiselle, that I was never more pleased at anything in my life than at meeting you the other day at the duchesse de la Feuillade's house. It was one afternoon, you remember, when you two were alone together and I intruded upon you. You even seemed slightly annoyed at being interrupted in your engrossing conversation. I did not attempt to conceal my gratitude, however, for the pleasure it gave me to see and speak to you again, and I think it would show a lack of appreciation and civility on my part if I didn't tell you I was a little hurt by your attitude.

In fact, mademoiselle, not to mince matters, you were not

[1] A play about this event, *Port-Royal*, by Henry de Montherlant has been enjoying success in Paris for several years.

given so many rare qualities and such a lovable nature entirely for your own satisfaction. They were given to you to use for the joy and pleasure of deserving mankind. Decorum and decency have much to thank you for, I venture to assert, and there is no one in the world better able than I to know how wonderful you are. If only I had the wit to publish abroad your worth as I have to recognize it I should attempt to enhance the exquisiteness of your reputation.

When I saw you again the other day I fell under your spell anew, and especially appreciate the fact that even after such a long absence you seemed as charming to me as if I had never lost sight of you, and also that you did me the honor of permitting me to visit you as if I had never ceased to do so.

I humbly thank you a thousand times, and beg that you will remember and not be annoyed at my gratitude.

Ninon began to feel the passing of time as much by seeing the change in her friends as by feeling it in herself. She had reached the age where people say: "You haven't changed a bit" and "You look remarkably young for your age." It had seemed it could happen to everybody else but not to her.

Madame de la Sablière had fallen in love with the young marquis de la Fare, which had in time dispelled her melancholy. She had written to Ninon: "The days when I see Monsieur de la Fare are my happiest days." Ninon had tactfully encouraged the affair, but she had secret misgivings. Marguerite was not a woman for light love. Soon the marquis began making love to other women and ridiculing constancy. When Antoine de Rambouillet died, leaving Marguerite free to marry her lover, La Fare was no longer so inclined. It was the second blow and almost more than she could bear. Ninon wrote to François d'Usson de Bonrepaus:

I have received a letter from Madame de la Sablière. The poor woman fills me with pity. I also see Monsieur de la Fare every day, and like the members of *parlement*, I never cease hearing the pros and cons. . . . I am sorry for them. Conscience is a cruel gift from heaven, and love causes more sorow than joy in the long run.

As far as I am concerned, I need nothing these days but comfort, and I am entirely on the side of the woman, who has earned my friendship and respect. I think the trouble is that she is alone too much.

She had met Bonrepaus at Madame de la Sablière's and they had become warm friends, corresponding when he was not in Paris. He was short, stout, with a provincial accent and a face that gave little indication of his real character. But Ninon had discerned that he was sensitive and a man of real ability. She was not wrong, for Colbert also recognized his qualities and he was soon placed in an influential position in the navy.

Ninon's son, Louis-François de Mornay, sieur de la Boissière, had been educated away from home, not only because it was the custom but because the house on the rue des Tournelles was hardly the place to bring up a child. As an illegitimate child he was in distinguished company, but as the son of a courtesan his position would, of course, have been untenable. Under her roof they would both inevitably have run into many conflicts and suffered many embarrassments. Ninon did, however, see him from time to time, and she always made sure he was well provided for.

At twenty-one he entered the Naval Academy at Toulon as a cadet. One day Ninon received word that her son had committed some folly which caused him to be degraded from his rank and lose a promotion he was about to receive. She wrote to Bonrepaus and asked that the young man be transferred from Toulon to Brest, where the western fleet was under Vice-Admiral d'Estrées, the son of the lover who had thrown dice for the paternity of the child that never was finished. Bonrepaus not only effected the transfer but obtained the young man's promotion. Ninon wrote him a letter of gratitude which ended: "You can be sure, monsieur, that in me you have a friend as devoted as she is useless."

No correspondence between mother and son has come to light. We know little of Louis-François. He loved music but could not perform, so he collected musical instruments and later in his life he would engage players to come to his home to play them. He became captain of a ship and eventually established residence at Toulon, but he never married. In 1690, when he was thirty-seven, his father legitimized him. A year later Villarceaux died and left him an income which the marquise de Villarceaux paid regularly. Dangeau wrote in his *Journal* on February 21:

> The king has learned this evening of the death of old Villarceaux. He had had a pension of eight thousand livres and the fox-hunting dogs, worth fourteen or fifteen to him.

Monsieur de Bonrepaus became Comptroller of Justice, Police and Finances for the Navy and was thus in a position to do many favors for Louis-François.

Ninon was not only grateful but deeply fond of the old man, and whenever he came to Paris they dined together, at his house or at hers. She would scold him if he went too often to see Mademoiselle de Scudéry. Sometimes he went on diplomatic missions to England or to Holland and then she faithfully sent him a gazette of the news of Paris.

Ninon did not forget her old friends. Marguerite de la Sablière, under the influence of Madame de Sévigné, had turned for solace to religion and charity. She had given up her home and moved into the Hôpital des Incurables where she led an austere life, with few visitors. Only Ninon, Bonrepaus and La Fontaine remained devoted, and went to see her often. Ninon met the fabulist there and was shocked to see how he had changed, wandering around and absent-minded. She wrote to Saint-Evremond:

> I know you would like to see La Fontaine in England, he is so little regarded in Paris, his head is so feeble. It is the destiny of poets, of which Tasso and Lucretius are evidence. I doubt whether there is any love philter that could affect La Fontaine; he has never been a lover of women unless they were able to foot the bills.

And to Bonrepaus she wrote:

> How I wish that Madame de la Sablière would return to her

own home. Her time would pass just as pleasantly in her own room as at the Incurables.

When in 1683 Colbert died, Ninon wrote a letter of condolence to Bonrepaus, knowing that he had lost a friend as well as a patron. The last letter she received from him was from La Hogue where he was preparing for the naval battle which the great Admiral Trouville was to wage, the result of which made Britannia rule the waves.

There is another letter from Ninon on record to someone unknown. In part, it reads:

My first action this morning was to go and hunt for that book at the top of the house. That was a good beginning for the day. Some people would say that I should not have thought of doing so, but it seems to me that we were not very kind to each other yesterday, and I have been reproaching myself on that account. I do not like friendships which begin with a rush and drop off as quickly.

It seems a little thing, but her step was less buoyant, her breath a little shorter, it required an effort to climb to a dusty attic . . . for attics surely have always been dusty . . . to hunt in a dim light among yellowing books, lingering among old memories evoked by a ribbon, a petticoat or a faded engraving.

Chapter LI

MADAME DE MAINTENON was indeed on her way up. According
to Montespan, "she gained the affection of Louis by friendly intrigue and fearless conversation." She continues:

> ... the king hardly ever saw me except a few minutes cere-
> moniously, before and after supper. He showed himself al-
> ways assiduous with Madame de Maintenon, who, by her ani-
> mated and unflagging talk, had the very profitable secret of
> keeping him amused. Although I venture to flatter myself that
> I am equally clever in the art of manipulating speech, I could
> not stoop to such condescensions.

"Stoop to such condescensions" is an odd phrase from a woman
who resorted to the use of love potions and powders of succession. The marquise de Maintenon had brought up Montespan's
children well and they loved her, possibly better than they loved
their mother. The queen liked her ... the poor queen who was
grateful for a kind word ... but the courtiers did not. They called
her Madame de *Maintenant*, Madam Now. She was an anomaly,
this paragon who had said: "There is nothing cleverer than irreproachable conduct."

Every schoolboy in France knows the story of the meeting of
the two women in the gardens of Versailles:

"Madame la Marquise," said Françoise, "I dreamed last night
that I was ascending a staircase which you were descending."

After an interlude long enough for Mademoiselle de Fontanges
to be loved by the king and poisoned, it is said, by Montespan,
Françoise gradually became the most important woman in France.

Court ceremony had reached its apogee. In the morning the

king was awakened about eight by the *First Valet de Chambre*. Then the *Grande Entrée* was admitted: the duc de Bouillon, Great Chamberlain and Chief Gentleman of the Bedchamber; the duc de la Rochefoucauld, Grand Master of the Wardrobe, followed by the masters of the wardrobe; valets, physicians, favorites and the king's nurse. While the barber was dressing the king's hair, the *First Entrée* was admitted: Readers, Comptrollers of the Plate, Physician in Ordinary, Royal Apothecary and a very few courtiers, among them Ninon's pupil Dangeau. The marshals and generals, dukes and princes awaited their turn outside.

The *grand appartement* where His Majesty supped was a series of salons decorated in the most luxurious splendor. Under the blazing lusters were tables for every form of gambling, and the ladies and gentlemen of the court in elaborate costumes and brilliant jewels milled around, gossiping, gambling, dancing, playing billiards, going into the Salon de Vénus where a collation of rare fruits was served. And the king, wandering in and out, shedding his beneficence, noticed if a single courtier was unduly absent.

But the God-given was a man as well as a king, and in some departments it was natural that he should slow down. Françoise induced His Majesty to give up dalliance and take up religion in a serious way. Huguenots were again persecuted, and the whole court followed the king's example and was converted. Lizalotte wrote: "To the devil with all this whining and psalm singing, aaa! iii!"

Gentle Marie-Thérèse died in July 1693, "the first sorrow" she had ever caused the king. Six months later, at midnight in a little chamber of the palace, with a few witnesses, His Majesty and the marquise de Maintenon were married. Françoise did not thereby become queen, but she exercised more influence than the queen and all the mistresses put together. Louis asked her counsel in private and acted on it in public. It was upon her advice that he revoked his grandfather's law of tolerance, the Edict of Nantes. And some years later the Council met in her apartments and agreed with her decision that the duc d'Anjou should accept the throne of Spain.

Louis teased his wife, calling her "Your Solidity," and referring to her furnishings, he said, "She will die of symmetry." He made her a present of Saint-Cyr, which she turned into an academy for young women of good birth and no fortune. It remained a fashionable school until the Revolutionists disbanded it.

Montespan had worn "gold upon gold, embroidered in gold." Maintenon wore solid black silk with long sleeves and fur bordering the skirt. A black scarf covered her high Fontanges coiffure and her neck.

During the three years that Montespan remained at court after the revelation of her crimes, the king did not address a word to her. That was the greatest punishment he could administer. Finally she left of her own accord.

The whole atmosphere of the court changed. The ribbons on the shoulders, the ostrich plumes, the ruffles of *clinquant* lace on the breeches were no more. La Bruyère wrote:

> The courtier of the past had flowing hair, was dressed in doublet and hose, wore wide boots and was a libertine. This is no longer the mode. He now wears a wig, a closely fitted coat, plain stockings and is devout.

The morganatic wife of the king evidently added the zeal of the convert to the puritanical elements of her native Calvinism.

Lizalotte read the manuscripts of Descartes and Leibnitz with a few congenial souls behind the backs of the king and Maintenon. She did not like the king's wife and called her "*die alte Zotte* [the old whore]."

But of Mademoiselle de Lanclos she held a high opinion:

> Now that Mademoiselle de Lanclos is old she leads a very austere life. She maintains, they say, that she would never have reformed if she, herself, had not realized how ridiculous the whole business was ... there is not a more *honnête homme* anywhere than Mademoiselle de Lanclos, and everyone says she is very modest in her behavior and speech, which my son is not.

Despite Monsieur's tendencies, he and Madame had a son,

Philippe, duc de Chartres, who later became Monsieur and the regent. He was one of Ninon's visitors and would sit at her feet listening for hours. His mother wrote:

> My son is a friend of hers. She is very fond of him and I wish he would visit her more often in preference to his other companions. She would inspire him with higher and more noble sentiments than they do.

Among the young men that Ninon was now inspiring with noble sentiments was a nephew of Charleval, a cousin of the king of Sweden, on a visit to Paris. Charleval had continued to be one of Ninon's dearest friends although she had never accepted him as a lover. Banier had heard about Ninon in his native land and asked his uncle to present him.

Charleval warned Banier that he would fall under Ninon's spell, and the young man, scarcely twenty, laughed at the idea. He bet a thousand *pistoles* that, no matter what blandishments the aging courtesan used, he would be unmoved.

Charleval presented him at one of the intimate afternoons, and without any "blandishments" Ninon won his heart. He paid his bet willingly and said that he did not believe Ninon was sixty-four and moreover it didn't matter what age she was. He preferred a mature woman, young girls bored him. He decided to pay her court and begged Charleval not to reveal the fact that they had made a bet.

Charleval couldn't resist telling Ninon. Perhaps he was a little jealous. He asked her to punish the impudent young fellow by "permitting him to reach the gates of Paradise but not to enter." Ninon agreed.

When Banier called the next day he found her alone, in an agreeable mood and attractive gown. He made ardent love to her, and when the moment arrived the gates of Paradise offered no resistance.

No sooner did Banier leave the house than he ran to his uncle in triumph, saying that Ninon loved him, he was the happiest man in the world. Charleval was not as surprised as he might have been.

It has been said that Jean Banier was Ninon's last lover.

Ninon in Her Later Years

Another young man who sat at her feet was Philippe de Clérambault, the son of her old friend and lover, the comte de Paluau, who asked her if he resembled his father in intelligence. "Not in the least," she replied, and then told a friend that the young man was so conceited he regarded it as a compliment. She arranged a meeting for him with a young lady, object matrimony, about which the young Clérambault wrote:

> I am very grateful to Mademoiselle de Lanclos. I think she is sufficiently my friend not to have given an impression of me that I can't live up to, and it comforts me to think that the first interview will take place in her presence. I am hoping that her presence will lend me courage, without either she or my judges perceiving it. You may be sure it will be a great advantage to me to have behind me the intellectual support of a person whose vivacity and good sense never fail, because I, myself, as you know, am not always guided by tact . . . you would be doing me a favor if you would send me news of Mademoiselle de Lanclos who has no friend who takes a livelier interest in what concerns her than I do.

Even young Grignan, the grandson of Madame de Sévigné, came, although he did not fall in love with her as had his grandfather and his uncle. When he later married into a middle-class rich family, his mother remarked at court: "It is sometimes necessary to manure the best of lands."

Chapter LII

ALTHOUGH she never crossed the Channel the name of Mademoiselle de Lanclos was on many English tongues. Not only Saint-Evremond but the French ambassador, the duc de Taillard, and the young marquis de Ruvigny spread her fame. When the duchess of Sandwich, daughter of the earl of Rochester, came to Paris her most prized possession was a letter of introduction to Ninon from Saint-Evremond.[1]

Saint-Evremond also sent a young doctor, Turretini, to Ninon. We know that Ninon was now approaching seventy, yet the letter shocks us a little:

> I have news of Monsieur du Boulay through an old lady of his acquaintance to whom Monsieur de Saint-Evremond gave me an introduction. She is called Mademoiselle de Lenclos and is very clever. Many distinguished people visit her daily. I go to see her occasionally and have met the abbé Châteauneuf there among others . . . at the same house I made the acquaintance of the charming Monsieur de Fontenelle, author of the *Dialogue des morts*, and of Monsieur de la Loubère, the new academician.

Every common friend who crossed the Channel purveyed letters and gifts, French wine from Ninon, English tea from Saint-Evremond. She wrote:

> I envy everyone who goes to England, because I should like

[1] Fifty years later Horace Walpole received a portrait of Ninon by Ferdinand Elle or his son which had been the property of the deceased Lady Sandwich.

to dine with you once more. How vulgar to long for a dinner. The mind may have great advantages over the body, but the body has its own little appetites which forever recur and serve to distract the mind from its sad thoughts.

You often used to laugh at my melancholy moods, but I have banished all that. When one is on the last stretch of life there is no time for melancholy. One should live each day for itself and be content with it. Nearby hopes, whatever you may say about them, are worth as much as distant future ones, and are more likely to be realized.

Nevertheless, her periods of melancholy increased, the inevitable regret of a person who had found life good and was loath to leave it. She remembered La Rochefoucauld saying that old age was a woman's inferno, and mentioned it in a letter. Saint-Evremond replied:

You are more *spirituelle* and intelligent than the young and lively Ninon . . . your life, my very dear one, has been too brilliant for it not to continue so to the end. So do not let the inferno of which Monsieur de la Rochefoucauld speaks frighten you. He was only trying to work off a well-premeditated maxim. Pronounce the word "love" boldly, and never let "old" cross your lips. What ingratitude to be ashamed to name love when you owe all your charms and graces to it. You were born to love all your life.

Lovers and gamblers have something in common: once a lover, always a lover.

A group of people had been working for the recall of Saint-Evremond to France, Ninon among the most arduous. Finally the official letter, written by Gramont, was sent to England. Saint-Evremond, to Ninon's great disappointment, refused to return. He could not bring himself to part with the duchesse de Mazarin, the beautiful Hortense Mancini, with whom he was in love. Her salon "for love and conversation" contained also a menagerie, and the dogs, cats, birds and monkeys wandered at will among the distinguished guests: Dryden, Temple, Pepys and a young Irishman named Jonathan Swift. Saint-Evremond had found a new country and a way of life that suited him. Moreover, although still in good health, he was nearly eighty, too late to uproot himself a second time.

Gramont had been his friend for many years, and when the count decided to write his memoirs, he sent for Saint-Evremond for advice. The book was eventually written by Gramont's nephew, Anthony Hamilton, and called *Memoirs of the Court of Charles II*. In it, Hamilton writes:

> As he [Saint-Evremond] arrived unannounced he placed himself among us without ceremony, but he could not forbear smiling at the respect with which we withdrew our chairs under the pretense of not crowding him.

Then they discussed the projected memoirs and Saint-Evremond said:

> "I approve your plan and I have not come to advise you on its execution. Arrange as well as you can the material you had collected for others and disregard the order of time or events; I would advise you, on the contrary, to choose the latter years of your hero for your principal subject matter; his earlier adventures are too remote to be quite so interesting in the present day. Make some short and light observations on the resolution he has formed of never dying and upon the power he seems to possess of carrying it into execution . . . do not embarrass your brains in seeking ornaments or turns of eloquence to paint his character; that would resemble strained panegyric; and a faithful portrait will be his best praise."

Ninon began to read Seneca as she had formerly read Montaigne. The Stoic philosopher seemed to fit in with her mood. Her spells of melancholy increased. She wrote Saint-Evremond:

> Sometimes I am tired of always doing the same things, and I admire the Swiss who throw themselves into the river for that very reason. My friends scold me for talking like this

and try to reassure me that life is good as long as one is happy and the mind is healthy. It is all very well for people whose bodies are still strong to talk that way, but I would choose a healthy body in preference to a healthy mind.

This mood frightened Saint-Evremond, who wrote at once trying to cheer her, praising her and recalling past pleasures, to which she replied:

Your letter has filled me with vain desires of which I no longer believed myself capable. The days pass in idleness and ignorance as our friend des Yveteaux used to say, and Time is destroying us and taking away everything we enjoy. You used to say I would die of overthinking, but here I am, trying to think of nothing and forgetting tomorrow what I did today.

Ninon had no special ailment. Her body was gradually wearing out. Once, when her condition seemed serious and her friends surrounded her anxiously, she opened her eyes and said, *"Vais-je expirer ou soupirer?"* She was making fun of the old *précieuses* who had proscribed the horrid word "die" and substituted "sigh."

The marquise de Sévigné, grown mellow, wrote:

Our charming Lenclos has such a cold that I am quite anxious about her; there seems to be a great deal of illness about. Madame de Frontenac has a feverish cold, a prevailing trouble which makes one quite fearful. Our poor Lenclos is very sadly too, suffering as she does from some kind of low fever which increases at night. A bad throat complicates matters and causes much anxiety to her friends.

and later:

Corbinelli [a distinguished lawyer] asks me about the new marvels taking place at Mademoiselle de Lenclos's house in the way of good company.

She assembles around her in her old age, whatever Madame

de Coulanges may say to the contrary, *both* men and women, but even if women did not flock to her side she could console herself, having had men in the good age for pleas [*dans le bel âge pour plaider*].

Obviously the marquise would have liked to visit the rue des Tournelles herself. Perhaps she was even beginning to regret her impermeable virtue.

Hardly a week passed without Ninon receiving news of the death of some friend or former lover. Elbène, La Rochefoucauld, Marguerite de la Sablière, Bonrepaus, Gourville, all preceded her in shuffling off this mortal coil. The Grande Mademoiselle and the marquise de Sévigné, too, were dead. She had written to the abbé de Hautefille: "Monsieur de Saint-Evremond and I shall live to write the epitaphs of mankind." These two survivors, watching from their respective shores the foundering of their world, clung closer together. The mail took a long time. The Channel was more of an obstacle than the ocean is today, and the mail coaches had hard going. A letter which Ninon wrote in October reached Saint-Evremond in December. He replied, wishing her a happy New Year, "a day on which those who have nothing else to give make up the deficiency by wishes."

Ninon wrote:

I was alone in my chamber, weary of reading, when someone exclaimed: "Here is a messenger from Saint-Evremond." You can imagine how quickly my ennui disappeared—it left me in a moment.

I have been speaking of you quite recently and have learned many things which do not appear in your letters—about your perfect health and your occupation. Joy, to my mind, indicates strength and your letter assures me that England promises you forty more years of life, for I believe that it is only in England that they speak of men who have passed the fixed period of human life. I had hoped to pass the rest of my days with you, and if you had possessed the same desire, you would be in France.

It is, however, pleasant to remember those we have loved,

and it is, perhaps, for the embellishment of my epitaph that this bodily separation has occurred.

I could have wished that the young ecclesiastic had found me in the midst of the glory of Nike, which could not change me, although you seem to think that I am more tenderly enchanted with him than philosophy permits.

Madame the duchesse de Bouillon is like an eighteen-year-old: the source of her charms is in the Mazarin blood.

Now that our kings are so friendly, ought you not to pay us a visit? In my opinion it would be the greatest success derived from the peace.

And Saint-Evremond:

I lived in those days under a kind regency; Paris and the court alike breathed but love and amusements. An indulgent policy smiled upon the desires of our innocent nature. Every fancy seemed a legitimate one; slight errors were then no crime, and dainty vices but everyday distractions.

Ninon:

I have twenty letters of yours, and they are read with admiration by our little circle, which is proof that good taste still exists in France.

Saint-Evremond:

When I was young I used only to admire the mind and cared less for the affairs of the body than I should have done. Now I am repairing the wrong I did as well as I can, both by the use I make of my body and by the respect and affection I feel for it.

In your case it was different. Your body counted for something to you in your youth, and now you are only occupied with what concerns the mind. I don't know, however, whether you are right to respect the mind so highly. One reads hardly anything that is worth the trouble of remembering, one says hardly anything that deserves to be listened to. But however enfeebled by age the senses may be, they still respond quite appreciably to whatever they come in contact with, and it would be wrong to try to mortify them. It may be that the mind is jealous of them because it thinks they have the better of it.

More and more Ninon was beset by priests trying to save her soul. The abbé Testu hoped to gain a miter thereby. Père Orléans, more sincere, took every opportunity to try to convert her and got nothing but arguments. Finally he cried in exasperation:

"Very well, mademoiselle, while you are waiting to be convinced, at least offer up your unbelief to God!"

She wrote to Saint-Evremond:

You know what fortune I could formerly have made by selling my body. I could do even better now by selling my soul. The Jesuits and the Jansenists are fighting for it. . . .

If I could only believe with Madame de Chevreuse that in the next world we should be able to converse with our friends, the thought of death would be actually pleasing.

Saint-Evremond was an intransigent atheist, and when he heard that Gramont had been converted he wrote Ninon:

Hitherto I have been content to be an honorable man, but now I see that something more is expected of me, and I only await your example to become religious . . . religion is the last of our loves, and although we imagine we are only concerned with the happiness of the world to come, we are in reality searching for a new delight in this.

Ninon was not quite so sure as Saint-Evremond. She had seen corruption and hypocrisy within the Church, but she had also known many pious people who were good as well. She read both Scripture and philosophy, she continually searched for something in which she could believe, and she remained to the last an agnostic.

When Charleval died it was a serious blow. She wrote:

Now Monsieur de Charleval is dead and I am so much affected that I am trying to console myself by thinking of the share you will take in my affliction. Up to the time of his death I saw him every day. His spirit possessed all the charms of youth, and his heart all the kindness and tenderness so desirable among true friends.

We often spoke of you and of all the old friends of our time. His life and the one I am leading now had much in common. Indeed, a loss like this is like dying oneself.

Saint-Evremond himself sustained a bitter loss when Hortense Mancini died. Ninon wrote him:

I feel this death as much as if I had been acquainted with the duchess. She thought of me in her last moments . . . what she was to you drew me to her.

In the autumn of 1690 Ninon met the abbé Nicolas Gedoyn, an academician of learning, young enough to be her grandson. He made no effort to conceal the fact that his intentions were not honorable. At first Ninon laughed at him and reproached him, but he could not be discouraged, and he came to see her every day. Finally she told him that she would yield in a month and a day. The abbé curbed his impetuosity and waited. When the happy day arrived, Ninon was as good as her word . . . better. Her lover was delighted and could not resist asking her why she had so arbitrarily picked that day.

"Because today is my birthday," she replied. "I wanted to prove to myself that I could entertain a lover at the age of seventy. Now run along and find someone nearer your own age."

The abbé Gedoyn was said to be Ninon's last lover, and no doubt he was, unless, of course, the stories spread about her and the abbé de Châteauneuf some years later are true.

Chapter LIII

THE turn of the century saw many changes. The new Place Vendôme, designed by Mansart, was beginning to replace the Place Royale as a promenade of fashion. The Cours-la-Reine was widened and planted with elms, and sometimes the pageant of carriages continued across fields and gardens to the Bois de Boulogne.

The quarter around the church of Saint-Germain-des-Prés housed more and more families of distinction who occupied the two *étages nobles*, while the upper stories were for artisans and the very top for the servants. The beautiful gardens of the Palais du Luxembourg, formerly the Palais d'Orléans, were now filled with gallants and ladies, strolling among the flowers and the marble statues. A young Flemish boy who had come to Paris to study art was copying Rubens in the palace, and when he looked down at the scene it impressed itself on his mind. His name was Antoine Watteau.

The Tour d'Argent, where Henry III had dined on his way home from the hunt, now introduced many complicated dishes, as well as forks to eat them with. Rotisseries and coffeehouses became better and more numerous; horse racing was imported from England, the owners riding as jockeys.

The streets were widened and paved and most of them lighted at night. The old gates became arches; Paris was no longer a fortified city. La Reynie promised "security, cleanliness and clarity," and, thanks to Colbert, the city was surrounded by a green belt. Nevertheless, there was still plenty of mud.

Paris now contained some six hundred thousand inhabitants who left their uncomfortable homes on the slightest excuse, to mill around the streets, to play the lotteries, congregate in the coffeehouses and celebrate the many holidays.

The peasants, as La Bruyère wrote, were "sullen animals, male and female, attached to the earth they dig up . . . and with a kind of articulate speech." They paid the tax to their lords and to the king and gave their tithe to the Church. Workers in what factories existed got six *sous* a day, artisans in towns twelve, and miners about fifteen. Yet there was a dawning of realization that these creatures were human beings. Fénelon told the king that instead of extorting money from them he should feed them and give them alms.

The century of Ninon and Saint-Evremond was ended. The next one was ushered in with war. Lieutenant General Villars had turned defeat in Germany into victory. The Palatinate had been devastated. The king said of Villars, "This little fellow springs out of the ground to be present wherever there is any firing." The "little fellow" became a marshal and a peer. He had saved France. He was the son of Villars-Oroondate whom Ninon had followed to Lyon. But Villars was defeated at Turin, and in 1704 the duke of Marlborough with Prince Eugene of Savoy administered a crushing defeat at Blenheim. The tide had turned and the great empire which Richelieu, Mazarin and Colbert had built was now beginning to crumble at its frontiers.

It was the custom to write epitaphs for people who were still alive, so their subjects might enjoy them. Saint-Evremond wrote an epitaph for Ninon:

> L'indulgente et sage Nature
> A formé l'âme de Ninon
> De la Volupté d'Epicure
> Et de la Vertu de Caton.

(Indulgent and wise Nature has formed the spirit of Ninon of the voluptuousness of Epicurus and the virtue of Cato.)

He also wrote an epitaph for his friend Gramont, two verses of which are:

We may once more see a Turenne;
Condé, himself, may have a double;
But to make Gramont o'er again
Would cost Dame Nature too much trouble.

Sworn enemy of all long speeches;
Lively and brilliant, frank and free;
Author of many a repartee;
Remember, over all, that he
    Was most renowned for storming breeches.

The last known letter of Saint-Evremond to Ninon reads, in part:

Never have I read such a common-sense letter as yours. I am eighty-eight and breakfast on oysters every morning. I dine well and certainly do not make a bad supper. The world makes heroes of men with less merit than mine.

The very last letter I receive from Mademoiselle de l'Enclos always seems to me to be better than the preceding ones.

. . . Your mind is becoming stronger and more fortified every day. I wanted to make a trial of mine [stomach] against that of Lady Sandwich at a banquet given by Lord Jersey. I was not the vanquished.

Everyone knows the spirit of Madame Sandwich; I see her good taste in the extraordinary esteem she has of you. I was not overcome by the praises she showered on you any more than I was by my appetite. You belong to every nation, esteemed alike in London as in Paris. You belong to every age of the world, and when I say that you are an honor to mine, youth will immediately name you to give luster to theirs. There you are, mistress of the present and of the past. May you have the right to be so considered in the future!

and added a verse:

L'esprit vous satisfait, ou du moins vous console:
Mais on préférait de vivre jeune et folle,

Et laisser aux vieillards exempts de passion
La triste gravité de leurs réflexions.

(Mental joys satisfy you, or at least they console you; but
one prefers to live young and reckless and leave to the old
men exempt from passion the sad gravity of their thoughts.)

Despite his constant quips about his appetite, his way of
whistling in the dark, Saint-Evremond knew the end was approaching and he kept forging ahead with his work, not a word
of which was published during his lifetime. On September 9,
1703, he died with a quip on his lips. He was buried in West-
minster Abbey with the inscription:

NONAGINTA ANNIS MAJOR OBIIT DIE
IX SEPTIMUS MDCCIII

Thereafter two volumes of his essays appeared. There were
such titles as: *Interest in Persons Altogether Corrupted; What
Sciences a Gentleman Should Apply Himself to; The Pleasure
That Women Take in Their Beauty; A Discourse upon the
Word "Vast,"* and many others.

There was also *To the Modern Leontium,*[1] who was no other
than Ninon de Lanclos.

In the introduction to the English translation of these works
Dryden wrote:

. . . there is not only justness in his conceptions which is the
foundation of good writing, but also a purity of language
and a beautiful turn of words so little understood by modern
writers . . .

and a good deal more that was high praise indeed.

Hamilton, Gramont's biographer, wrote an epitaph which
reads in part:

No more shall Evremond incite us,
That chronicler whom none surpasses

[1] A disciple of Epicurus who added beauty to her intellectual attainments,
who was the friend of all the great people of her day and who incurred
the anger of many philosophers by writing a treatise against Theophrastus.

Whether his grave or gay delight us,
That favorite of divine Parnassus
Can find no word in dark Cocytus;
From that sad river's fatal bourne,
Alone de Gramont can return.

His ancient studying cap he wore,
Well tanned of good Morocco hyde,
The eternal double loop before,
That lasted till its master died.

Ninon's life was now really empty. She struggled to overcome the lethargy which set in, to fulfill the few engagements she made. Her mind was still alert, but she was very, very tired.

Chapter LIV

ONE day the abbé de Châteauneuf, also said to be Ninon's last lover, brought her some verses written by his godson, the ten-year-old François-Marie Arouet, who was the son of her notary and called Zozo. In the *Life of Voltaire* Tellentyre writes:

> She received the child in the midst of her brilliant circle with the infinite tact and kindness which have made her as immortal as her frailties. His bright, quick answers, his self-confidence, his childish store of information delighted her.

Voltaire, whose memory was sometimes faulty, and who showed remarkable ingratitude, wrote many years later:

> When I was about eleven the abbé de Châteauneuf took me to Ninon's house one day. I had written some very poor verses which were apparently not bad considering my tender age; this lady had formerly been acquainted with my mother, who was herself a great friend of Châteauneuf. Anyhow, he seemed to delight in introducing me to her. It was an open house for the abbé, who had, so to speak, concluded by his love intrigue the more exciting stages of Ninon's life. His nature was not one of those in which the attributes of youth are needed to intensify the desire, and the delight he experienced in Mademoiselle de Lenclos's company, in her conversation and general demeanor, had affected him just as her beauty was wont to attract in years gone by.

Then he tells of the episode of the abbé Gedoyn as if it had happened with Châteauneuf and continues: "My first acquaintance with Ninon came a few years later. She had the kind fancy of mentioning me in her will." His memory again was at fault. Born in 1694, Voltaire was eleven when Ninon died. Many years later from Potsdam he repeated the episode in a letter to a member of the Berlin Academy, adding:

> She encouraged me to continue my poetic writings. Really, she would have been wiser had she urged me to leave such things strictly alone. It is, after all, but a poor trade, and the wretched breath of fame creates too many enemies to do ought but embitter one's life.
>
> Look at Ninon's career; she never wrote verses, but enjoyed life and increased the pleasure of others, and that is surely far preferable to the things I have done in mine.

Voltaire wrote other things about Ninon, including the story of her supposed affair with Cardinal Richelieu. He said she was "full of maxims of an austere philosophy." He discussed her at Sans-Souci with Frederick the Great, who asked many questions about her.

A short time after Zozo's visit Ninon made her will and left him a thousand francs "for books." Châteauneuf said, "She saw in him the germ of a great man."

Old age for a pure voluptuary becomes intolerable; his greatest sources of pleasure have let him down, leaving nothing but cold memories for boasting. Ninon, it is true, had yielded to some of the calls of the flesh with abandon, but from her youth the delights of the mind had held equal sway, and when she was old she reaped her reward.

Saint-Evremond had said that the best reason to be resigned to death was that one could do nothing about it. And yet it is hardest to bear for people who have been happy. She continued to read Seneca. Perhaps the Roman philosopher's preoccupation with death accorded with her own mood.

Her servants adored her, her friends remained devoted . . . those that remained. Her mind was clear, and she continued to read, to write, to see a few chosen people, and she retained all her teeth. Her son was provided for and her house in order. Her will had been signed on December 19, 1704. She had nothing to do but wait.

Toward the end, to please her friends, or to insure her right to burial, or perhaps to be on the safe side, she permitted herself to be taken to Saint-Paul's by the Mesdames de Vaubert, Nancré and Ollier. There she confessed to Father Brunet. She apparently satisfied him as to her sincere repentance, for she received extreme unction. She then took to her bed.

On the night of the seventeenth of October 1705, she could find no sleep. Words were forming in her head as she tossed on her hot pillow. Marguerite and Catherine had red eyes when they served her.

Sister Marie watched at the bedside, expecting the spirit to leave the flesh any moment. Before dawn Ninon seemed to rally. She asked the nun to get a pen and write for her. Sister Marie assumed it was another confession or a codicil to the will. Nothing of the sort. Ninon dictated a poem:

> Qu'un vain espoir ne vienne point s'offrir
>> Qui puisse ébranler mon courage.
> Je suis en âge de mourir,
>> Que ferais-je ici davantage?

(Let no vain hope be held out to make my courage waver. I am of age to die, what is there left for me to do here?)

She then closed her eyes and lay still. From time to time Sister Marie held a mirror to her lips. When it was removed unclouded the nun felt for the pulse that was no longer beating. She crossed herself, said a prayer and then opened the door. The sleepy *valet de chambre*, Lapière, fell into the room.

The following day Ninon was buried at the parish church of Saint-Paul with little pomp or circumstance. She had left only ten *écus* for her funeral "so that it may be as simple as possible."

TESTAMENT OF ANNE DE LANCLOS

IN THE NAME OF THE FATHER, THE SON AND THE HOLY GHOST.

As God has granted me the grace of having a free mind, these are my last wishes; I give to the poor of this parish two hundred francs, to my confessor, Monsieur Brunet, fifty francs to read fifty masses for the repose of my soul. For my burial, ten *écus* so that it may be as simple as possible.

I give to M. de Gourville, nephew of the late M. de Gourville, for the obligations which I owe his uncle, my house in which I live, and because I have always and personally loved him. If the quality of universal heir is necessary to legalize this will, I request him to accept it as it cannot be an expense for him, as my assets are free from debts and from claims of relatives.

I give to my valet La Pierre three thousand francs, to his sister, who is my chambermaid, two thousand francs, to the girl who serves below, Marguerite, two hundred francs, to Catherine, who also works downstairs, sixty *livres*, to Sister Marie Provaut sixty *livres* to enshroud me. I forgot to say that I forbid la Piere and his sister to wear mourning for me; if I wanted that I would leave them the means for it. I give to Nielle Emero,[1] who is somewhat related to me and who needs it, two thousand five hundred *livres*, and to the widow Ferrier, another relative, two thousand five hundred *livres*. I humbly request M. Arouet very kindly, for the sake of his friendship for me, to undertake the execution of my will and to allow me to leave to his son, who is at the Jesuits, one thousand francs for books; this is a kindness for which I shall be much obliged to him. I give and bequeath to the abbé de Trianon-Lagrange a contract of sixteen thousand francs on the *gabelle* of the City Hall; I beg him to dispose of it according to the use I wish to make of it. I have forgotten to give to Nielle Emero two dresses which are the newest I have and a skirt of her choice, and to the widow Ferrier a dress and a skirt which will suit her, one of my lace headdresses of her choice to Nielle Emero, asking her not to go into

[1] A second cousin.

mourning for the sake of the little legacy I am leaving her, and the same order for the widow Ferrier. Made the nineteenth of December, 1704.

signed: Anne de Lanclos

I beg M. Arouet to see that my servants are nourished for six weeks.

Appendix A

LA COQUETTE VENGÉE

My dear Niece (said Eléanore to Philomène)

When you are in Paris beware of making acquaintance with every kind of man, and do not enter into conversation indiscriminately. Choice will not prove a difficulty, and whatever you do, avoid the company of philosophers. I quite see that this is gibberish to you, but with a little patience you will soon grasp my meaning.

When your brother Dorilas was at college, you often saw at your home a certain man who bowed himself into a room with strange gestures, who laughed at everybody and seemed to speak all languages except our own. His hair was unkempt, his beard untidy, his collar unfastened and soiled, his frock stained and his mantle ragged. Do you remember your irresistible fit of laughter at dinner one day when he told the footman who was pouring out wine for him that he must put on his hat, otherwise he would accept nothing at his hands? And this with such long-winded compliments that he might have died of thirst had not your father taken pity on him! You must recollect him; he it was who taught Dorilas philosophy and was himself a philosopher, but he is not the kind of man to whom I now refer.

Then you have often heard people talking about a certain abbé who lives near here. He leads a very retired life and thinks of no one but himself. He refuses to make friends with anyone lest he should be called upon to take any trouble for them, and he shrinks from society because of the intrigues and worries it involves. He loves his books and his dogs, the latter even more than the former, and nothing else. Whenever this man has formed the topic of conversation we have heard people call him a philosopher, but this again is not the sort of man I mean.

There are others who love society, but only that of men like themselves, among whom they feel free to do and say just what they like; these are greedy philosophers, frequenters of taverns, who drink incessantly because they maintain that they are never happy unless they have drowned or dulled their wits; when these are too keen they play their owners sorry tricks, forcing them to make melancholy reflections, and are altogether fatal to peace of mind. Such philosophers as these are a warning to us.

When I tell you to avoid philosophers, I do not refer to students, to hermits, nor to freethinkers, who declare their opinions openly. The men of whom I am thinking are those disguised pedants who wear short coats and have a somewhat fresher complexion than the others, because they live in sheltered places and are never exposed to dust or sunshine . . . "*philosophes des ruelles*" who dogmatize from the depths of a comfortable armchair; gallant philosophers who talk incessantly about love and have absolutely nothing lovable about them.

You cannot imagine what a nuisance such people are. When I first came to Paris fresh from the country, every newcomer was welcomed, provided he talked to me; thus it was that I became acquainted with one of those creatures who happened to come to a house where I was visiting one of my cousins. He was very quietly dressed, wearing neither ribbons nor laces, and I am not sure that he even had a tasseled girdle. His hat was rather shiny and had a small band; he wore silk stockings without a crease in them; his cloak hung from his shoulders, his tunic was buttoned up, showing neat cuffs at the wrist, and he carried his Grenoble gloves in his hand.

There was nothing foppish about him; a wink, a smile or a gesture made up for all those artificial mannerisms that really mean so little.

He received so hearty a welcome from the eldest son that his mother said: "My son is charmed to see you," and turning to the rest of the company, among which were many ladies, she added, "This is Mr. So-and-so." I did not think that the ladies took much notice; I fancy they were too deeply engrossed in the conversation, which his arrival had interrupted, to think of bowing to him. I knew him by name, for young men of my acquaintance who had been to Paris had mentioned him to me on their return to the country. He took a chair beside me while the discussion regarding a certain marriage in high life was resumed; neither of us said a word; I was silent, having nothing to say, and he did not speak because the subject displeased him. He, however, fancied we were both silent for the same reason, and after some time remarked in a low voice, "We are neither of us interested in the main topic of conversation, but we may choose another without interfering with it, especially as these ladies are talking so loud that they are bewildering one another and making such a noise they cannot possibly hear us."

I made some reply and he said something else, and so we went on; but I purposely used some odd words and expressions so that he thought me a provincial; whereupon he began to ply me with a number of questions about my home; he wanted to know my name, and all about my family, the books I had read, etc. He had plenty to say against Balzac, Voiture and all the writers of Letters, Plays and Morals; for, as he remarked: "People are cowardly enough to give up all solid knowledge for the sake of a mere phrase." He grew so elequent on this topic, and spoke with such warmth, that he frequently clenched his fist in his excitement. Finally he declared that if he were permitted to visit me I should learn more in a month than all those triflers could teach me in my whole life. There would be no subject with which I could not at once become familiar, for a few words from him would enable me to draw a thousand conclusions and give me material for endless conversations.

He came to see me not long after, as he had promised, and I bought some books of the kind called "tables"; whenever he called he explained their use to me, until this became my sole occupation and I began to neglect everything else. His visits and my studies continued thus for over a year; I had plenty of leisure and as yet knew nothing of the world, but eventually I was obliged to receive visitors every day and every hour, so that I no longer saw him except in company of others.

One day Polyxène was calling on me with her brother, who is the wittiest, cleverest man I ever met. Philidor said to him: "Sir, you have come at an opportune moment; you have taught Eléanore so much philosophy that she drives us distracted. I remarked to her that a faithful love was the most beautiful of all virtures. She answered proudly that I confused virtue with passion, that love was a passion, not a virtue, and that a passion does not become a virtue by reason of its duration, but is only a prolonged passion. She said a hundred things of the same nature. I am quite exhausted, and I entreat your help."

"How can I help you?" he replied. "I am altogether on Eléanore's side. She has shown you the source of the mistake common among men, of assuming that a passion is often really a virtue or a vice because men do not recognize the number and the nature of the passions. All this," he added, "is explained in two tables." He took up the book which lay near, and having turned to the table of passions, gave it to Philidor to read.

"What," said Philidor, "is this all that can be said about the passions, those powerful impulses which agitate our lives? Here is indeed a great ocean confined in a very small space. You condense your work admirably. Why, there is only one line about love! What a pocket divinity! If one line is enough to supply the needs of all lovers, it must be a remarkably long one. The seeker after knowledge on this subject must certainly be endowed with powerful intellect! 'Love is an impulse of the appetite toward a satisfaction of the senses, considered absolutely.' This knowledge will make me doubly gallant; I shall be possessed of many more attractive qualities; many more grand ideas to display in my conversation. There is nothing more beautiful nor so complete as love. Yet this book represents it as a perfectly dry skeleton, bereft of all attractions of color and curve. If the whole of this man's philosophy resembles this, my opinion of it is that it is a poor and meager monarch whose tables are very inadequately supplied."

My philosopher was inclined to be angry with Philidor, so

to put an end to a conversation which was becoming acrimonious, I took my lute and played some sarabandes. Philidor, with his usual energy, danced them all.

Then the conversation turned upon dancing and I thought I had succeeded in averting a dispute when Polyxène, out of pure malice, asked me if my book contained a table on the dance.

"Sir," said Polyxène to the philosopher, "for my sake you must construct one."

"That is quite easy," said Philidor, "I shall save him the trouble. I shall first put down some general remarks to show the necessity and utility of the dance. Then I shall define it thus: 'The dance is a series of rhythmical movements of the body to the sound of a voice or an instrument; these are simple or complex, rising high or bending low.' Then I shall enumerate the different kinds: the *sarabande*, the *branle*, *courante* and ballet. I shall describe the various steps, the gliding, the slow, the swift and the hopping. Good-by to all dancing masters. Whoever reads my table when it is finished will become a perfect dancer.

Polyxène laughed heartily, but my philosopher went away in a huff. I ran after him and in the antechamber made the best excuses I could. He said he was not in the least shocked, that Philidor was but a young man, fresh from college, who wanted to amuse himself; that unless he was very much mistaken his sister was an arrant coquette, and that he saw plainly that he would be unable to influence me in the future; he begged me to dispense with his advice, and added that he would send me in his stead a former pupil who knew his system as well as he did himself.

I thanked him a thousand times for all his kindness to me and we parted. All this is a prelude to a much more amusing story.

Although my philosopher only discussed the subject of tables, definitions and divisions, he was agreeable in this respect, that he was quite content if one listened, and he exacted nothing from me or any other woman he met but attention to his conversation, which was really its due.

This was not the attitude of his friend, whom Philidor called the Master of Ceremonies. He played the gallant and was evidently anxious to practice the love he preached; he sighed frequently and sang songs, of which he said he had composed both words and music. He was jealous of other men and criticized all they said. There was no one with whom he agreed. They were all ignorant and stupid. Even our own sex, which is sacred and inviolable among honorable men, was no more priviliged in his eyes. He sat in judgment on all the different beauties, and took upon himself to criticize the character and humor each possessed with such insolent presumption that to hear him one would have thought we had no qualities but those with which he thought to endow us.

All this was the cause of a great conspiracy among the men and women who frequented my house. Nothing was said about it to me because they knew that I should have been sorry for him and should have spoiled the plot by revealing it to him.

By means of continual watching, they found out the hours at which he visited me so that it was an easy matter for them to surprise him in my room. They arrived all together, and I had never received such a numerous company before. Everyone was exceedingly polite to him at first, so much so that I was quite astonished. They called him to his face "the incomparable, the inimitable, the most gallant, witty, versatile and polished of men" until he hardly recognized himself. He was asked to give a short lecture, whereupon he expounded the eight beautitudes, interrupted by exclamations of "Fine! Splendid! Admirable!"

He was next invited to sing, and although he made hideous efforts and his convulsions and contortions were almost akin to those of an epileptic . . . although his voice was contemptible and wretched as his face was evil and melancholy, yet the audience exclaimed there was no longer any need of Lambert and his sister.[1]

There followed a continuous stream of congratulations when the song was ended. Then Polyxène showed him a love letter which she had received, but he would not even read it. He said

---

[1] Michel Lambert was the musician mentioned by Boileau in his third satire, and by La Fontaine in one of his fables. He was the father-in-law of Lulli.

these were but trifles which could only amuse small minds; everyone agreed with him, and granted that man was born for greater things.

Never was philosopher more contented and self-satisfied, and because it was Polyxène who flattered him the most, he had the audacity to approach her and make some pretty speeches. She received these in such a manner that he pressed her closer still, took her hand, touched her arm, and finally, pretending to whisper in her ear, he kissed her. Polyxène in turn boxed his ears soundly.

This was the signal for the conspirators, and they all fell upon him. One punched his nose, "That's for the lovesick philosopher"; another thrust a pin into him, "That's for the lovesick musician"; a third struck him on the ear, "That's for the lovesick poet." I did what I could to save his philosophy, music and poetry thus severely attacked on all sides. All I could do, however, was to drag him out of the crowd and open the door for him to fly. He cried out loudly as he went: "Coquettes, coquettes, I shall know how to avenge myself."

I heard that when he died, either of his wounds or of despair, among his papers was found a severe diatribe against women, written under the name of Aristandre, which was published by his heirs at their own expense.

I am sorry that this misfortune should have happened to him at my house, but I must consider myself to blame for having been so weak as to admit philosophers within my doors, men who destroy the peace of the most refined, chivalrous and agreeable gatherings, by introducing into them calumny, slander and confusion.

My niece, be guided by my advice and beware of such men.

Thus spoke Eléanore to Philomène, who partly understood and, reading between the lines, guessed the rest.

Appendix B

THE abbé de Châteauneuf . . . said to be her last lover . . . wrote
Ninon's epitaph:

> Il n'est rien que la mort ne dompte.
> Ninon, qui, près d'un siècle, a servi les amours,
> Vient enfin de finir ses jours.
> Elle fut de son siècle et l'honneur et la honte.
> Inconstante dans ses désirs,
> Délicate dans ses plaisirs,
> Pour ses amis fidèle et sage,
> Pour ses amours tendre et volage,
> Elle fit régner dans son coeur
> Et l'extrême débauche et l'extrême pudeur,
> Et montra ce que peut ce triomphant mélange,
> Des charmes de Vénus et de l'esprit d'un ange.
>
> A la vie elle eut grande foi,
> Pour ne rien mettre à l'aventure,
> Elle ne crut point à la future.

(There is nothing that death does not overcome. Ninon, who
for nearly a century has been the handmaiden of love, has
finally finished her days. She was both the honor and the
shame of her century. Inconstant in love and discriminating
in her pleasures, for her friends she was faithful and wise,
for her lovers, tender and fickle. In her heart there reigned
the extremes of debauchery and modesty, and she manifested
the triumph of the union of the allure of Venus and the
mind of an angel. She had great faith in life but would

270

trust nothing to chance, and did not believe in the future at all.)

Love seemed to her merely a matter of the senses; an instinctive feeling which neither presupposes any merit in the object by which it is inspired, nor demands any gratitude. In short, it is a caprice of a certain duration which often ends in disgust and repentance. Abbé Châteauneuf in *Dialogues on the Music of the Nations*

The old loved her from their memory of the past, but not so much from the memory of her charms as of her virtues. The young loved her for the grace and the beauty they still saw in her . . . it was her fortune to draw to herself the most worthy people of the court and of the city, but she drew only the worthy, and no one would have forgiven himself for wounding her in anything. There grew up a natural bond, an intimate friendship among all those who were intimate with her: they esteemed and loved each other naturally on that account.   Abbé Fraguier

Thus it is not strange that she should have enjoyed such a measure of esteem, and the number of her distinguished friends increased apace even though her physical charms were on the wane; material delights were replaced by the more refined pleasure of intellectual relationships. Ninon was conversant with all the intrigues of the former and present courts. Shocking or otherwise, her conversation was always fascinating, and she herself was disinterested and faithful to the highest degree; indeed, in spite of many indiscretions she came to be looked on as virtuous as well as remarkably honest.

Her friends rarely asked her help in vain; she never refused her name as a guarantee in important transactions, and she kept treasures left in her charge as she did many secrets with which she was entrusted.

She thus had for friends all who were most select and

most lofty at court, so that it became the fashion to be received by her . . . there was never any gambling or loud laughter or disputes or arguments on religion or politics, but a great deal of wit of the most delicate quality, old and new anecdotes, bits of charming gossip, but with never a trace of malice. . . . Ninon's conversation was delightful. She was disinterested, reliable, secret, could be counted on to the very last . . . and all these qualities gained her a reputation and a consideration that were altogether unusual. Saint-Simon

Ninon was a girl of wicked conduct and of good company. Ninons are as scarce in this world as are Corneilles. It was reserved for the century of Louis XIV to produce the great and the marvelous in both genres. Saint-Foix

He [Goethe] continued the conversation and spoke of the celebrated Ninon de l'Enclos, who, in her sixtieth year, and in all her beauty, lay apparently on her deathbed, and with most perfect composure comforted those who stood around it, saying: "What does it matter after all? I leave more mortals behind me." However, she lived to the age of ninety, after having, until her eightieth year, made happy or desperate hundreds of lovers. Eckermann's Conversations with Goethe

The Frenchwoman whose independence seems to us the most like that of a man is perhaps Ninon de Lenclos, seventeenth-century woman of wit and beauty. Paradoxically, those women who exploit their femininity to the limit create for themselves a situation almost equivalent to that of a man; beginning with that sex which gives them over to the males as objects, they come to be subjects. Not only do they make their own living like men, but they exist in a circle that is almost exclusively masculine; free in behavior and conversation, they can attain—like Ninon de Lenclos—to the rarest intellectual liberty. The most distinguished are often surrounded by artists and writers who are bored by "good" women.   Simone de Beauvoir in *Le Deuxième Sexe*

But it remained for Sainte-Beuve, over a century later, to render the highest praise of all:

From Montaigne to Charron to Saint-Evremond and to Ninon, and on again from Ninon to Voltaire, there is but a hand's breadth . . . thus great minds form connecting links throughout the course of the ages.

Appendix C

INVENTORY AFTER DEATH

Belongings of Anne de Lanclos, from October 21, 1705. Notes of Maître Fontana, notary in Paris, 10 rue Royale.

CELLAR

First of all 8 loads of wood, taken and estimated at 12 livres per load, totaling at this price ninety-six livres   96 Livres

300 fagots estimated at   12 "

5 cartloads coal taken at   12 "

KITCHEN

One pothanger [*crémaillère*], shovel, pincers, two large hand-irons, one spit with its stone weights and its ropes, one skewer, one grill, one dripping pan, two dishwarmers, one cast-iron kettle, one frying pan and one for frying chestnuts, one fire screen, one fish bowl, all in iron, estimated at   8 livres

One urn with its cover and tap, one jam basin, one dishpan, one cover and basin to cook potatoes, one coffeepot, one small sieve, three candlesticks and one tilt hammer, all in red copper, estimated in all, including a saucepan, at   30 livres

One small round dishwarmer, one small frying pan, two other medium frying pans, a small candlestick with handle, all estimated at   3 livres

One sideboard serving as larder, of oak wood and teak wood, two other open larders in white wood, a small saltbox, four old chairs, two of white wood rebottomed and two others covered in old tapestry, all estimated at   4 livres

One mortar in white marble with wooden brush   30 sols

A quantity of 30 lbs. of pewter taken at 13 sols per lb.   19.10

UNDER THE ENTRANCE

One sedan chair lined with yellow striped satin and three striped taffeta curtains, three fine glass windows with their fastenings, estimated at   80 livres

One screen of white wood trimmed with green serge at the door of the kitchen, an iron hook to hang meat, valued and estimated at   50 livres

IN A LITTLE ROOM ON ENTERING THE APARTMENT OF THE SAID DECEASED ON THE FIRST FLOOR LOOKING INTO A COURTYARD

Item, a small couch of oak wood with a straw mattress, one mattress filled with horsehair, a bed and bolster of ticking filled with feathers and a coverlet in tapestry of Bruges, three small stools in oak, upholstered with horsehair and covered with matching tapestry, a walnut table on its stand furnished with a drawer, a large center table of dark wood, a walnut wardrobe with two doors garnished with brass wire at the top and with key, all at   30 livres

Item, three Flanders tapestries with scenery showing four alder trees, a window curtain of solid-color cotton cloth, estimated at   40 livres

Item, one utility chair in beech wood, nine pieces of ceramic used to decorate the mantelpiece   40 sols

A clock with movement and carillon, in ebony wood case with a front in gilded copper made by Théodore Denize of Paris, estimated   10 livres

IN A LARGE ROOM IN THE ABOVE-MENTIONED FIRST FLOOR LOOKING OUT ONTO THE ABOVE-MENTIONED STREET WHERE THE LATE OWNER DIED

Item, an iron grill ornamented with four copper balls, an iron (polly) shovel and tongs, a bellow, all estimated at   10 livres

A couch with low feet of oak with its bottom reinforced, a mattress, box spring filled with horsehair, a cotton twill mattress filled with wool, a big bed and bolster of ticking, a blanket of white wool, another embroidered by Mareuil, a counterpane likewise embroidered by Mareuil, the couch surrounded by two large curtains, two half-curtains, back and side, slopes and valances of striped taffeta with little squares in flounces, a cover composed of two large curtains, two half-curtains of red taffeta, the baldachin of the bed furnished with a four-post canopy and four large covers of similar striped taffeta in little squares, estimated at   100 livres

Four window curtains and a "portière" in two pieces of the same taffeta in little squares, six chairs, four of which have arm-rests with low backs in gilt wood, the ends stuffed with horsehair covered in red material with their dust covers in the same taffeta in small squares, a large utility armchair, two other arm-chairs also covered with tapestry of needlework and stuffed with horsehair, another armchair in walnut stuffed with horsehair, covered with red plush, two other small armchairs of black wood with small back stuffed with horsehair, covered with satin embossed on a green background, the whole estimated at

120 livres

Item, a small day bed in dark wood with its base, a mattress stuffed with wool, a small bolster of ticking stuffed with feathers, a mattress stuffed with horsehair, the bolster covered with the same taffeta with little squares similar to that of the cover, a small cover of the same taffeta, a front of oak covered with red satin, two little stools of oak upholstered with horsehair, covered with satin, two little tables of which one in cedar wood and the other in oak, covered with Turkish tapestry, estimated in all 25 Livres

Item, one cedar-wood table on its stand with drawer, desk like-wise in cedar with 18 little drawers, two round side tables of the same wood, another large one of dark wood and a small one in walnut; a small desk of wood and gilt wood composed of six drawers and its top, a music-stand of walnut, two little Chinese tables, two little chests likewise in Chinese wood, taken and esti-mated at   40 livres

A large mirror 26 *poulces* [1] by 18 wide with its border likewise in mirror, two other little mirrors of about 16 by 18 *poulces* also

[1] One *poulce*: approximately one inch.

with borders of mirror, a chimney pier glass in two pieces with
its border of wood containing about 36 *poulces* of *lon* [?] estimated at   100 livres

Item, eight screen sections painted with foliage   6 livres

Item, five little paintings on canvas of flowers in their gilded
wood frame, estimated at   18 livres

Another painting on canvas representing the Virgin, the Infant
Jesus and Saint-John in its gilded wood frame, estimated at
                                                                20 sols

Seven pictures on canvas representing portraits in gilt frames,
estimated at   6 livres

A little desk for putting books, of cedar wood with *fil de laton*
[?] closed with key   3 livres

Four pieces of faïence, an urn and two small flagons, estimated
at   30 sols

IN THE PANTRY, SECOND FLOOR

An oaken closet with two doors, closed by key, two pitch-pine
tables, two armchairs and a chair stuffed with horsehair, one
covered in leather and the other two in yellow cloth   50 sols

IN THE DRESSING ROOM ON THE SECOND FLOOR

An old lowboy cupboard in oak with key, two doors and an
old trunk   20 sols

IN THE ANTECHAMBER OF THE SECOND ROOM LOOKING ONTO SAID STREET

A four-door cupboard in walnut with key, an old coffer or
square cabinet, covered with black leather, an old armchair, a
chair in dark wood upholstered with horsehair and covered with
yellow cloth, six other armchairs of similar wood also upholstered
in horsehair, covered with similar cloth, an old table of oak, a
carpet of tapestry of Bergame, a small table for chess, a brass
tray   12 livres

IN THE ROOM

A bellows, an oak chest, a painted table on its stand with one
drawer, a painting on canvas with foliage and a figure in gilt

frame, a small buffet in wood *rapporté* with 11 drawers and key; the front of the drawers is of tortoise shell, a small round table, estimated at   8 livres

A couch with short legs with its straw mattress, a mattress, a sack stuffed with horsehair, a bed and bolster in ticking filled with feathers, a blanket of white wool, two welcomes of cotton and wool with green background, a small counterpane of printed calico [*indienne piquée*], the said couch having two curtains; another small couch with short legs with its box spring, a mattress stuffed with horsehair, a bed and bolster of ticking filled with feathers, a white wool blanket, estimated at   30 livres

A wooden panel covered with green serge in the first room 20 sols

(*Two hours out for lunch*)

IN THE STORAGE ROOM ON THE THIRD FLOOR LOOKING ON SAID STREET

One folding bedstead, a frying pan with copper bottom mounted on an iron stand, a large and a small faïence pail, two pots in faïence, four sections of an Indian screen, a table in tortoise shell on its stand, a spinet in walnut case, a small oaken table, on which were four screen sections covered with Indian material, a similar door, two chairs in dark wood, a round table of white wood, a lowboy in oak, with two doors and key, a small bench fitted with strips and covered with green cloth, estimated at 25 livres

A dozen strips of red gauze with little squares, a valance of embroidered gold damask lined with red taffeta composed of two large curtains and two half-curtains, covers and ruffles of similar material with its imperial, four large curtains in red taffeta for windows, estimated   80 livres

Two pieces of Flanders tapestry forming a valance of about 8 *aulnes* [2] with cloth bands   100 livres

IN A HEREUNDER INVENTORIED CUPBOARD IN THE ROOM LOOKING ON SAID COURT

Eight white linen chemises trimmed with Malines lace at the cuffs and collar   25 livres

[2] One *aulne*: approximately a yard.

Seven other chemises in white linen without sleeves and trimmed with a little lace at the collar   15 livres

Four pairs of wristbands in linen with sundry lace of fine Malines or Flanders   35 livres

A garniture of Malines lace   25 livres

Two bombazines [3] and a headdress in linen trimmed with heavy lace, a pair of sleeves for the night, an old bed jacket of twilled cotton, 11 handkerchiefs to blow the nose in batiste   4 livres

18 other handkerchiefs also in batiste, 9 others of rough linen   10 livres

Four armchair dust covers, green and golden yellow   3 livres

CLOTHES FOUND IN A CUPBOARD ON THE SECOND FLOOR

A taffeta mantle with skirt also in taffeta, covered with pigeon-breast material   50 livres

A skirt in white damask with flowers, another skirt in white satin striped with bands in yellow and other colors, a petticoat of white satin embroidered with dots and bands of purple, a house robe of Indian material lined with crimson taffeta with black stripes and a skirt of striped cloth with embroidered bouquets   30 livres

A gauze scarf, another gauze scarf, a little white satin petticoat, embroidered at the bottom with flowers, another petticoat of gros de Tour, with red and white stripes, a corset, a foot cover-let of treebark [4], embroidered, stuffed with cotton   3 livres

Seven pairs of sleeves of white linen embellished with Malines lace, two old bed jackets, an English apron, two little bombazines, three stitched nightcaps, a peignoir trimmed with old lace, a toilet apron, an old dressing gown trimmed with an old lace, a bonnet   16 livres

A petticoat of watered silk embroidered at the bottom, lined with a little cotton material, a quilt of white satin embroidered with flowers and imitation gold   30 livres

[3] *Bazin:* can also be dimity.
[4] *Escorce:* bark or shavings used to stuff pillows to give a pleasant scent.

A little foot-robe of Indian material 25 sols

5 bed sheets of coarse linen with two *letz* [?] 10 livres

Four pairs of white linen bed sheets considerably worn 16 livres

Two dozen embroidered linen napkins with tablecloth in the same material; two other napkins also of embroidered linen, worn 25 livres

A window curtain and six little linen napkins 6 livres

A small foot-robe of Indian taffeta stitched and lined with red taffeta, a pillow filled with feathers, covered with checked taffeta, another pillow filled with feathers, covered with painted cloth, a small *canapé* covered with Bruges satin, a little divan with its box spring, a mattress of horsehair and a small mattress filled with wool, a small bed and bolster of gray linen filled with feathers, covered with Bruges satin, a small China table, a fire screen and a front of embossed China satin, a small English casket on a little olivewood table decorated with gilded copper plaques, closing with key 40 livres

About 10 *aulnes* [ells] of Bruges satin tapestry running around the said room, four little sections of a screen in linen painted with figures and estimated with 2 toile curtains at 50 livres

12 little pictures, that is 10 on canvas and two engravings of different sizes representing various persons and landscapes with gilt wooden frames 8 livres

40 pieces of porcelain constituting the decoration of the mantelpiece 50 livres

A petticoat of red and yellow striped satin with a border of silver at the bottom, lined with white taffeta, another petticoat of satin with white background and striped with red and with little bouquets, lined with white taffeta; another petticoat of white watered silk lined with taffeta, also white, a house robe of striped satin, yellow, violet and coffee-colored, lined with black taffeta; another house robe of satin with a blue background, covered with bouquets, lined in black taffeta; another house robe of red and green striped satin lined with green taffeta, another house robe of Indian material lined with gold yellow taffeta, a little jacket of white satin with flowers   60 livres

A thermometer and a barometer   10 livres

60 volumes of books in folios and quartos and in twelfths bound in calf and parchment treating of different subjects   40 livres

SILVER VESSELS

6 candlesticks, two square and 4 small in the *cabinet de toilette*, two pitchers, a basin, a covered bowl, a saltcellar, a candle snuffer with its stand, an inkstand and a sandbox all in Paris hallmarked silver weighing 24 marcs 5 ounces taken at 31 livres per marc according to the edict of the king

163 livres 7 sols 6 denies

An oval basin, a large platter, two medium and one small platter, a dozen plates for fish, 5 spoons, 5 forks and 5 knife handles also in Paris hallmarked silver taken at 32 livres 7 sols 6 deniers per marc, all weighing 43 mares   1392 livres 2 sols 6 deniers

CASH

Item, 140 écus at 3 livres 17 sols, and 38 livres in pieces of 10 sols, amounting in all   570 livres

INDEX